THE MAKING OF WALES

JOHN DAVIES

Llywodraeth Cynulliad Cymru
Welsh Assembly Government

I Anna ac Ian

First published in 1996 by Sutton Publishing
This edition published in 2009 by The History Press
The History Press, The Mill, Brimscombe Port, Stroud, Gloucestershire, GL5 2QG
www.thehistorypress.co.uk

British Library Cataloguing in Publication Data.
A catalogue record for this book is available from the British Library.
ISBN 978-0-7524-5241-8

Production editing by Diane Williams and Bill Zajac
Design by Ceri Staziker
Maps and plans by Cartographics, Welsh Assembly Government
Typesetting by Cadw, Welsh Assembly Government
Origination by The History Press
Printed in the UK by J F Print Ltd., Sparkford, Somerset

CONTENTS

Preface and Acknowledgements

This book first appeared in 1996. Since then, much has happened in Wales, and therefore I was invited to prepare a revised and updated edition. Over the last thirteen years, an increasingly sensitive attitude towards the natural and the built heritage has developed, leading to a far deeper understanding of the making of Wales. Indeed, it has been suggested that to see the one heritage in a different context from the other is an outdated concept which should be replaced by a concern with integrated ecosystems. Furthermore, to think in terms of whole landscapes highlights the fact that, in seeking to understand the story of people, the only document we have which illuminates that story in its entirety is the landscape itself.

Changes in agriculture have altered the appearance of vast swathes of the Welsh countryside, and the country has been endowed with new iconic buildings, the Millennium Stadium in Cardiff, the National Waterfront Museum in Swansea and the Great Glasshouse at the National Botanic Garden among them. Yet an emphasis upon recent changes and new buildings can obscure the fact that 'everything', as W. G. Hoskins put it in 1955, 'is older than we think'. He was directing his argument specifically against the notion — then widely held — that the countryside looks the way it does chiefly as a result of the parliamentary enclosures of the late eighteenth and early nineteenth centuries. Hoskins pushed back the date of major landscape making by over 600 years and emphasized in particular the role of the assarters — the tree clearers — of the twelfth and thirteenth centuries. The tendency now is to push everything much further back. In 1986, Oliver Rackham demonstrated that the landscape of the Lizard Peninsula in Cornwall 'has altered little in a thousand years', and recent work on Welsh upland regions such as Ardudwy has revealed a landscape which has only marginally changed over the last two thousand years.

The reshaping of the landscape of Wales began in the Mesolithic era and accelerated hugely in the Neolithic, Bronze and Iron Ages. Thus, huge strides in that reshaping had been taken long before Wales tiptoed into the historical record in the first century AD. To a great extent, therefore, the making of Wales is a prehistoric phenomenon and thus the names of its early makers are wholly unknown to us.

Even with the dawn of history, the paucity of written records means that the makers of Wales remain anonymous. We can surmise that the Roman frontier in Wales was planned by Julius Frontinus, the governor of the province of Britannia from AD 74 to 78, but we do not know the names of those who dug the initial ramparts and ditches at Gelligaer, built walls at Caerleon and paved the hundreds of miles of Roman roads. Even when documentation becomes more plentiful, the actual makers continue to elude us. We know that Master James of St George was instrumental in the construction of Edward I's great castles, that Telford and Jessop designed Pontcysyllte, and that Lanchester, Stewart and Rickards designed Cardiff's City Hall, but who dug the foundations and who applied the mortar? To write of the makers of Wales is to pay tribute to a vastly long succession of users of axes, spades and trowels, to shapers of timber, to quarriers of stone and slate, and, in more recent times, to drivers of bulldozers and mechanical diggers. We can name hardly any of them. Yet they are commemorated, for the landscape itself is their memorial.

In preparing this edition of *The Making of Wales*, my first debt is to Diane Williams, Cadw's publications manager, whose attention to detail has been exemplary and whose patience has been much appreciated. I am also appreciative of the contribution of Bill Zajac. I wish to thank Cadw's director, Marilyn Lewis, who suggested that there should be a revised version of the 1996 edition. The text was read in whole or in part by Judith Alfrey, Richard Brewer, Stephen Burrow, Astrid Caseldine, Toby Driver, Nancy Edwards, Ralph Griffiths, Sian Rees, Richard Suggett, Peter Wakelin and Elizabeth Walker, and I am grateful for their constructive suggestions. The book was designed by Ceri Staziker, the maps and plans were prepared by Peter Lawrence, and the index was compiled by John Kenyon, who, with Christine Kenyon, assisted with the proof reading. At The History Press, Jo de Vries has been supportive throughout.

Above all, as always, my greatest debt is to my wife, Janet Mackenzie Davies, and to my children. To dedicate the book to my elder daughter and her husband is a special delight.

Opposite: Cardiff Bay, once a busy coal port, is today the heart of Wales's devolved government (© Crown Copyright (2009) Visit Wales).

PROLOGUE

The Blorenge near Abergavenny is the place to start. This mass of heather, bracken and whinberries thrusts out above the Usk Valley; it marks the north-eastern corner of the south Wales coalfield and dominates the only area where the one-time coal valleys are in close — although often uneasy — contact with rich agricultural land.

The twenty-first century is very visible here, for the Blorenge offers a view of the labour-intensive efforts to transform the Heads of the Valleys road into a motorway. The twentieth century has also left its mark; at the beginning of that century, the A40 was a leisurely highway, but, at the century's end, the road was a dual carriageway which gashed its way across the green lushness of central Monmouthshire. The second half of the nineteenth century is here too: the Newport to Hereford railway (1854), the Big Pit on the upper reaches of the river Llwyd (sunk to its present depth in 1880) and Forgeside, Blaenavon, where Gilchrist and Thomas pioneered the smelting of phosphoric ores (1878). So is the first part of that century: the Blorenge overlooks the great cirque of Llanwenarth, where evidence of the vanished community celebrated by Alexander Cordell is immediately apparent. Equally apparent is the location of the tramroad which slid down the mountain to the canal below; the canal is still there and I can see holidaymakers clambering over the decks of the barges moored at the Govilon quay. And a very different early nineteenth century is represented beyond Abergavenny where Clytha House, Wales's finest Greek revival country house, edges into view.

The eighteenth century has left memorable imprints, including the landscaped park at Coldbrook and those of the side streets of Abergavenny which 1960s planners fortunately neglected to demolish. The seventeenth century had its demolishers too; far away to the east lie the ruins of the great Yellow Tower of Gwent, partially undermined following the Civil War. The demolition marked the final demise of an old world, and the arrival of a new world is represented by the erection in the 1690s of chapels at Llanwenarth and Abergavenny, harbingers of a great building crusade. Evidence of the sixteenth century is less immediately obvious; but it is there, for many of the substantial farmhouses which dot the landscape of Monmouthshire stand on sixteenth-century foundations.

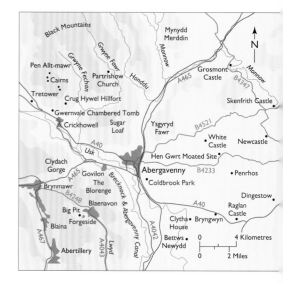

The Blorenge and its surrounding landscape: a map illustrating places mentioned in the text (Cartographics, Welsh Assembly Government. Derived from digital data supplied by Lovell Johns, Oxford).

Opposite: The view from the Blorenge near Abergavenny offers just one panorama of the Welsh landscape — a landscape upon which at least two hundred generations of human beings have left layer upon layer of impressions. This scene shows Abergavenny set in the valley of the Usk. It was the Roman Gobannium, and subsequently a medieval market borough, established in the wake of the Norman Conquest. Abergavenny has remained a flourishing market centre in this corner of Monmouthshire through to the present day.

The Iron Age hillfort of Crug Hywel, situated atop Table Mountain (© Crown: Royal Commission on the Ancient and Historical Monuments of Wales, AP_2005_1847).

The Gwernvale chambered tomb, north-west of Crickhowell, was used by Neolithic people for communal burials about 3650 BC. During its excavation in the late 1970s, archaeologists discovered that the site had an even longer history, finding evidence of earlier Neolithic buildings and artefacts and stone tools of Mesolithic hunter-gatherers.

Despite the partial ruination of the great fifteenth-century Yellow Tower, the fortified palace of the Herberts at Raglan remains a dramatic symbol of the wealth and power of the lords of the March. A more appealing reminder of fifteenth-century Wales lies in the hills to the north. The Grwyne joins the Usk below the mistletoe-encrusted trees of Cwrt-y-gollen and the line of the valley of the Grwyne Fawr can be followed until it melts into the blue haze of the Black Mountains. Just below the haze lies Partrishow Church, with its splendid rood screen; the church is not visible from the Blorenge, but to know that Partrishow is there and to imagine it brings a rich contentment. The Blorenge offers a fine view of Abergavenny Priory, the necropolis of some of the leading lords of the south-eastern March, its fourteenth-century tower standing serenely in a whirl of traffic. The earlier medieval centuries are represented too, with masonry castles at Abergavenny, Crickhowell and Tretower, and a rash of mottes and ringworks, among them Bryngwyn, Penrhos, Newcastle, Bettws Newydd and Dingestow.

Over thirty parishes are visible from the Blorenge, and more than twenty of them bear *llan* names. Some commemorate the great saints of Christendom — Mary, Peter and Michael among them — but the majority honour saints of early Welsh Christianity, with Cadog, Teilo and Dewi in the lead. These *llannau* indicate the desire, from the fifth century onwards, to imprint the landscape with the names of the founders of Christianity in Wales. That Christianity emerged from the Roman occupation, and there, on the banks of the Usk, at the foot of the Blorenge, lies *Gobannium*, the Roman fort controlling the point where the Usk emerges from its narrow valley into the plain.

To the north-west, there is another fortification — Crug Hywel on Table Mountain — an Iron Age hillfort overlooking the confluence of the Grwyne Fawr and the Grwyne Fechan. And beyond, in serried ranks up to the summit of Pen Allt-mawr, are cairns, the burial places of the Bronze Age people who settled in these noble uplands. But the features which dominate the view from the Blorenge are fields — thousands of them — and hedgerows — hundreds of miles of them. As Oliver Rackham put it: 'To convert millions of acres of wildwood into farmland is unquestionably the greatest achievement of our ancestors'. The turning of the forests of the Usk Valley and its flanking hills into fields was a long, long process. It began 6,000 and more years ago and there, beyond Crickhowell, I can see the grave of some of the pioneer field creators. This is the Gwernvale chambered tomb, erected by Neolithic people, and used as a burial site about 3650 BC.

Thus the view from the Blorenge offers a panorama of a palimpsest — a landscape upon which at least two hundred generations of human beings have left layer upon layer of impressions. The countryside has traditionally been considered wholly natural, in contrast with the artificiality of the town. Yet there is nowhere in twenty-first-century Wales which is in any sense primeval. Everywhere the results of the labours of human beings are evident. In consequence, the notion of the naturalness of the countryside has been replaced by an insistence that, by the twentieth century — and indeed, long before the twenty-first century — the countryside is as much an artefact as is a town. Rural Wales, like urban and industrial Wales, it is argued, is the

product of the human makers of Wales. This argument can give rise to the belief that, as the landscape is made by people, there is no limit to what people can do with it, for to modify the landscape is merely to continue a long and hallowed tradition. Yet the panorama from the Blorenge is not solely the result of human ambition and design. It has come into existence through the interaction between the natural world and human activity. Furthermore, its major features are vastly older than any human activity, for this landscape was in the making long before — millions of years before — the first human set foot upon it. The Old Red Sandstone, which underlies the soil in the borderlands of Monmouthshire and Powys, was laid down between 370 and 415 million years ago. Thus, while the argument that the countryside is an artefact is an important antidote to the anti-urban bias implicit in many landscape studies, it is an argument which should be tempered with humility. Human beings are the co-makers of the landscape; in addition, they are its custodians — custodians not only of its beauty but also of its meaning.

I walk down from the Blorenge to the upper reaches of the Clydach Gorge, a place resonant with meaning. On the way, I suck the juice of the mountain's fat whinberries and nibble the grain of the wayside wild oats. At the top of the gorge, reddish water rich in iron drips from the rock and a narrow vein of coal emerges on the cliff side. I drink the iron water and chew a little of the coal.

I am in communion with the land.

The Clydach Gorge, near Brynmawr, is now a place of great natural beauty, but the remains of ironworks — such as these of the Clydach Ironworks begun in 1793–95 — limekilns and workers' housing reveal that it was an area of industrial activity from the late seventeenth to the nineteenth century. It also served as an important link between the iron-producing uplands around Nantyglo and the Brecknock and Abergavenny Canal, which was constructed between 1797 and 1812 and crosses the lower mouth of the gorge. The routes of several horse-operated tramroads and the later Merthyr, Tredegar and Abergavenny Railway can still be traced from surviving terraces, bridges and tunnels.

THE EARLIEST MAKERS

PALAEOLITHIC AND MESOLITHIC WALES

The landscape upon which the original makers of Wales made their mark was that which emerged following the retreat of the glaciers, over 12,000 years ago. There had been human beings in Wales long before the last of the ice ages, known as the Devensian (120,000 to 12,000 BC), for human teeth discovered at Pontnewydd Cave near St Asaph are considered to be 225,000 years old. The cave is the only site of the Lower Palaeolithic era yet discovered in Wales and is the most north-westerly of its period in Europe. Wales's only indubitable site of the Middle Palaeolithic period is Coygan Cave, near Laugharne. Here Neanderthals left their stone axes some time between 64,000 and 36,000 BC. The most remarkable site of the Upper Palaeolithic period is Goat's Hole Cave in Gower, the burial place of the 'Red Lady of Paviland'. The 'Red Lady' is in fact the skeleton of a young man, who lived around 27,000 BC. He was buried with a number of ivory ornaments in earth strongly impregnated with iron oxide, the first example in Wales — and, indeed, in Europe — of a rich ritual burial which would eventually loom so large in the archaeological record. From broadly the same era, there is evidence of human activity at Ffynnon Beuno and Cae Gwyn, caves near Tremeirchion in Denbighshire. It consists of flint implements — a scraper, a spear and two chisels — more delicate and specialized than those used by earlier peoples.

In about 21,000 BC, the Devensian ice age entered its most severe phase, and for the following 8,000 years the whole of Wales, apart from the southernmost fringes, was covered with ice. The inhospitable climate meant that the fringes did not have human inhabitants; thus there was a hiatus in human settlement until around 13,000 BC, after which people returned to Wales. However, the cold era that followed brought about a millennium (about 10,500–9500 BC) during which Wales was almost bereft of human beings. It was only at the end of that time that continuous human settlement probably began in Wales with the start of the Holocene or the early Mesolithic period. Settlement is believed to have been the result of movement across the land bridge between Britain and mainland Europe; by 6500 BC, however, Britain was an island.

The climate improved rapidly following the final retreat of the ice. From about 7000 to 2500 BC, average annual temperatures were a degree or two

Approximate dates

Lower Palaeolithic:	Earliest people–120,000 BC
Middle Palaeolithic:	120,000–35,000 BC
Upper Palaeolithic:	35,000–9500 BC
Mesolithic:	9500–4000 BC

A Palaeolithic handaxe of about 125,000 BC found at Rhossili on the Gower Peninsula. The object was a chance find, but it provides some evidence for the very earliest presence of people in the Welsh landscape (© National Museum of Wales).

Opposite: Goat's Hole Cave on the south Gower coast, the burial place of the 'Red Lady of Paviland'. The lady was in fact a man aged about 25 who was ceremonially buried in the cave around 27,000 BC.

Footprints representing at least three Mesolithic people who walked across the mud of the Usk Estuary. These people probably belonged to one of the bands of Mesolithic hunter-gatherers who had begun to take advantage of the rich natural resources available around the shores of Wales at this time (© National Museum of Wales).

Below right: An outline chronology of landscape development in Wales.

Below: The distribution of known Palaeolithic and Mesolithic sites in Wales.

Celsius higher than they are today. This period was characterized by the growth of trees. Pollen analysis allows the chronology and geography of tree growth to be worked out in remarkable detail. Juniper established itself first, followed by birch, pine, hazel, elm, oak, alder, lime and ash. Cors Caron on the Teifi was the first place in Wales to be examined for pollen and is a key site in the history of pollen studies. Radiocarbon dating enables archaeologists to assert that hazel trees first grew at Tregaron in about 9200 BC. Much of Wales came to be covered by a thick canopy of trees. Open grassland was restricted to the very highest land, thus robbing the reindeer and the bison of their feeding grounds. Their place was taken by a far less gregarious woodland fauna — red deer, wild boar and wild oxen.

This was the setting for the Mesolithic people of about 9500 to 4000 BC. Mesolithic sites far outnumber those of the Palaeolithic period, indicating not only the destruction of the latter by ice sheets, but also suggesting that the more favourable climate of early postglacial times permitted a greater density of population. Many of the Mesolithic sites discovered in Wales so far are near the present coastline, but, as many low-lying areas were drowned following the retreat of the ice, it is likely that numerous sites, particularly of the early part of the period, now lie beneath the sea. Large sites of the Mesolithic era include that at Nab Head, near Marloes in Pembrokeshire, which has yielded stone implements, including evidence of a workshop manufacturing stone beads, perhaps the earliest indication of a trade workshop in Wales. Beads of Pembrokeshire origin have been found as far afield as Waun Fignen Felen in the Tawe Valley.

The pollen record suggests that some tree clearance might have occurred in parts of Wales during the Mesolithic period, probably the result of the deliberate use of fire to create forest glades, thus modifying the landscape. Later during that era, when the Welsh uplands experienced increasingly heavy rainfall, the combination of treelessness and waterlogging led to a rampant growth of peat which, even without further human intervention, would have inhibited the growth of trees. The Mesolithic burnings were probably the first

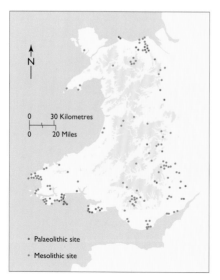

N

| 0 | 30 Kilometres |
| 0 | 20 Miles |

• Palaeolithic site

• Mesolithic site

Calendar Years	Climatic Period	Archaeological Period	Climate	Vegetation	0% Trees 100%
1000	Sub-Atlantic	Modern Medieval Early Christian Romano-British	Global warming Little Ice Age Medieval warm period Climatic deterioration	Reafforestation Forest shrinkage	
AD/BC			Warmer	Oak-birch-beech-alder	
1000		Iron Age Late Bronze Age	Climatic deterioration		
2000	Sub-Boreal	Middle Bronze Age Early Bronze Age		Mixed oak forest and alder woods	
3000		Neolithic			
4000			Climatic optimum	Elm decline	
5000	Atlantic			Mixed oak forest and alder woods	
6000					
7000	Boreal	Mesolithic		Hazel-oak-birch-elm-pine woodland	
8000			Climatic amelioration		
9000	Pre-Boreal		Rapid warming	Pine-birch-juniper-willow	

major example of the impact on the landscape of the human makers of Wales. The Blorenge, which is about 1,800 feet (550m) above sea level, was almost certainly forested in the mid-Mesolithic age. It is now moorland, as are great tracts of upland Wales. The moorlands are generally considered to be a wholly natural landscape, but they are essentially people-made, although the process of making them extended well beyond the Mesolithic period.

While climatic change in Britain — and in Europe generally — led to the forest cultures of the Mesolithic people, the reaction elsewhere was different. In the Near East, where higher temperatures led to the spread of deserts, the reaction was to invent agriculture. The early farmers of the Near East practised slash-and-burn tactics, which rapidly exhaust the fertility of the soil. They were therefore obliged to move, and archaeologists posit a gradual movement of farmers from Anatolia to Greece and the Danube Valley and eventually across Europe, reaching Britain by about 4500 BC. By growing crops and tending animals, human beings can sustain themselves in far greater numbers than could the hunter-gatherers of the Mesolithic period. In a few generations, the incoming farmers might well have had descendants numerous enough to overwhelm the sparse Mesolithic inhabitants. Some archaeologists have suggested that the westward moving farmers may have been speakers of Indo-European languages. Although the suggestion has been much attacked, it is conceivable that the ancestor of Brythonic or British (the language spoken in southern Britain at the time of the Roman invasion, itself the ancestor of the Welsh language) was spoken in this island over 6,000 years ago.

While the hunter-gatherers were capable of landscape modification, agriculturalists are, almost by definition, landscape makers; thus, by the fourth century BC the transformation of Wales was gathering pace.

The promontory at Nab Head, near Marloes in Pembrokeshire, the most celebrated Mesolithic site yet discovered in Wales. Excavations here have yielded masses of stone implements used by the fishing and hunting community which occupied this site as a base for exploitation of the coastal landscape. In this view, an Iron Age promontory fort can be seen on the right of the headland (© Crown: Royal Commission on the Ancient and Historical Monuments of Wales, 905545-18).

THE MAKERS BECOME FARMERS

NEOLITHIC WALES

Until the late 1950s, the Neolithic period — the age of farmers lacking metal — was considered to have lasted for about 400 years (about 2300 to 1900 BC). The radiocarbon-dating revolution has resulted in the realization that the Neolithic Age was coming to an end at the time when once it was thought to begin. It lasted from about 4000 to 2400 BC; thus the Neolithic makers of Wales operated over a far greater time span than was once thought, and their impact should be visualized as a series of slow but cumulative changes. As both pastoralists and cultivators, the Neolithic farmers would have needed open spaces on a far greater scale than had their hunter-gatherer predecessors. Thus the attack upon the wildwood accelerated. The earliest cultivators were likely to have been gardeners rather than farmers and had little beyond occasional clearings, but by about 3000 BC exploitation became more intense as the population increased and as grazing by animals inhibited tree regeneration. Hence some clearings evolved into extensive open spaces.

Unlike their predecessors in the Palaeolithic and Mesolithic periods, the Neolithic people made extensive use of implements of polished stone. On softwoods, a polished stone axe can be as effective as steel. In an experiment in Denmark, three men using stone axes cleared 600 square yards (500 sq m) of birch wood in four hours. The volcanic rocks of Wales were a useful source of raw material for the making of axes. There was quarrying in Mynyddoedd y Preseli, but the most significant site is that of Graig Lwyd on Mynydd Penmaenmawr, east of Bangor. There was much activity there around 3000 BC, when the earliest quarrymen of Gwynedd were shaping the hard stone into rough-outs. Axes of Penmaenmawr stone have been found in many parts of Britain and their distribution suggests the ability of the people of the Neolithic period to organize trade on an extensive scale.

Further proof of the wide-ranging contacts of the Neolithic communities is provided by their most celebrated activity — the building of megalithic tombs. They were built as stone chambers enclosed in a mound of soil and stones; where the covering has been eroded away, the stone structure stands starkly, and often dramatically, as at Pentre Ifan above the Pembrokeshire coast — the most immediately recognizable of Wales's prehistoric monuments, and the first ancient monument in Wales to receive statutory protection.

Opposite: The megalithic chambered tomb of Pentre Ifan, set on the edge of Mynyddoedd y Preseli in Pembrokeshire. It is one of more than 150 such tombs raised by the Neolithic people of Wales.

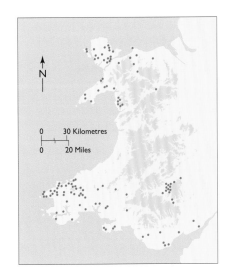

The distribution of Neolithic chambered tombs in Wales. The variety in their form of construction suggests there was eventually a number of regional Neolithic cultures across the Welsh landscape.

The megalithic tomb at Tinkinswood in the Vale of Glamorgan belongs to the Cotswold-Severn group of such monuments. The chamber, which is covered by the largest capstone in Britain, was originally enclosed within a trapezoidal mound with projecting wings that created a forecourt, probably used for ritual purposes. Over 900 fragments of human bone, from at least fifty individuals, were recovered in and around the chamber.

Wales has over a hundred known megalithic tombs. The variety in their construction suggests that by the middle of the Neolithic period there were in Wales a number of regional cultures. In the south-east, tombs such as those at Tinkinswood and St Lythans in the Vale of Glamorgan have affinities with those in neighbouring English counties and belong to the so-called Cotswold-Severn group. Those of the western coastlands are more various, but the most assured are the 'portal dolmens' with high stone doorways and huge capstones like the tomb at Tan y Muriau on Llŷn and those at Dyffryn Ardudwy south of Harlech. Such tombs are related to those in south-east Ireland, while the magnificent passage grave at Barclodiad y Gawres (The Giantess's Apron) on the island of Anglesey resembles the great tombs of the Boyne Valley in Ireland. The distribution of the Anglesey, Llŷn, Merioneth, Pembrokeshire and Vale of Glamorgan tombs indicates that their builders were accustomed to sailing the western sea routes. The remarkable group of tombs in upland Breconshire, tombs lacking a marine context, raise fascinating issues.

The tombs were used for communal burial. Tinkinswood contained parts of at least fifty individuals, too many to have been fitted into the tomb all at the same time, and suggesting that it had been used as a depository for elements of skeletons that had been defleshed elsewhere. Some tombs may have been in use for generations, while others were open for a far briefer span of time. That at Nicholaston in Gower provided no access after the construction of the mound, indicating that it been built for a single interment.

The face of one of those buried at Penywyrlod near Talgarth has been reconstructed; if alive today, his handsome features would make him very welcome as a son-in-law. Yet, to call the structures tombs may be to overstress their funereal role. Bodies were certainly placed in them, but as they were the centres of communal ritual, they had wider functions. Often sited at locations where the cairn dominated the scene, they can be considered to be statements of landownership — 'a sepulchral title deed in stone'.

It is believed that the tombs were the work of fairly egalitarian clans and that the cromlech, to use a more traditional term, was the focus of the life of a community of a few dozen families, although it would have been built through the joint efforts of several such communities. It is estimated that at least two hundred men would have been needed to crown the Tinkinswood cromlech with its capstone — the largest in Britain.

The inventiveness needed at Tinkinswood underlines one of the chief characteristics of human endeavour from the time of the building of the megalithic tombs to the era of the construction of Gothic cathedrals. For millennia, ritual, not necessity, was the mother of invention. Ritual was also the mother of art, for among the earliest evidence in Wales of artistic impulses are the patterns carved on stones at Barclodiad y Gawres.

That less inventiveness was expended on more necessary structures, such as dwellings, is evident from the paucity of evidence of where the cromlech builders lived. A very rare example of a Neolithic dwelling was found at Clegyr-Boia near St Davids, where two huts of timber and daub with wall footings of stone have been excavated. The scarcity of known Neolithic settlements does not in itself mean that our knowledge of them will always be slight, for hardly one in a hundred of the potential sites has as yet been excavated.

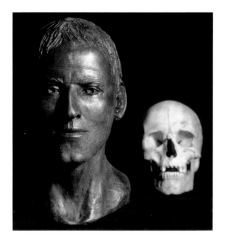

The face of a Neolithic maker of Wales; this facial reconstruction was based upon the skull of a man dating from about 3500 BC excavated at Penywyrlod chambered tomb near Talgarth (© National Museum of Wales).

Barclodiad y Gawres (The Giantess's Apron) is a magnificent passage grave related to similar structures in the Boyne Valley in Ireland. Several of the stones that make up the walls of its chambers are decorated with lightly pecked geometric designs — some of the earliest evidence of artistic impulses found in Wales. The tomb, which is covered by a restored mound, stands in a spectacular coastal location overlooking Trecastell Bay on the island of Anglesey.

THE MAKERS DISCOVER METALS

EARLY AND MIDDLE BRONZE AGE WALES

If the Neolithic period is defined as the era of communities of farmers using stone tools, then it did not come to an end in Wales until well after 2000 BC, when some metal tools probably came to be within reach of the entire population. But there were metal objects in Wales from about 2400 BC onwards — objects made of copper initially, and later, as it was realized that copper is hardened by the addition of tin, objects made of bronze.

The coming of bronze was traditionally believed to mark the settlement of Britain by a new people, the 'Beaker Folk', so called because of the highly distinctive type of pot in use among them. By the later twentieth century, however, views had changed. While archaeologists agree that a different racial type — robust and broad skulled — may be found in many of the burial sites containing beakers, it is now believed that there were no mass invasions; rather were there inward movements of small groups of people which were not sufficiently numerous to threaten the existence of locally established communities. Until fairly recently, the dominant feature of the prehistory of Britain was believed to be a sequence of invasions, for changes in material culture were seen as the result of a succession of migrations. The current tendency is to deprecate the notion of abrupt change and to emphasize the continuance and development of existing society. The increasing number of individual rather than communal burials, however, suggests that by about 2000 BC society was becoming more hierarchical, with a growing distinction between ceremonial and burial sites. Yet communal burial was already in decline in the late Neolithic period, and the existence of henges, especially the early example at Llandegai near Bangor, indicates that the extensive ritual sites of the early Bronze Age had precedents over a thousand years earlier.

In terms of the making of Wales, the main significance of the Bronze Age is that the transformation of the landscape was being continued and intensified. The growing importance of metal tools would have enhanced the domination of people over the landscape, and in Wales evidence for the exploitation of natural mineral resources is increasing with the acknowledgement that the early copper mines on the Great Orme were among the most extensive in Europe, and that the workings on Copa Hill in Cwmystwyth were on a scale and of a sophistication unsuspected a decade or two ago.

In this reconstruction of a cist burial from Brymbo in north-east Wales, the skeleton of an early Bronze Age maker of Wales is seen accompanied by a 'beaker' and a flint flake knife — perhaps symbols of his rank and status in life (© National Museum of Wales).

Opposite: These prominent standing stones at Penrhos Feilw on Holyhead Island, Anglesey, were doubtless of ritual or memorial significance in the Bronze Age landscape.

The landscape of the upper Brenig Valley contains a wide range of Bronze Age cairns, barrows and ritual monuments, forming a cemetery which appears to have been of great significance from about 2000 to 1500 BC. This ring cairn on the edge of the Brenig reservoir was reconstructed after excavation (© Mick Sharp Photography).

Much new evidence serves to strengthen the belief that the landscape was more highly developed and that society was more structured than was previously believed. Above all, population densities were probably much greater; indeed, they may well have been a hundred times higher than the levels suggested a generation ago. Population growth puts pressure on land. In the favourable climate of the early and middle Bronze Age (about 2400 to 1200 BC) new settlements could be created by pushing cultivation up to ever higher altitudes. Today, it seems incredible that cereals had once been grown near the source of the river Brenig in the Hiraethog Mountains over 1,600 feet (500m) above sea level; yet pollen analysis shows that wheat and barley were harvested there in the middle Bronze Age. The upland settlements where the crops were grown were abandoned as a result of the deteriorating climate of the late Bronze and early Iron Ages, and the monuments their inhabitants created have therefore survived relatively unscathed. This is also true of the high ground above the coastal fringe of Merioneth (in Ardudwy, and on the slopes of Cadair Idris), in the valleys of Breconshire and on the Glamorgan ridges. Thus an appreciation of the work of the Bronze Age makers of Wales means visiting sites on the high moorland. Dartmoor has been described as a complete Bronze Age landscape. The same could be said of many areas of upland Wales.

The upper Brenig Valley offers the finest display, partly because detailed work in the mid-1970s, prior to the creation of the Brenig reservoir, uncovered almost the totality of the monuments. This underlines a fundamental fact about archaeology: what we know depends not upon what there is, but upon where we have looked. In other parts of Wales — the Garn Fawr and Strumble Head area of Pembrokeshire, for example — the little work that has been done suggests an even greater richness of prehistoric monuments than was found in the Brenig Valley, but the full exploration of that richness may be a task that will have to be left for future generations.

As with chambered tombs, many cairns were located in places where they dominate the landscape. This is evident in the Kerry Hills, the moors above the Elan Valley and Mynyddoedd y Preseli, in particular Foeldrygarn, where three large cairns stand out against the sky. Some Bronze Age memorials are marked by tall, isolated monoliths up to 13 feet (4m) high — at Cefn Graeanog near Llanllyfni, for example, or at Battle near Brecon. Concentrations of such standing stones — sometimes, but not always, in conjunction with burials — have a distribution pattern which provides further evidence of Bronze Age upland settlement. In terms of standing stones, Wales has nothing to offer comparable with the astonishing remains at Carnac in Brittany where there are almost 3,000 menhirs. Nevertheless, the circle of twenty stones at Cerrig Duon near the source of the Tawe or that of sixteen stones at Gors Fawr in Mynyddoedd y Preseli offer an evocative experience to the seekers of the Bronze Age makers of Wales.

Yet, the apparent richness of evidence from the uplands can distort our understanding of the density of prehistoric settlement. More evidence survives in the uplands because the intensive agriculture practiced in the lowlands has obliterated there the immediately recognizable signs of the labour of prehistoric, and indeed of later, peoples. The increasingly sophisticated methods available by the later twentieth century, in particular aerial photography and geophysical surveying, have revolutionized the study of prehistoric lowland settlement. That is particularly true of the recent work on the fertile lowlands of Walton near New Radnor, where a wealth of monuments extending from the Neolithic period to the Middle Ages has been discovered. Bronze Age Walton may have been one of the most densely populated areas of Wales, a notion which gains credibility from the admirable interpretation of the site exhibited at the Radnorshire Museum in Llandrindod.

Some interpreters of Bronze Age communities have argued that, by about 2000 BC, much of southern Britain consisted of a series of quasi-states with clearly defined borders. Great monuments such as Silbury Hill and Stonehenge suggest that the most powerful of such states were located on the Downs of Wessex. The eighty bluestones at Stonehenge were conveyed there from Mynyddoedd y Preseli, suggesting perhaps that the mountains had mystical significance. Recent work at Carn Menyn may have pinpointed the exact origin of the bluestones.

Wales offers virtually no evidence of human settlements of the early and middle Bronze Ages, although it is possible that burial cairns were constructed over what had previously been habitations. The closest we can get to the domestic life of Wales's Bronze Age people is their burnt mounds — stones used to heat pools in which meat was probably cooked, although the pools may have been the Bronze Age equivalent of a sauna. Among the best examples are those east of Clynnog-fawr and on Cefn Bryn in Gower. But if evidence of the settlements of the people of the early and mid-Bronze Age is rare, that would not be the case in the following era, an era that has produced plentiful evidence of the dwelling places of the inhabitants of Wales.

Tools and weapons made of bronze became increasingly common in Wales from about 2000 BC. This example of an early Bronze Age 'flanged' axe comes from Kilgwrrwg, near Chepstow (Newport Museum and Art Gallery).

Saith Maen, an impressive row of seven stones, stands high on a mountainside above the valley of the river Tawe. Many of the Bronze Age monuments of upland Wales have survived relatively undisturbed since the deteriorating climate of the late Bronze and early Iron Age led to the abandonment of once fertile regions (© Crown: Royal Commission on the Ancient and Historical Monuments of Wales, DI2006_0772RI).

THE MAKERS CREATE FORTIFICATIONS

LATE BRONZE AGE AND IRON AGE WALES

Hillforts, far and away the most impressive constructions of the prehistoric makers of Wales, were considered until recently to belong to the last few centuries of prehistory. They were believed to have been constructed by the Celtic peoples who, it was claimed, had colonized Britain from about 600 BC onwards and that they represent new defence methods necessitated by the use of iron weapons. Once again, radiocarbon dating has brought about a revolution, and it is now accepted that the earliest hillforts predate the alleged Celtic colonization and the Iron Age by several hundred years. It is undeniable that a Celtic language or languages were widely spoken in southern Britain in the last centuries of the pre-Christian era, but, in conformity with the rejection of the notion of mass invasion and abrupt change, the present tendency is to consider that Britain became Celtic in speech as a result of what has been described as 'culminative Celticity' rather than mass migration.

The need for elaborate defences was probably the result of climatic change. In the centuries after about 1250 BC, average annual temperatures fell by up to 2 degrees Celsius, ushering in the Sub-Atlantic climatic period by 650 BC which has lasted until today. The change led to a shortening of the growing season, particularly at higher altitudes. Heavier rainfall brought about increased flooding in the lowlands; marshes multiplied and alluvial changes occurred in river valleys. Peat formation further undermined the viability of upland communities. Communities faced with a contraction in their agricultural land are likely to assert their territorial rights by building fortifications to defend them. The back-breaking toil involved in constructing the greater hillforts of Wales points to the existence of hierarchical societies having leaders with the power to force others to labour for them. The distribution of hillforts indicates a movement away from the higher altitudes to the margins of river valleys, locations convenient for the exploitation of fertile lowlands and for a continued but less intense use of the uplands.

There are almost six hundred hillforts in Wales, over a fifth of the British total. They vary greatly in design and size, and it may be indiscriminating to use the same term to denote all of them. While some great hillfort defences were designed to withstand actual attacks, evidence suggests that many more were intended simply to intimidate neighbours and ward off potential attacks

Opposite: The hillfort of Tre'r Ceiri, near the summit of Yr Eifl, on the Llŷn Peninsula in north-west Wales. It is one of the country's most remarkable prehistoric sites, and a superb testament to the Iron Age makers of Wales (© Crown: Royal Commission on the Ancient and Historical Monuments of Wales, AP_2007_0224).

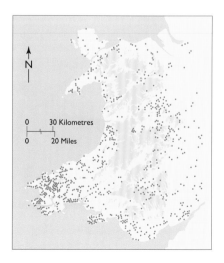

The distribution of late Bronze Age and Iron Age hillforts in Wales and the borders.

through the appearance of impregnability. A fifth of the surface area of Moel y Gaer on Halkyn Mountain has been stripped, revealing roundhouses dating from around 800 BC; some two hundred years later, a further group of roundhouses was built, together with a number of rectangular buildings. Many hillforts offer evidence of such storage facilities, which may have been used by dominant elites to gather in and redistribute the local food surplus, roles which would have added to their power. Surveys of others of the great hillforts of the north-east, particularly those on the Clwydian Hills, have given rise to the belief that each fort was the focal point of a well-defined area. Several of the Clwydian hillforts have yielded groups of roundhouses; indeed, some, in particular Moel y Gaer on Halkyn Mountain, contained streets of houses laid out almost on town-planning principles, proof that the economy in the last centuries of prehistory, in some parts of Wales at least, was capable of sustaining semi-urban communities

North-east Wales has the greatest concentration of large hillforts, but it is the north-west that contains the country's most remarkable prehistoric hilltop fortification. That is Tre'r Ceiri near the summit of Yr Eifl, 14 miles (22km) south-west of Caernarfon. Its surrounding wall still stands up to 13 feet (4m) high, and within it are the ruins of over 150 stone dwellings; some of them belong to the Roman period, although the settlement's origins are dated to about 200 BC. In the south-west, Garn Goch, near Llangadog, is a spectacular stone-walled settlement; even more remarkable is Foeldrygarn in Pembrokeshire, where the three massive Bronze Age cairns already mentioned are enclosed within a large Iron Age fort. However, the prevalent pattern in the south-west is a multiplicity of smaller forts; the area has over 150 which are little more than 1.5 acres (0.5ha) in extent. Among the smaller hillforts of the south-west is Castell Henllys, east of Nevern, a well-fortified site containing reconstructed huts. The most dramatic of the smaller forts are the cliff castles or promontory forts, formed of sometimes quite massive dykes and ditches across coastal promontories and often occupied

Roundhouses at the small hillfort of Castell Henllys, near Nevern, where an Iron Age settlement has been recreated as an exercise in experimental archaeology (© Mick Sharp Photography).

Above: Llyn Fawr above the Rhondda was one of several lakes in Wales which appear to have been of sacred significance to the Iron Age makers of Wales. A hoard of iron and bronze objects was discovered in peat deposits at the site (© Crown Copyright (2009) Visit Wales).

Right: One of the earliest and rarest iron objects found in Wales is this sword fragment from the Llyn Fawr hoard of metalwork (© National Museum of Wales).

Not all the settlement sites of late Bronze Age and Iron Age Wales show up as hillfort enclosures. This 'cropmark' at Rhiwau, near Llawhaden in Pembrokeshire, shows the line of a small defended inner enclosure, perhaps occupied by a farmstead. The surrounding larger outer enclosure may represent the 'home fields' or a protected stockyard (© Crown: Royal Commission on the Ancient and Historical Monuments of Wales, 955010-58).

for many centuries. Perhaps the most remarkable is at Flimston, west of St Govan's Head, where the fort is perilously poised above vertiginous cliffs. The Iron Age was a time of regional contrasts in settlement types, and adaptation to the different landscapes of Wales. Very rare timber-built Iron Age rectangular buildings were unearthed in recent years on the intertidal mudflats of the Gwent Levels at Goldcliff. Containing animal stalls and cattle hoofprints, these prehistoric byres are thought to represent a seasonal practice of cattle movement down from the hills to graze coastal pastures.

Several of the large hillforts have yielded evidence that iron was smelted and worked within their confines. One of the earliest iron objects found in Wales is a sword dating from about 700 BC, discovered in Llyn Fawr above the Rhondda. It was probably thrown into the lake as a votive offering, for the inhabitants of Iron Age Wales found sanctity in lakes and rivers rather than in people-made ritual structures. Objects found at Llyn Cerrig Bach in Anglesey include metalwork decorated with La Tène motifs, an art form associated with the finest flowering of Iron Age Celtic culture. About 150 pieces of metal were recovered from the lake; some were of bronze, but many were of iron — slave chains, farmers' tools and plain bars of metal among them.

The availability of iron led to the manufacture of iron axes capable of felling the hardwoods of the valley bottoms. Pollen evidence from the Ystwyth Valley indicates extensive clearing of the valley floor in the last centuries of prehistory. By then, over half the woodland canopy which had first come into existence in the Mesolithic period had ceased to exist. A folk memory of the clearances may be preserved in the early medieval Welsh story, *Culhwch ac Olwen*: 'Do you see that great thicket out there?… I want it uprooted and burned on the ground down to cinders and ashes for manure; I want it ploughed and sown'.

The size of the Skomer fields, seen here from the air, probably reflects the ploughing methods of the Iron Age makers of Wales (© Crown: Royal Commission on the Ancient and Historical Monuments of Wales, 2001/CS/0664A).

Below: A sketch plan of the Iron Age field boundaries and house sites on the Pembrokeshire island of Skomer.

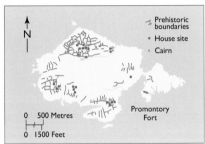

Clearances meant creating fields, such as those that survive on the island of Skomer. There, the stone banks of Iron Age, and possibly earlier, fields are immediately apparent, as are the lynchets — the steps formed when soil loosened by cultivation creeps downhill to pile against a field boundary. Similar tracts of ancient field lynchets and walls, many with their origins in prehistory, survive along the west-facing coastal hills of Wales from St Davids Head and Mynydd Carningli in Pembrokeshire, to the hills of Ardudwy between Barmouth and Harlech and to the mountain slopes above Llanfairfechan in Gwynedd. As on Skomer, the fields are very small. They probably reflect early ploughing methods — the use of the light ard which ripped the soil rather than turning the sod. The Welsh word *cyfair* means the area which can be ploughed in a day, and the so-called 'Celtic fields' may consist of a series of *cyfeiriau*.

The British Iron Age is conventionally considered to span the years from 600 BC to the first century of the Christian era. Yet to seek the terminal date is futile, for so useful has iron proved to be that the Iron Age has continued until today. The technology available to the people of the last centuries of prehistory would be the basis of life for many centuries to come, until indeed the material circumstances of the Welsh people were transformed in the last two hundred years. The makers of late prehistoric Wales were heirs to millennia of social, economic and technological development. And then came the Roman occupation, when Wales, for the first time, creeps into the historical record.

This superb example of late Iron Age Celtic art comes from a collection of metalwork found at Tal-y-llyn, near Dolgellau. The decorative plaque bears a pair of human faces linked by a common neck (© National Museum of Wales).

WALES AND ROME

THE MAKING OF WALES FROM THE FIRST TO THE FOURTH CENTURIES

The Roman invasion of Britain was launched in AD 43. Wales came under attack in AD 47, and a year later Ostorius Scapula and his forces had reached the banks of the Dee. Sources show that north-east Wales was then inhabited by the Deceangli tribe; the north-west and much of central Wales was the home of the Ordovices, while the territory of the Cornovii extended to the central borderlands; the south-west was inhabited by the Demetae and the south-east by the Silures. The five known tribal groupings of Wales had probably been evolving over many centuries.

Within four years of the invasion, the south and east of Britain had become part of the empire, but the campaign to subjugate the inhabitants of Wales was not successfully concluded until AD 78/79. Much of the country had in fact been occupied by AD 60, but it had only been partially garrisoned. The collapse of the Roman plan for the full conquest of Wales at this time was the result of various factors, among them the revolt of Boudicca. The subsequent delay of almost two decades meant the country had to be virtually reconquered in the late 70s. Temporary marching camps constructed by the Roman forces on campaign represent the initial impact made by the Romans upon the land of Wales. One of the earliest was probably at Rhyn Park near Chirk, and its size indicates that a greater military force may have been used to subdue the Deceangli than is suggested by the historic record. Two other impressive examples may be seen at Y Pigwn, east of Llandovery, where a 37-acre (15ha) camp is overlaid by another of 25 acres (10ha).

As the conquest proceeded, more permanent fortifications were constructed. Among the earliest — built in the mid-50s AD — were those built at Clyro and Usk. The most ambitious building project of the Romans in Wales began about AD 74 with the establishment of the legionary fortress at *Isca* (Caerleon). Extending over 50 acres (20ha), the fortress could accommodate up to 6,000 legionaries and in its north-west corner are the only Roman legionary barracks still visible in Europe. Even more impressive is the amphitheatre just outside the walls. About 200 years after its foundation, Caerleon seems to have been largely abandoned, but it proved inspiring even in ruin. In 1188 Gerald of Wales (d. 1223) wrote of it with awe; in 1405, the French forces supporting Owain Glyndŵr allegedly made a detour to visit the amphitheatre, long believed to be King Arthur's Round Table;

The amphitheatre of the Roman legionary fortress of Isca (Caerleon) seen from the air. Situated on the banks of the Usk, the fortress was designed to accommodate up to 6,000 legionaries. In the Middle Ages the amphitheatre was believed to be King Arthur's Round Table (Skyscan Balloon Photography for Cadw).

Opposite: Caerwent, the Roman Venta Silurum, is still encircled by its walls, which stand to an impressive height in many places. The town was the tribal capital of the Silures, the Celtic tribe that had controlled south-east Wales before the arrival of the Romans and had fiercely resisted the invaders.

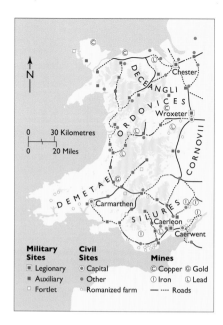

Above: A map of Roman Wales showing all known military sites and the principal civilian settlements and Romanized farmsteads.

This inscribed stone from Goldcliff records that legionary soldiers were involved in building an earthwork on the Gwent Levels, perhaps part of a process of land reclamation (© National Museum of Wales).

Right: This geophysical survey plot of part of Dinefwr Park, near Llandeilo, shows the superimposed outlines of two Roman forts. The larger, outlined in red, was probably established in the AD 70s, but was soon abandoned. The smaller fort, outlined in blue, probably dates from the late first century AD and was occupied longer (National Trust/Stratascan).

Tennyson, when writing *The Idylls of the King*, stayed at Caerleon in order to absorb its atmosphere.

The establishment of the fortress was merely a part of the impact of the Roman Empire upon the lower Usk Valley and south-east Wales. Soon there was a *vicus* (a civil settlement) outside the walls, a quay on the Usk and a *territorium* from which the fortress drew its raw materials. Legionaries may well have transformed the landscape; a stone found at Goldcliff, 3 miles (5km) east of Uskmouth, records that the century of Statorus Maximus built a length of earthwork. Their labour was possibly part of the process of reclaiming and draining the Gwent Levels, work which has produced Wales's supreme example of a handcrafted landscape.

Caerleon was one of the two hubs of the Roman frontier in Wales; the legionary fortress at Chester was the other. They were linked to a network of auxiliary forts, the sites of some of which are yet to be found. The discovery of a sequence of forts in Dinefwr Park, near Llandeilo, created much excitement in 2003, and the increasing realization that the Romans penetrated deeply into what is now Pembrokeshire has led to the belief that a fort may yet be found on the banks of the Western Cleddau. The auxiliary forts were built to accommodate infantry, cavalry or mixed regiments up to 1,000 strong, and were therefore much smaller than the legionary fortresses. A mere 4 acres (1.6ha) was enclosed within the walls of *Segontium* (Caernarfon), a fort which remained occupied until the 390s, long after most of the others had been abandoned. Yet, the auxiliary fort itself was only part of the impact the network had upon the landscape. Many forts

had a *vicus*; there was even one at Tomen-y-mur (Trawsfynydd), the only auxiliary fort in Britain also to have an amphitheatre. Caersws had an extramural temple and bath house; outside *Segontium*, there was Hen Waliau (probably a storehouse for marine supplies), a mithraeum, a guest house, a kiln and a cemetery, and on a hill adjoining Castell Collen (Llandrindod) there were eighteen camps built for training purposes — the largest group in the Roman Empire.

Roads linked the forts and it is perhaps above all as road constructors that the Romans should be remembered among the makers of Wales. Their roads continued to be the vital links between Welsh communities for many centuries after the collapse of their empire; indeed, much of the A48, the chief road across Glamorgan until the coming of the motorway, is superimposed upon its Roman predecessor. Yet, by emphasizing the role of Roman roads, it is possible to imply that a well-developed system of land communication did not exist before their coming. That is misleading, for the Neolithic trader

The characteristic playing-card shape of the Roman auxiliary fort of Segontium is shown in this aerial photograph. Founded in the wake of the Roman conquest of Mona, the Isle of Anglesey, in AD 77 to accommodate up to 1,000 infantrymen, the fort was garrisoned for more than 300 years. The memory of the Romans' presence here on the banks of the river Seiont passed into Welsh legend and it seems to have been consciously invoked by King Edward I when he invested nearby Caernarfon Castle with Roman imperial symbolism.

The Roman forts of Wales were linked by a network of metalled roads. Sarn Helen is the name by which long stretches of the Roman roads of Wales have traditionally been known; this view shows a section of road between Coelbren and Brecon Gaer (© Crown: Royal Commission on the Ancient and Historical Monuments of Wales, DI2008_0320).

The Paulinus inscription at Caerwent provides confirmation that the Roman town was the capital of a civitas. *Its community was self-governing, its officers meeting in an impressive 'town hall' within the centre of the Romanized settlement.*

carrying axes from Graig Lwyd must have trodden a trackway, and some of the Bronze Age standing stones are believed to have marked long-distance routes over high passes. Bwlch y Ddeufaen, the pass which provides access to the lower Conwy Valley, was a veritable prehistoric highway, to judge by the richness of the Neolithic and Bronze Age monuments which adjoin it.

To emphasize Roman achievement in other fields may also be to denigrate the achievements of earlier makers of Wales. Although the industrial activities of the Romans — particularly gold mining at Dolaucothi, tile making at Holt and lead/silver mining at Machen and elsewhere — had implications for the landscape, it should not be believed that they were particularly innovative. Overall technical improvements there may have been, but recent work at Copa Hill in the Ystwyth Valley shows that mine-drainage systems and the exploitation of copper sulphide ores in 2000 BC compared favourably with the mining methods of the Romans.

A true innovation of the Romans in Wales was the town. The territories of the Silures and the Demetae were recognized as self-governing communities (*civitates*) with their own provincial capitals — that of the Silures at *Venta Silurum* (Caerwent) and that of the Demetae at *Moridunum* (Carmarthen). There is no incontrovertible evidence that Carmarthen was a *civitas* capital, but Roman planning left a deep impression upon the landscape, for the boundaries of *Moridunum* can still be discerned in the layout of the modern town. At Caerwent, the town's walls, built apparently in the later third century, still stand up to 16 feet (5m) high, although most of the dressed stone has been removed up to arm's reach. In its heyday, Caerwent had a population of perhaps some 3,000; despite its small size, it had all the appurtenances of a Roman city — a *forum-basilica* complex, bath houses, temples, shops, inns and a number of grand houses with mosaic floors, brightly painted walls and underfloor (hypocaust) heating. By the early twenty-first century, the huge majority of the inhabitants of Wales were town dwellers; thus, in terms of the making of Wales, town making is second only to field making. It is a process which began at Caerwent.

The Roman planned city had its rural counterpart. That was the villa, the centre of an estate — a mansion, Roman in style and comfort. The villas hitherto discovered in Wales are concentrated in southern Monmouthshire and the Vale of Glamorgan, where the fine example at Llantwit Major has been excavated. About two dozen sites in Wales are on occasion described as villas, but most of them are in fact Iron Age farms which have undergone varying degrees of Romanization. Whitton, near Bonvilston, is perhaps the best excavated example. The villa owners were the pioneers of a more progressive agriculture; they introduced capitalist farming, a development assisted by the army's demand for grain. They encouraged heavier ploughing and contributed to the making of Wales by introducing new flora and fauna. It is possible that cultivated oats, apples, cherries, carrots and parsnips were unknown in Wales before the conquest, and it is fairly certain that it was the Romans who introduced turnips, leeks, grapes, walnuts and sweet chestnuts. A less welcome newcomer was the black rat, the carrier of bubonic plague, a creature which must rank high among the unmakers of Wales.

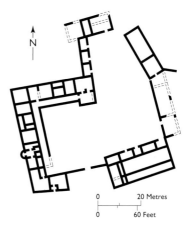

Above: In Wales, villas or mansions in Roman style are known chiefly from the south-east. They served as centres of extensive rural estates. The best known example is that at Llantwit Major in the Vale of Glamorgan.

In the remoter parts of north and west Wales, it would appear that the native inhabitants had only slight and intermittent contact with things Roman. Here at Din Lligwy in Anglesey, although Roman pottery and coins have been found, the settlement and buildings remained essentially late Iron Age in style.

The areas of Wales upon which the imprint of Rome can be clearly discerned constitute a small part of the country. Half a dozen partly Romanized farms have been discovered in the south-west, but in mid- and north Wales the native stone-built hut groups, which are numerous in the uplands of Gwynedd and on Anglesey, are in a tradition which stretches back to the Bronze Age. Nevertheless, these farmsteads could have supplied the Roman army with agricultural produce. Where excavation has taken place, most have yielded a range of Roman pottery and occasionally coins and other artefacts. Such objects have been found at Din Lligwy on Anglesey and at the Breidden hillfort, near Welshpool. However, the hut group at Cors y Gedol in Merioneth, although occupied during the Roman period, has yielded virtually nothing of Roman provenance. It would thus appear that the inhabitants of the remoter parts of Wales had only slight and intermittent contact with things Roman. That would seem to be confirmed by the fact that Romanization was not thorough enough in Wales to ensure that the inhabitants abandoned their native language in favour of that of the conqueror. This is what happened in France, Italy and the Iberian Peninsula, where, after the collapse of the empire, most of the inhabitants are found to be speaking forms of Latin which would evolve into French, Italian, Castilian, Catalan and Portuguese. Although in Wales some knowledge of Latin survived the fall of the Roman Empire, the country's native inhabitants continued to speak Brythonic or British, a Celtic language which would evolve into Welsh.

The face of 'Roman Winter' in Wales: a detail of the 'Seasons' mosaic excavated at the Roman town of Caerwent in 1901 (Newport Museum and Art Gallery).

EARLY CHRISTIAN WALES

THE MAKING OF WALES FROM THE FIFTH TO THE ELEVENTH CENTURIES

The half a millennium following the collapse of the Roman Empire in the west was a vitally formative period for Wales and for the Welsh people. The country came to be geographically defined by the extent of the English conquests; its people were converted to Christianity, and the location of Christian places of worship made a fundamental contribution to the making of Wales; an early form of the Welsh language evolved, the language of the great majority of the place-names of Wales, place-names which are one of the basic building blocks of the country. Wales evolved from a region on the mountainous fringe of a remote Roman province into a recognizable political and cultural entity, an entity heavily influenced by peoples sailing the western sea routes, the Irish and, later, the Vikings among them. Whatever name is given to the immediate post-Roman centuries — early Christian or early medieval (the older 'Dark Ages' which originated during the eighteenth-century Enlightenment has little to recommend it) — the period was crucial in the making of Wales.

The removal of Roman political authority around the end of the fourth century left power in the hands of local rulers or chieftains and their warbands, sometimes reinforced — as in Dyfed, Brycheiniog and Gwynedd — by arrivals from Ireland and, possibly, southern Scotland. In the sixth century, the cleric, Gildas, castigated several of the 'tyrants' in Wales and in south-western England, some of whom were at least second-generation rulers.

The seat of another chieftain or ruler of the period was excavated in the 1950s at Dinas Powys near Cardiff. His settlement was sited on a promontory defended by earth-and-rubble ramparts and ditches cut into the bedrock. The only evidence found of buildings revealed that they were of timber, and were essentially unimpressive. But the ruler of Dinas Powys was able to provide his followers with feasts of beef and pork, no doubt tribute taken from the peasantry in return for his 'protection'. He and his retainers enjoyed the contents of amphorae filled with wine and olive oil brought through Mediterranean and Atlantic trading networks from Asia Minor and the Aegean. At feasts, the chieftain was able to use tableware from what is now the west coast of Turkey, from Tunisia and from western France, together with glass beakers also imported from France. His jeweller produced fine metalwork, including brooches decorated with enamel and millefiori glass.

The seat of an early Christian chieftain is known at Dinas Powys near Cardiff. These fragments of glass from the site were imports from mainland Europe (© National Museum of Wales).

Opposite: The removal of Roman political authority at the end of the fourth century left power in early Christian Wales in the hands of local rulers or chieftains. The rock of Dinas Emrys in Snowdonia, the bluff seen at the centre of this view, appears to have been the seat of one of these rulers. Excavations have revealed evidence of a defended site occupied in the fifth and sixth centuries.

The importance of woodland management in early medieval Wales is reflected in the contents of Welsh lawbooks. This illustration of trees represents coppicing (left) and lopping (right), and comes from a thirteenth-century manuscript (By permission of The National Library of Wales, Peniarth Ms. 28, f. 22).

In the porch at Llanwnnws church, Cardiganshire, there is an early Christian inscribed stone. The church site may well be ancient, and now stands in splendid isolation. There was once perhaps a surrounding bond village which has disappeared (© Crown: Royal Commission on the Ancient and Historical Monuments of Wales, 95-CS-0437).

Similar imported amphorae and glass are known from other fortified seats of early Welsh chieftains — at Hen Gastell in western Glamorgan, for example, and at Deganwy at the mouth of the river Conwy, the traditional stronghold of Maelgwn Gwynedd (d. 547), one of the rulers castigated by Gildas.

The sources suggest that Wales had a more impoverished society in the immediate post-Roman centuries than it had had in the Iron Age. Metalworking continued, as at Dinas Powys, but there is no suggestion that masterpieces similar to those of the La Tène era were created. No attempt was made to construct anything on the scale of the prehistoric hillforts. Dinas Powys, for example, is some 2.5 acres (1ha) in extent; the larger of the two Iron Age forts at Garn Goch, covers 27 acres (11ha). The decline in material culture in the fifth century is generally ascribed to the collapse of the economy following the downfall of the Roman Empire and to the ravages caused by barbarian attacks. There is some evidence of other adversities, including plague epidemics and a deterioration in the climate. Yet, as pollen studies do not suggest a massive return of woodland, the inhabitants of early Christian Wales were at least capable of maintaining the open spaces won by their predecessors over the millennia. Domesday Book, which provides details of the settlement pattern in parts of the Welsh borderland in 1086, implies that only 16 per cent of what became eastern Flintshire consisted of forested land.

Some nineteenth-century historians maintained that early Christian Wales was inhabited by semi-nomadic people and known sites of permanent settlement belonging to the era are scarce because they hardly existed. Topographical studies and analysis of the documentary evidence — in particular the earliest substrata of the Welsh lawbooks — have led to a different conclusion. Society did have a limited nomadic element, for in late spring a proportion of the population moved with their flocks and herds from the *hendref* (the winter home) to the *hafod* (the summer home). The shape of the *cantrefi* (hundreds) — in Glamorgan, for example — indicates the essential unity of highland and lowland. A society which practises transhumance is not necessarily nomadic, for it can have settled roots in the lowlands. A nomadic society does not grow crops. The querns (hand mills) found at sites such as Dinas Powys, Dinas Emrys and Dinorben prove that grain was an integral part of the diet, and lynchets created by post-Roman ploughing have been discovered adjoining the hut group at Tŷ Mawr, near Holyhead.

The Welsh countryside today is generally a landscape of dispersed settlement, but that may not always have been the case. The lawbooks discuss the responsibility of a householder if fire spreads from his house to that of a neighbour, an indication of the existence of nucleated settlements. It is now believed that the majority of the inhabitants of Wales in the immediate post-Roman centuries, and, indeed, in the Roman and immediate pre-Roman centuries, were *taeogion* — unfree cultivators of the soil — and that the free population — the *bonheddwyr* (those with *bon* or honourable ancestry) — would not constitute a significant proportion of the population for centuries to come. The *taeogion* dwelt in *taeogdrefi* (bond villages), where they worked under the direction of the *maer* to supply food rents for their masters. Some of the older churches may well have been built in the centre of *taeogdrefi*. A note in the margin of the eighth-century *Lichfield Gospels*, which were on the altar of the church at Llandeilo Fawr in the early ninth century mentions Gwaun Henllan (The Meadow of the Old Church). The church referred to is that of Llandybie; the church of St Tybïe is located at the centre of a substantial village, but many of the ancient church sites of Wales now stand in splendid isolation, indicative, perhaps, of the decay and disappearance of the bond villages which once surrounded them. This suggests that medieval settlement patterns had roots going back to the Iron Age, and it has been argued that continuity in settlement is far greater than most historians have been prepared to admit.

Continuity in settlement is indicated by the location of the religious centres established by the early leaders of Welsh Christianity. St Illtud settled near the Roman villa at Llantwit Major (Llanilltud Fawr), and St Dochdwy near that at Llandough. Churches came to be built adjoining Roman structures at Caerleon, Caerwent, Carmarthen, Caerhun, Gelligaer, *Segontium* and elsewhere. From the sixth or seventh centuries, the Welsh Church became predominantly monastic, though it is important to remember that it was an integral part of Christendom. The old term 'Celtic Church' is misleading, since it can imply that the Welsh Church was in some way separate from the wider Christian faith. The layout of the religious houses of early Christian Wales is likely to have followed the tradition of the eastern Mediterranean and the monasteries were therefore eremitic (the monks living separately) rather than coenobitic (the monks living in a community) — the pattern which came to characterize the monastic life of Latin Europe. The monastery

The eighth-century Lichfield Gospels, *also known as the* Book of St Teilo *or the* Gospels of St Chad, *were in the possession of the church of Llandeilo Fawr in the ninth and tenth centuries. Numerous marginal notations not only provide valuable information about the possessions of the church and its surroundings, but also constitute early evidence of written Welsh (Dean and Chapter of Lichfield Cathedral, Ms. 1).*

From the sixth or seventh centuries, the Welsh Church became predominantly monastic. The parish church at Llantwit Major (Llanilltud Fawr) preserves the memory of the important monastery of St Illtud (© Crown Copyright (2009) Visit Wales).

Opposite: The late ninth- or early tenth-century Cross of Conbelin is the largest and most elaborate of such Welsh disc-headed slabs. Both faces of the cross and all four sides of the base are richly decorated and a Latin inscription records that 'Conbelin set up this cross'. It is one of several early crosses and inscribed stones from Margam and the immediate vicinity, and their concentration indicates that Margam was an important Christian centre long before the foundation of the Cistercian monastery there in the twelfth century. These important early carved stones have been collected together in the Margam Stones Museum.

would probably have consisted of a church surrounded by the cells of individual monks. As the buildings were made of wood, pre-Norman church buildings of Wales have left no readily detectable trace. The monastery of St Illtud at Llantwit Major and that of St Cadog at Llancarfan were among the most important. In northern Powys, St Tysilio presided over the monastery at Meifod; the present-day 5.4-acre (2.2ha) Meifod churchyard occupies the site, which served as the necropolis of the kings of Powys. Other churchyards — Llandeilo Fawr, Llanynys, Clynnog-fawr, Llangurig and Glascwm — also represent the sites of ancient monasteries.

The chief tangible remains of early Christian Wales are its inscribed and sculptured stones. There are over 500 of them dating from the fifth to the eleventh centuries. The earliest of them, which probably marked graves — some 140 in all — demonstrate clear links with both Ireland and with Christian communities in mainland Europe. Some, particularly those erected in the south-west, bear inscriptions in Old Irish, written in the ogam script — a lettering system of straight or diagonal lines cut at the angles of stones. Other stones carry the Latin *filius*, 'son of', important in a tribal society where genealogy and ancestry were of paramount importance. A stone from Penmachno claims to have been put up in the time of the Roman consul Justinus, whose consulship in AD 540 was used in the Lyon area of France as the baseline for a dating system. Among the most appealing of Wales's early inscribed stones is that at Llangadwaladr church in Anglesey, where King Cadfan of Gwynedd, who died around 625, is described as 'the wisest and most renowned of all kings' (*Catamanus Rex sapientissimus opinatissimus omnium regum*). Later stones usually lacked inscriptions, bearing as they did no more than a simple cross. From the eighth century onwards more elaborate crosses came to be erected. These include the monument erected in the ninth century near Llangollen in memory of King Eliseg of Powys, who died in the later eighth century. Towards the end of the first Christian millennium Wales was endowed with a series of remarkable stone crosses which were skilfully carved with interlacing patterns and with figural scenes indicative of contacts with Ireland and the Vikings and, to a lesser extent, with Anglo-Saxon England.

The concentrations of monuments at major Christian centres such as Llantwit Major, St Davids, Llanbadarn Fawr and Margam (where the stones museum, established in 1932, is under Cadw's care) suggest that most of them were erected under the auspices of churches. Some of them commemorate secular figures. Llantwit Major, which is believed to have been the necropolis of the royal house of Glywysing, has several memorials to secular rulers, including one to King Rhys, which was erected by his son, Hywel, who died in 886. The crosses at Penally, Nevern, and Carew (all in Pembrokeshire) represent the apogee of the art of the early Welsh stone carvers; those at Nevern and Carew are by the same sculptor. While elaborately carved stones are rarer in the north, that known as Maen Achwyfan at Whitford in Flintshire, with its pagan Scandinavian iconography, is indicative of Viking settlement in the area.

Carved stone monuments offer some evidence of the whereabouts of Welsh rulers after death, but little has come to light concerning their

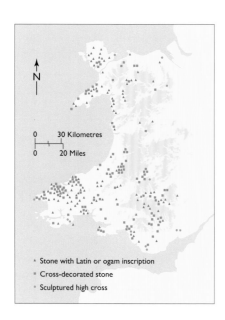

N

0 — 30 Kilometres

0 — 20 Miles

* Stone with Latin or ogam inscription
* Cross-decorated stone
* Sculptured high cross

The distribution of early Christian inscribed and decorated stones in Wales.

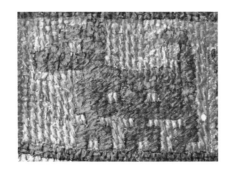

A reconstruction of a fine ninth-century textile associated with the crannog in Llangorse Lake. It seems to have been part of a woman's dress (© National Museum of Wales).

The artificial island or crannog in Llangorse Lake was the probable seat of the kings of Brycheiniog around AD 900.

whereabouts when they were alive. The hillforts at Dinas Powys and Deganwy provide information about the dwellings of the Welsh rulers of the immediate post-Roman period, but evidence for later centuries is very slight. Of the major kingdoms of early medieval Wales, tradition maintains that the ancestral seat of the dynasty of Gwynedd was at Aberffraw, of Powys at Mathrafal and of Deheubarth at Dinefwr. Excavations at Mathrafal have as yet proved disappointing; the royal seat at Aberffraw may have been built over as late as the 1950s, and the original Dinefwr seat may lie beneath the later stone castle. Thus, virtually nothing can be said about the residences of rulers such as Rhodri Mawr (d. 877), Hywel Dda (d. 949/950) and Maredudd ab Owain (d. 999). Work on the site of the seat of the kings of Brycheiniog — the crannog at Llangorse Lake — is proving to be more promising; woven fabric from the site suggests that the royal house of Brycheiniog enjoyed a sophisticated material culture. The crannog is located on an island in the lake, where the water is little more than 3 feet (1m) deep. The island, which was connected to the shore by a causeway, was artificially extended by piling soil upon a timber-and-wattle-framed raft and was enclosed by a palisade. Tree-ring studies suggest that considerable work was undertaken

on the site between about 860 and 910. The crannog is the only one as yet discovered in Wales and is similar to many of those in Ireland. Thus, it seems likely that links between Ireland and Brycheiniog, for which there is considerable evidence from the fifth and sixth centuries, were still significant four hundred years later.

Although landscape evidence relating to the activities of the early rulers of Wales is slight, other evidence indicates that the dynasties to which they belonged were remarkably stable and were powerful enough to ensure that the Vikings, who occupied large parts of Ireland, Scotland and England, only succeeded in establishing minor colonies in Wales. Among Wales's most intriguing settlements of the last years of the first Christian millennium and the early years of the second is that at Llanbedrgoch in Anglesey, where excavations from the mid-1990s onwards have revealed what is widely believed to be evidence of a Viking presence — perhaps intermittent — from the late ninth to the late eleventh century.

By far the chief visible tribute to the power of the Welsh rulers is Offa's Dyke, the most impressive monument constructed in Britain in the second half of the first Christian millennium. The dyke, built under the aegis of Offa, king of Mercia from 757 to 796, was an admission that the English were unlikely to be able to extend their power to Wales. If the entire earthworks traditionally known as Offa's Dyke are considered integral parts of a single concept — an assumption contested by many archaeologists — then Offa's intention was to provide Mercia with a well-defined boundary from Prestatyn to Chepstow, a distance of 150 miles (240km). The dyke is a series of sections rather than a continuous line; there is a gap at its northern end, natural barriers such as rivers were used on occasion, and, in the south, the earthworks are short stretches, particularly in those areas where English settlement had penetrated the natural forest of the region. In total, the earthworks represent a barrier 80 miles (130km) in length.

At its most impressive, Offa's Dyke is up to 20 feet (6m) high. It can be seen at its best near Chirk, where its course coincides with the present border between Wales and England. Almost equally striking is the stretch east of Montgomery, where again the dyke marks the present border, and that around Knighton, where there is an admirable dyke interpretation centre.

When constructed, Offa's Dyke broadly denoted an ethnic frontier that had been in existence for at least a century. The frontier did not prove to be stable, for the Anglo-Saxons penetrated westwards across it into Powys and may have established a settlement at Rhuddlan. Gruffudd ap Llywelyn (d. 1063), the only ruler to win authority over the whole of Wales, penetrated eastwards across the dyke and won extensive territories, particularly in the north-east. Yet, during Gruffudd's reign, other forces were gathering strength. In 1053, Ralph, the Norman nephew of the English king, Edward the Confessor (1042–66), became a powerful figure in Herefordshire. He built earthwork castles in the county, an activity hitherto unknown in Anglo-Saxon England. One of them was at Womaston, south of Presteigne, less than 110 yards (100m) west of the present Wales–England border; it was to prove to be a fateful act.

A coin of Offa (757–96), the Anglo-Saxon king of Mercia who undertook to define his frontier with neighbouring Welsh kingdoms through the construction of what has long been known as 'Offa's Dyke' (© National Museum of Wales).

Assuming that all the sections which bear his name were raised under the aegis of Offa of Mercia, the king was responsible for a total of 80 miles (130km) of dyke. This section is near Chirk Castle. The dyke played an important part in shaping the perception of the extent and identity of Wales (© Crown: Royal Commission on the Ancient and Historical Monuments of Wales).

THE IMPACT OF THE NORMANS

THE MAKING OF WALES 1070–1170

In the making of Wales, the contribution of the Normans was among the most enduring. The aggressive impulses of the Anglo-Saxons had ebbed away by the time they reached the Welsh uplands. Those of the Normans did not, for the Normans, perhaps more than any other of the peoples of medieval Europe, were colonists by instinct and inheritance.

During the tenth century, the Anglo-Saxon kingdom of England attained a remarkable degree of consolidation, and, following his victory at Hastings in 1066, King William I (1066–87) won such mastery over it that, within twenty years of his accession, he was able to order the compilation of Domesday Book — a detailed survey of landholders and landholding in England and some Welsh border territories — proof of the thoroughness of the Norman Conquest. Power in Wales was far more decentralized, and destroying the power of the native Welsh dynasties proved a protracted and piecemeal business. Initiated by border lords, but increasingly undertaken by the Norman kings and their Angevin successors, the process took over two hundred years.

The long conflict left a profound impress upon the landscape of Wales. The key to the advance of the Normans in Wales was the castle. Their aggression took the form of a four-pronged attack — upon Gwent from Hereford, upon Powys and Deheubarth from Shrewsbury, upon Gwynedd from Chester and upon the kingdom of Morgannwg from across the Severn Estuary, and in each case the aggressors sought to convert victory into permanent domination through the construction of castles.

William fitz Osbern (d. 1071) and his son Roger, during their brief tenure of the earldom of Hereford (1067–75), proved to be vigorous commissioners of castles. Among their castles were those at Monmouth and Chepstow, the keys to the fitz Osberns' conquest of the kingdom of Gwent. The early Norman castles were of the motte-and-bailey or ringwork variety and built using earth and timber. A ringwork consisted of a bank and ditch enclosing a circular area containing wooden buildings, while a motte-and-bailey castle was an earthen mound, surrounded by a ditch and with an adjoining fortified bailey. Some of Wales's most imposing stone castles — Kidwelly, Laugharne and Llansteffan among them — were originally ringworks. The motte at Cardiff was located within the one-time Roman fort; almost 36 feet (11m) high, it was the largest

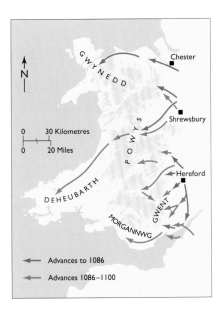

Early Norman aggression in Wales took the form of attacks on several fronts from bases on the Welsh border, and from across the Severn Estuary.

Opposite: The Norman great tower at Chepstow Castle was long believed to have been built by William fitz Osbern (d. 1071), who established the castle on the limestone cliffs above the river Wye to command the lowest crossing point into Wales. However, recent research indicates that his stronghold was probably constructed of earth and timber, and that the stone-built tower was raised at the command of one of the early Norman kings, perhaps William the Conqueror (1066–87) himself.

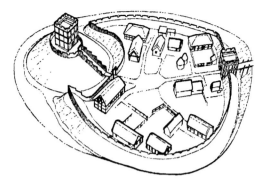

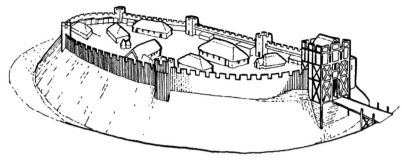

Above: Most of the early Norman castles in Wales were of the motte-and-bailey variety. The motte was a great earthen mound, topped with a tower of wood. It was surrounded by a ditch, with an adjoining fortified bailey.

Above right: The Normans also erected ringwork castles — a substantial bank and surrounding ditch enclosing an area which contained wooden buildings.

The distribution of earthwork castles (mottes and ringworks) in Wales.

motte built in Wales. Most of Wales's two hundred and more mottes were less than half that height, but even lower structures could overawe and provide permanent evidence of the might of the conqueror. Each motte was topped by a tower built of wood, a material chosen partly because a freshly raised mound cannot bear the weight of masonry, and partly because a timber structure can be erected cheaply and rapidly — a motte-and-bailey castle could be completed in as little as eight days. However, one of the Norman castles in Wales was a stone construction almost from its inception. By the late eleventh century, the narrow ridge above the Wye at Chepstow had been crowned, not by a wooden tower, but by a stone-built hall-keep. Its style is very similar to broadly contemporary work in Normandy, such as the hall-keep at Falaise, the birthplace of William the Conqueror. Indeed, while the original earthwork castle at Chepstow was probably commissioned by fitz Osbern, the hall-keep may have been built at the command of King William himself.

Initially it seemed as if the invasion would rapidly bring the whole of Wales under the control of the Normans. Even Gwynedd, protected by the ramparts of Snowdonia, seemed ripe for conquest, for the Normans swept across it and constructed an impressive motte at Aberlleiniog, at the south-eastern extremity of Anglesey. However, the invaders had overreached themselves, for, as a result of the Welsh risings of the 1090s, their sphere of influence in the north came to be restricted to a narrow strip along the estuary of the Dee. In mid-Wales, their losses were even more striking, for there the Welsh successes culminated in 1095 with the capture of Old Montgomery Castle (Hen Domen), the launch pad of the invasion of Powys. The rising was almost as successful in the south-west, where the Normans were driven from all their strongholds with the significant exception of their castle at Pembroke. Parts of the south-east were also convulsed with revolt, but there the insurgents failed to capture the castles.

The success of the Welsh uprising, although not complete, forced the Normans to conclude that, unless they devoted disproportionate resources to the subjection of Wales, they would have to be content to permit Welsh rulers to hold sway over much of the country. Thus, the twelfth century saw the emergence of three zones in Wales. The north-eastern borderlands around Hawarden and Mold, the vicinities of Montgomery and Radnor, the lower Wye and Usk Valleys, the Vale of Glamorgan, Gower, the area south of Carmarthen, and southern Pembrokeshire were all firmly under Anglo-Norman domination. Gwynedd, Powys, Ceredigion and Ystrad Tywi (most of the later Carmarthenshire)

continued under Welsh dynasties. In between lay the upper Wye, the uplands of Brycheiniog, Gwent and Glamorgan, and northern Pembrokeshire, areas over which the Anglo-Normans exercised spasmodic control.

The regions firmly under Anglo-Norman control became known as *Marchia Wallie* (the March of Wales); those under Welsh rule were *Pura Wallia*, while the intermediate areas were part sometimes of the one *Wallia* and sometimes of the other. The division had implications for the making of Wales. Although the rulers of *Pura Wallia* began to build castles — Trallwng (Welshpool), near the later Powis Castle, built by Cadwgan ap Bleddyn by 1111, was perhaps the earliest of them — *Marchia Wallie* was the true domain of the castle, at least in the century following the launching of the Norman invasions. Little now remains of the fortified buildings erected in Wales during that century. The vast majority of the castles built in Wales and its borders never consisted of anything more than wooden structures. As their timber has long rotted away, they feature on the landscape as earthworks rather than as buildings. A minority — those which developed administrative and domestic roles as well as a long-term military function — were rebuilt in stone. Thus, a stone shell keep — a rare structure in Wales — had taken the place of the wooden tower at Cardiff, at least by 1158, when it was attacked by Ifor Bach; Gerald of Wales (born in 1145) spent his boyhood within the stone walls of Manorbier Castle, and Rhys ap Gruffudd (the Lord Rhys, d. 1197) had by 1174 erected a castle of 'masonry and mortar'

The earliest documentary reference to Manorbier Castle in Pembrokeshire dates from 1146. The earliest masonry structures at the site could belong to this period, though the curtain walls probably date from about 1230.

Cardiff Castle was planted by King William I in 1081 during his only visit to Wales on what was ostensibly a pilgrimage to St Davids. The timber fortifications atop the motte had been replaced by a stone shell keep by 1158. The existing gate tower was added to the keep around 1300.

By 1165, Cardigan had passed into the hands of Rhys ap Gruffudd (d. 1197), the Lord Rhys, ruler of the principality of Deheubarth. He encouraged the growth of the borough and rebuilt the castle in stone. According to tradition, the castle was the location of the first eisteddfod, held under the patronage of the Lord Rhys in 1176. In this aerial view of Cardigan, the castle appears as the green mound in the foreground and the medieval core of Cardigan clusters tightly around it (© Crown: Royal Commission on the Ancient and Historical Monuments of Wales, 99/CS/1023).

at Cardigan. Little of the building work which would have been familiar to Ifor Bach, Gerald and Rhys is now visible, for, in the late twelfth and the thirteenth century, strategically placed castles were subjected to vast programmes of rebuilding.

As well as being the domain of the castle, *Marchia Wallie* was also the first region of Wales to experience the rebirth of the town. There is some evidence to suggest that the origins of the urban settlement at Monmouth may lie in the pre-Conquest period when it was part of the Welsh kingdom of Gwent. In about 921 the Anglo-Saxons established the short-lived burh of Clwydmouth (Cledemutha), possibly, but not certainly, at Rhuddlan. However, the extensive planting of towns in Wales did not occur until the coming of the Normans. By 1170, Wales had about fifty settlements with at least some pretensions to urban status, the great majority of them in the regions under secure Anglo-Norman control. Yet, by then towns were not unknown in *Pura Wallia*. The borough of Cardigan, which had come into the possession of Lord Rhys of Deheubarth by 1165, was fostered by its new ruler, and in Gwynedd and Powys quasi-urban communities were coming into existence. The towns of late eleventh- and twelfth-century Wales were very small compared with what they would be in the heyday of urban settlement in the late thirteenth century. In 1086 Rhuddlan had eighteen burgesses, and in the 1090s the burgesses of Brecon lived, not in a settlement distinct from the castle, but in the outer bailey of the castle itself.

The towns, like the castles, were not immediately protected by masonry; Carmarthen, in the 1230s, was perhaps the first borough in Wales to be provided with stone walls. Yet materials other than stone — palisades, banks and ditches — could provide elaborate defences. Norman Rhuddlan was surrounded by extensive earthworks enclosing a total of 35 acres (14ha). The invaders were aware of the vulnerability of their urban plantations in Wales. At the height of medieval town building, 86 per cent of the towns of Wales had defences, compared with 38 per cent in England, and in Wales, unlike in most of England, burgesses were obliged to undertake military service. The boroughs created in Wales in the late thirteenth century had a regular plan, but planned towns were an aberration rather than the norm. Indeed, most of the towns of early twelfth-century Wales probably consisted of little more than a single street leading from the town gate to the castle.

The primary role of the borough was to serve the needs of the castle garrison. The greater the success of the invaders, the less the garrison was needed, and towns which did not attain a role beyond the military were doomed to failure. The town's secondary, and eventually its primary role was to serve as a centre of specialization and exchange in what was an overwhelmingly agricultural economy. In what came to be the county of Monmouth, a network of towns came into existence, each serving a hinterland about 6 miles (10km) in radius. Thus Usk, 9 miles (14km) from Trelleck, 10 miles (16km) from Monmouth and from Abergavenny, 13 miles (21km) from Newport and 14 miles (22km) from Chepstow, could sustain some semblance of urban life. A similar pattern emerged in the Vale of Glamorgan and in the lordship of Pembroke, and ultimately in other parts

of Wales. In the thirteenth century, many of the urban settlements received charters of privilege which formally made them boroughs.

In the twelfth century, town dwellers hardly constituted 5 per cent of the population. Although the innovative forces represented by the boroughs were of great significance, *Marchia Wallie*, and, even more so *Pura Wallia*, were overwhelmingly rural. As with castles and boroughs, so also with the countryside, the Normans left an enduring mark. Along with the castle, the key to the success of their incursions was the knight, a mounted warrior who gave allegiance and military service to his lord in return for material support, usually in the form of an estate. The lands firmly under Anglo-Norman control became a patchwork of knights' fees, a development which went far to obliterate earlier territorial divisions. The power of the incomers was further strengthened by encouraging substantial colonization of their newly won lands by peasants — from England in the main, but also from Flanders and France, and also from parts of Wales itself. The colonists stamped their traditions on the land. The Flemings brought their skills as sheep rearers to the region around Haverfordwest. English migrants to the Gower Peninsula were among those who brought with them the open-field system. The impact of that system on the landscape can best be appreciated at the Vile, near Rhossili, where land extending over 950 acres (385ha) is still divided into bundles of strips hardly more than 1.25 acres (0.5ha) in area. Where colonists were numerous, Welsh place-names gave way to those of the newcomers. Wales has 350 early examples of place-names with the suffix '-ton', of which 155 are in Pembrokeshire, 74 in Glamorgan, 35 in Monmouthshire and 25 in Flintshire. Many of the settlers were villeins — unfree tenants working the manorial land for their lord. They brought with them the arable traditions of the English lowlands, and crop raising was further encouraged by the

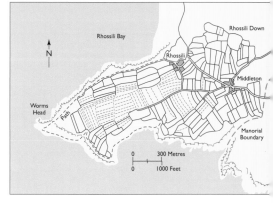

Throughout the Norman period, Wales remained an overwhelmingly rural country. From the early 1100s, the Gower Peninsula, for example, became a patchwork of knights' fees, with nucleated villages at the centre of manorial open fields. At Rhossili, on the south-west corner of the peninsula, the remains of an open-field system — known locally as 'the Vile' — can still be seen. As the aerial photograph reveals, the strip pattern of fields remains very distinct. The map, based on an original of 1780, shows the 'fossilized' medieval layout, with the fields still communally occupied (Photograph © Crown: Royal Commission on the Ancient and Historical Monuments of Wales, 95/CS/1206).

Drawings of two household officials — the groom (top) and the cook — from one of the earliest surviving manuscripts of the Welsh lawbooks, which dates from the thirteenth century. Although the traditional ascription of the laws to the tenth-century ruler, Hywel Dda, must be questioned, they undoubtedly embody time-honoured practices for the regulation of a Welsh princely household. They provide invaluable information on the personnel who served the prince and the organization of life in the llys *(By permission of The National Library of Wales, Peniarth Ms, 28, f. 6r).*

Below: North-west Wales, showing the commote boundaries. Each local division had a llys *or court, one of a number of seats of the ruler.*

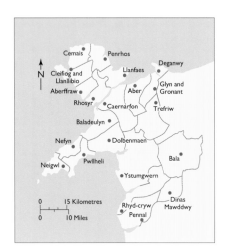

demands of an increasing population, a development aided by the milder climate of the two centuries after 1080. Thus, corn mills proliferated; almost all of them were the lord's property, a factor which greatly contributed to his power over his peasantry.

The area directly colonized under the Normans constituted but a small part of the country. Welsh patterns of landholding continued in existence, even in lowland Gwent, the Vale of Glamorgan and the Gower Peninsula. They were overwhelmingly dominant in upland Gwent and Glamorgan and were, in the twelfth century, wholly unchallenged in Gwynedd, Ceredigion and in most of Powys and Ystrad Tywi. In native Wales, the older local unit, the *cantref* — theoretically an area containing a hundred settlements — was giving way to the smaller unit, the *cwmwd* (the commote). Each had a *llys* or court, one of a number of seats of the ruler. Several of these survive in place-names — Llysfasi, the *llys* of the commote of Llannerch in Dyffryn Clwyd, for example — but archaeological evidence is sparse as yet.

Fascinating work has been done at Rhosyr in Anglesey, although what has been found there is more relevant to the age of Llywelyn ap Iorwerth (d. 1240) than to that of Gruffudd ap Cynan (d. 1137) and Owain Gwynedd (d. 1170). The *llysoedd* of rulers such as Gruffudd ap Cynan probably consisted of an enclosure containing a group of timber buildings, the most prominent of which was the *neuadd* (the hall), in which the court officials so meticulously described in the Welsh lawbooks served their ruler and where he entertained his nobility with feasting, music and the declamations of his poets.

Near the *llys* dwelt the ruler's hereditary servile class, the *taeogion*, and they worked their strips of land under the close supervision of their masters. The land of the free population, the *bonheddwyr*, also tended to become fragmented, for each son of a freeman had an equal right to the property of his father. Writing in 1603, George Owen of Henllys in Pembrokeshire described the consequences of gavelkind (the equal division of land among sons): 'The whole countrie was brought into smale peeces of ground and intermingled upp and downe with another, so as in every five or six acres you shall have ten or twelve owners'.

While the Norman incursions led to new kinds of settlement in places such as Pembroke and the Vale of Glamorgan, they also resulted in much dislocation in those regions which swung back and forth between Anglo-Norman and Welsh control. Other regions, Gwynedd in particular, enjoyed greater stability, especially under the rule of Gruffudd ap Cynan and his son, Owain Gwynedd, and Gruffudd's biographer described the extensive establishment of orchards and gardens. Increasing prosperity could undermine age-old practices, as could the embryonic money economy which came with the growth of towns. Above all, the population increased; indeed Wales by 1300 may have had as many as three times the number of inhabitants it had had in 1070.

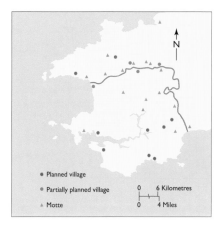

There is sound evidence to suggest that a number of villages in south Wales were deliberately planted by the Norman conquerors. This map shows the extent of such planned villages in Pembrokeshire, with the loose frontier between Anglo-Norman and Welsh areas marked (After Jonathan Kissock).

Templeton in Pembrokeshire was almost certainly a planned village planted by the Norman conquerors. Elements of its regular form can still be seen (© Crown: Royal Commission on the Ancient and Historical Monuments of Wales, 90-CS-565).

In the transformation of Wales, a powerful role was played by the Church. The Norman incursions coincided with the surge for reform which swept through the western Church in the late eleventh century. The Normans were godly in their way, faithful to the papacy which had blessed their venture in England. To enthusiastic reformers — to some native Welsh rulers as well as to Norman lords — the distinctive features of the Welsh Church, the product of centuries of isolation, were abhorrent. The monasteries had married abbots and hereditary offices; the bishops were neither members of a defined hierarchy nor pastors of clearly demarcated dioceses; the building of great stone churches, work already afoot in Normandy and England, had not begun; the country lacked monasteries obedient to the *Rule of Saint Benedict*, the most powerful of the influences giving unity to Latin Europe.

By 1170, Norman power and influence had gone far to correct these perceived deficiencies, and as a result religious houses had been created and territorial units had been established which were among the most important contributions to the making of Wales. Up to a dozen Benedictine priories were established. Chepstow, the earliest, probably founded by William fitz Osbern before his death in 1071, has massive piers characteristic of Romanesque architecture at its most monumental. Ewenny, founded by the de Londres family, lords of Ogwr, in 1116–41, is perhaps the finest example of Romanesque architecture in Wales. It is the only Benedictine priory in Wales not built within or adjoining a Norman borough, and its fortress-like architecture seems to echo Norman insecurity. It was a cell of the great Benedictine abbey of Gloucester, and Gloucester's abbot advised the prior of Ewenny to 'strengthen the locks of your doors and surround your house with a good ditch and an impregnable wall', proof of the suspicion of the Welsh harboured by the promoters of the first phase of Latin monasticism in Wales.

All the Benedictine houses of Wales were cells of abbeys outside Wales. In addition, the revenues of Wales's pre-Norman monasteries — the *clas* churches — at least in southern Wales, were bestowed upon churches elsewhere. A similar fate befell many local Welsh churches, for the Normans

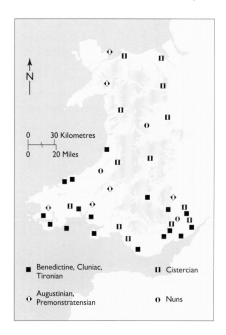

The distribution of medieval religious houses in Wales.

Opposite: The presbytery of the priory church at Ewenny reveals the quality of the very finest Romanesque architecture in Anglo-Norman Wales.

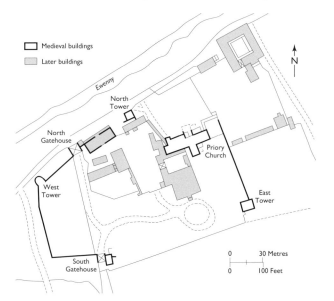

The Norman conquerors of Wales brought with them the order of Latin monasticism with which they were familiar: Benedictine priories were established, often in the new boroughs and in the shadow of the invaders' castles. Ewenny was an exception, built as it was away from both town and castle. However, like all medieval religious houses, the church and principal monastic buildings were surrounded by a substantial precinct.

The sumptuous arch between the sanctuary and the Lady Chapel at Llandaff Cathedral was commissioned by the first Norman bishop, Urban (1107–34). An excellent example of Romanesque architectural ornamentation, it was created by masons familiar with contemporary work at Hereford and Gloucester.

Below: The shrine at Pennant Melangell in the Berwyn Mountains dates from about 1160, and is a remarkable Romanesque survival (© Mick Sharp Photography).

carried out a massive disendowment of the Church in Wales. They also demoted native Welsh saints, with St Tathan giving way to St Stephen at Caerwent, St Teilo yielding precedence to St Peter at Llandaff and St David losing some pre-eminence to St Andrew at St Davids.

There were more constructive aspects to the activities of the Normans. The Benedictine priories are not the only buildings in Wales offering examples of Romanesque architecture. At Llandaff, the work of the diocese's first Norman bishop, Urban (1107–34), survives in the fine arch between the sanctuary and the Lady Chapel, but, at St Davids, the substantial cathedral erected during the episcopate of Bernard (1115–48) was demolished when rebuilding started in 1182. Some of the local churches in those areas early colonized by the Normans still contain appealing Romanesque features, St Mary's, Marcross, with its spirited zigzags, among them. The impressive architectural style introduced from mainland Europe also appealed to native Welsh patrons, and thus the Romanesque heritage of Wales may also be found in regions far from the centres of Norman power. His biographer states that Gruffudd ap Cynan caused Gwynedd to be strewn with churches as the firmament is strewn with stars. The church of Llanbadarn Fawr near Llandrindod has a strange early twelfth-century tympanum featuring two leaping lion-like creatures and a doorway rich in fantasy. Even more remarkable is the shrine at Pennant Melangell in the heart of the Berwyn Mountains; dating from about 1160, nothing comparable to it has survived anywhere else in Britain.

The religious fervour which sprang from the efforts to reform the Church gave rise to new monastic orders. By 1170, the order of Cluny had two houses in Wales; so did the Black Canons, the observers of the *Rule of St Augustine*, while the order of Tiron had three. Among the Augustinian houses was Llanthony, the most beautifully located of all the monasteries of Wales, its church a superb example of the transitional phase between Romanesque and Gothic. Far more numerous were the daughter houses of the monastery of Cîteaux in Burgundy. Wales was eventually to have thirteen Cistercian houses; seven of them had been established by 1170, among them Whitland and Strata Florida, the first of the new-founded religious houses of the era to receive the patronage of a native Welsh ruler. Unlike the Benedictines, who settled under the shadow of the power of the invaders, the Cistercians chose to build their

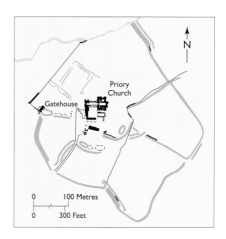

Above: The church, cloister and monastic buildings at Llanthony were surrounded by a large precinct, now defined by earthworks.

Below: Set in the Vale of Ewias, 'no more than three arrow-shots in width', the Augustinian priory of Llanthony is perhaps the most beautifully located of all the monasteries of Wales.

The massive simplicity of the nave at Margam Abbey gives eloquent expression to the principles of austerity central to the early Cistercian ideal. The Cistercians advocated a return to the strict observance of the Rule of St Benedict, *which had emerged as the dominant model for western monastic life, and denounced as frivolous distractions the exuberant carvings and fantastic grotesques often found decorating Benedictine monasteries in the first half of the twelfth century. Margam was founded in 1147 by Robert of Gloucester, lord of Glamorgan.*

monasteries 'far from the concourse of men'. Not only were they seekers of solitude, they were also creators of solitude, for they were not beyond depopulating the districts in their immediate vicinity. Of the Cistercian houses of Wales, the fabric of half of them has almost totally disappeared; the remains of the others, however, are among the most important indicators of the architectural achievements of the medieval makers of Wales. Among them is Margam Abbey. Founded in 1147, the nave of the abbey church bears eloquent testimony of the austerity of the early Cistercian ideal throughout Europe. The patrons of Cistercian abbeys endowed them with great tracts of land; Strata Florida, for example, came to own vast swathes of territory in the upper Teifi and Tywi Valleys. The land was well suited to sheep rearing, and, for centuries, the flocks of the Cistercians were an important feature of the Welsh economy.

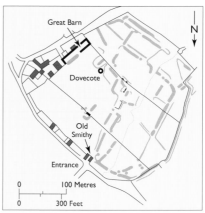

The key to Cistercian agricultural success was their system of grange farming. Wherever possible, their lands were consolidated in cohesive granges exploited from a single farm. Monknash, in the Vale of Glamorgan, is one of the best preserved grange centres in the country. This plan and the aerial photograph show the extent of the surviving buildings and earthworks. Up to 850 acres (350ha) of Cistercian land belonging to Neath Abbey surrounded this grange (Photograph © Crown: Royal Commission on the Ancient and Historical Monuments of Wales, 98/CS/0519).

Alongside the growth of the new monastic orders was the recasting of the territorial organization of the Welsh Church. By 1170, the four dioceses of Wales had clear boundaries and their bishops were part of a defined hierarchy recognizing the archbishop of Canterbury as metropolitan. The boundaries drew on old traditions, and they therefore had a significance beyond the ecclesiastical; diocesan boundaries, for example, frequently coincided with changes in dialect and in legal and social practices. The process of defining the basic ecclesiastical units — the parishes — proved more protracted. It was afoot in the Vale of Glamorgan by 1100 but up to two centuries would elapse before it had been completed throughout Wales. A parish represented a territory capable of maintaining a priest, and the network of parishes which eventually came into existence generally reflects the settlement pattern of twelfth- and thirteenth-century Wales. Thus, while the Vale of Usk around Brecon was divided into a large number of parishes rarely exceeding 1,500 acres (600ha), many of the parishes of upland Glamorgan could be up to 20,000 acres (8,000ha) — an issue of importance in later centuries when industrialization caused a vast increase in the numbers dwelling in those uplands. Originally created to serve the Church, parishes developed secular roles, serving as units of local government, taxation, relief of the poor and the compilation of population statistics, roles that continued to be of significance well into the twentieth century.

By the 1170s, the invigoration of society which had been gathering pace over the previous century was increasingly apparent. Towns were moving towards their medieval apogee and there was a marked increase in the amount of agricultural land available as assarting was intensified. With work soon to begin on the great round tower at Pembroke, Wales was moving into an era during which the country acquired buildings of international significance. The High Middle Ages was to see a heroic struggle to establish a viable Welsh polity; ironically, it was the failure of that struggle which endowed the country with its most iconic buildings.

To a varying degree, sheep rearing was significant to the economy of all thirteen Cistercian abbeys of medieval Wales. Vast upland sheep ranches existed in some areas, with sheep-cotes spread throughout the landscape. This fourteenth-century manuscript illustration shows a man and woman tending sheep. The early Cistercians would have employed their lay brothers to tend their flocks (© Board of The British Library, Additional Ms. 42130, f. 163v).

THE HIGH MIDDLE AGES

THE MAKING OF WALES 1170–1348

Between 1170 and 1348 the developments apparent in the early twelfth century became increasingly marked. With the continuing rise in population, rural settlement intensified, resulting in a vast expansion in the exploitation of the waste. Urban settlement burgeoned, with new towns being created and existing ones adding to their inhabitants. Romanesque architecture evolved into early and Decorated Gothic, the styles of most of the monasteries of Wales and many of the country's parish churches. The era saw the climax of castle building, for, with the exception of Raglan, all the great castles of Wales belong to the period 1170–1348. The definition and intensification of lordship, over land as well as over men, continued apace. In *Pura Wallia*, it led to the rise of the power of Gwynedd under Llywelyn ap Iorwerth (d. 1240) and Llywelyn ap Gruffudd (d. 1282), proof that there existed in medieval Wales the basic constituents of a Welsh polity.

Underpinning the power of the rulers of Gwynedd was the commotal system. Each commote — over twenty in all — had a *llys*, the centre in which dues were collected and justice was administered and where the peripatetic ruler stayed occasionally and entertained his leading subjects. One of the most exciting advances of recent years has been the discovery of the location of the *llys* at Rhosyr, the *caput* of the commote of Rhosyr in south-western Anglesey.

Opposite: Criccieth Castle, sited on a rocky promontory projecting into the waters of Cardigan Bay, was one of a number of stone castles built by the prince of Gwynedd, Llywelyn ap Iorwerth (d. 1240). Its twin-towered gatehouse was a sophisticated defensive feature for its day.

Above: This finely carved head of a crowned ruler may represent Llywelyn ap Iorwerth. It was discovered at Deganwy Castle, where Llywelyn undertook substantial building works (© National Museum of Wales).

An aerial view of the excavated remains of Llys Rhosyr, the centre of administration for the commote of Rhosyr in south-western Anglesey. Both Llywelyn ap Iorwerth and his grandson, Llywelyn ap Gruffudd (d. 1282), would have stayed at Rhosyr during their travels around the principality of Gwynedd (© Crown: Royal Commission on the Ancient and Historical Monuments of Wales, AP_2005_0151).

An aerial view of the village of St Brides Wentlooge, on the Wentlooge Levels to the west of Newport. The village stands at the edge of drained and reclaimed peat deposits. The process of drainage and land management was already underway in the Roman period. The channels were maintained throughout the Middle Ages, with additional areas drained and reclaimed (© Crown: Royal Commission on the Ancient and Historical Monuments of Wales, 2001/CS/1468).

Surveys and partial excavation of the site have revealed the stone foundations of rectangular buildings, among them, no doubt, the *neuadd* (hall) in which Llywelyn ap Iorwerth issued a charter in 1237 and in which the princes and their closest associates listened to the poetry of the court poets. Further work on the site is likely to reveal the entire setting of the life of a *llys* as described in the Welsh lawbooks, and should provide knowledge concerning the 600-acre (220ha) *maerdref* where the *taeogion* laboured to produce the food consumed in the lavish feasts held in the *neuadd*.

The effort to create a Welsh polity reached its climax in 1267, when Llywelyn ap Gruffudd won recognition as prince of Wales; his ambitions received a severe blow in 1277 and were utterly destroyed in 1282–83. Llywelyn's principality became the royal counties of Wales, with which the heir to the English throne was later invested. Yet the marcher lordships, whose raison d'être was to act as a *cordon sanitaire* between the kingdom of England and the territories of the Welsh rulers, continued in existence, and thus the division of Wales, first apparent in the late eleventh and early twelfth centuries, was perpetuated.

Of all these developments, the most significant in terms of the history of the Welsh landscape was the intensification of rural settlement, a feature of both Anglo-Norman and native Wales. In the March, place-names containing the element 'New-' became increasingly common — Newton Nottage in the lordship of Glamorgan, for example, and New Moat in that of Pembroke. The creation of new settlements involved a determined attack upon woodland, causing the thirteenth century to represent the climax of medieval assartment. In Anglesey, so great were the efforts of the assarters that the island was virtually denuded of trees. The right to assart was almost a condition of existence; when King Henry III (1216–72) seized much of north-east Wales in the 1240s, that was the right its inhabitants were chiefly concerned that the king should confirm.

Land could also be won for farming through drainage schemes. The monks of Tintern drained parts of the Caldicot Levels and the tenants of the lord of Gwynllŵg undertook similar work on the Wentlooge Levels.

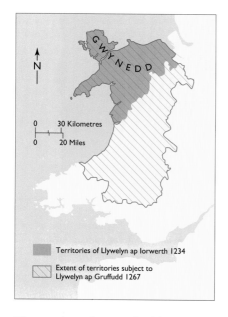

GWYNEDD

N

| 0 | 30 Kilometres |
| 0 | 20 Miles |

▨ Territories of Llywelyn ap Iorwerth 1234

▧ Extent of territories subject to Llywelyn ap Gruffudd 1267

The map shows the strength of the royal house of Gwynedd under Llywelyn ap Iorwerth (d. 1240) and Llywelyn ap Gruffudd (d. 1282). The reassertion of Welsh authority under these two gifted rulers and the response this provoked in the marcher lordships led to a climax in castle building across Wales.

Eventually the Gwent Levels would have 40 miles (64km) of wide ditches, 85 miles (138km) of narrow ditches and 750 miles (1,200km) of gutters — Wales's most remarkable example of labour-intensive landscape manipulation.

The ruling class was determined that some areas should not be brought under cultivation, for the chief delight of its members was the chase, and by establishing hunting parks they contributed to the preservation of ancient landscapes. The Norman lords of Abergavenny created a great park including much of the Sugar Loaf Mountain, and William de Braose (d. 1290), lord of Gower, surrounded 500 acres (200ha) at Parc le Breos with a 4-mile (6.4km) fence. Other areas were lost to cultivation through natural disasters. Coastal erosion created sunken forests at Newgale, and blown sand inundated Kenfig and part of Merthyr Mawr, as well as extensive areas of south-west Anglesey. Around 1300, Kenfig was a flourishing borough with up to 800 inhabitants; it had been virtually abandoned by 1470. A particularly interesting area of inundation is Stackpole Warren, where the sand has preserved a landscape offering evidence of occupation from the Mesolithic era to the Middle Ages.

Hunting parks, beloved by the ruling classes, were a prominent feature in the Welsh landscape of the High Middle Ages. This huge ditch was part of the enclosure defining the great park created by the lords of Abergavenny on the flanks of the Sugar Loaf Mountain.

Excavations at Cefn Graeanog near Clynnog-fawr recovered evidence of a substantial twelfth- to thirteenth-century farmstead, comprising a house, barn, stable and byre (Gwynedd Archaeological Trust).

Above: Rabbits were prized as a delicacy in the Middle Ages, and raised within the protective confines of warrens. Pillow mounds in which they could easily burrow, like that shown here in the early fourteenth-century Luttrell Psalter, were specially created for their husbandry and can still be identified in the landscape (© Board of the British Library, Additional Ms. 42130, f. 176v).

With the granting of extensive upland areas in Wales to the Cistercians, large parts of these lands became the domain of sheep. This map highlights the lands of Strata Florida Abbey, but also shows other Cistercian estates in south Wales.

Much of the new farming land was devoted to arable cultivation. In the 1290s, three quarters of the taxpayers of lowland Llŷn grew corn, mainly in the form of oats. The large barn built at Cefn Graeanog near Clynnog-fawr is evidence of the growing role of cereals, and successive versions of the Welsh lawbooks provide increasingly detailed instructions concerning joint ploughing, a necessity on land held in intermingling strips. Despite the rise in cereal growing, Wales remained a country of mixed farming. Central to the economy was the rearing of cattle — the drawers of ploughs as well as a source of milk, meat and leather — and it is the cattle rearers, above all, who have ensured that the Wales we have inherited is largely a land of meadows and pastures. Although few of the early medieval pastures were enclosed, Wales was eventually to become very much a country of hedged pastures, and some of these hedges may be very old indeed. Hooper's theory — that the age of a hedge may be determined by the number of species of trees and shrubs it contains — is considered to be unreliable where western Britain is concerned. However, further hedge studies may permit many of the hedges of Wales to be dated with a degree of accuracy, and it is likely that some at least date back to the High Middle Ages, or even earlier.

The traditional role of the uplands had been to provide summer grazing for cattle, but with the granting of extensive estates to the Cistercians, large parts of them became the domain of the sheep. Sheep are admirably designed to prevent the growth of trees. Goats are even more effective, and they were a significant element in the livestock — the so-called wild goats of Snowdonia preserve the characteristics of medieval breeds. Rabbits, introduced into Britain by the Romans and perhaps reintroduced by the Normans, are also eager grazers. Appreciated as a delicacy, pillow mounds — piles of easily burrowable soil — were created for them. Other additions to the diet included pigeons, which were also prized for their manure — the raw material of

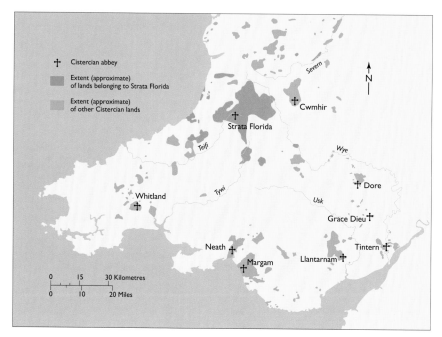

Above: Wales has some 140 known examples of moated settlement sites, with the majority of them constructed between 1200 and 1325. In most cases, the moated island housed a manorial or sub-manorial residence, and the moat served as a symbol of the owner's status, though they were also a source of fish. Hen Gwrt in northern Monmouthshire is a well-preserved example.

This splendid thirteenth-century columbarium or dovecote at Cadoxton Court, Barry, is a reminder of the significance of pigeons in the medieval diet (© Crown: Royal Commission on the Ancient and Historical Monuments of Wales, C2003/198/2).

saltpetre, which was a vital component of gunpowder; there is a splendid columbarium or dovecote at Cadoxton Court, Barry, and there are numerous examples particularly in the villages around Haverfordwest and Pembroke. Fish was an essential food. Wales has some 140 moated sites, a significant number of them in Maelor Saesneg. Most of them were constructed between 1200 and 1325 and were primarily status symbols; they were also a source of fish, as were the Wye weirs owned by the monks of Tintern.

The rural expansion of the High Middle Ages coincided with a remarkable increase in the number of towns and of town dwellers. Town planning in medieval Wales entered its last phase in the wake of the wars of King Edward I (1272–1307). Aberystwyth, Flint and Rhuddlan, established after the war of 1277, were the first of Edward's foundations. At Aberystwyth, an area of some 50 acres (20ha) had been enclosed by walls by 1280. Flint, protected by a bank and palisade rather than a wall, had a remarkably regular layout reminiscent of the bastides of Gascony. Its six parallel streets and one cross route can still be traced today. Rhuddlan, like Flint, was not a walled town, but the earthworks which defended its northern corner are still visible.

After the war of 1282–83, Edward was far more ambitious, for in the 1280s his builders constructed walled towns which rank among the most remarkable in Europe. Pride of place must be accorded to Conwy, where the town walls are among the most splendid of the achievements of the makers of Wales. Stretching for some 1,400 yards (1.3km), defended by twenty-one towers and pierced by three double-towered gateways, they are a far more

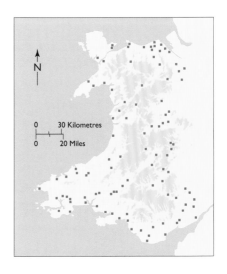

The towns of medieval Wales.

The apogee of medieval town planning in Wales followed in the wake of the wars of King Edward I. Pride of place must be accorded to Conwy, where the town walls and castle were raised in a frenzied building programme in the 1280s. The layout and street plan were determined at the outset, and seen from the air it is clear that the town walls continue to determine the shape of the borough today.

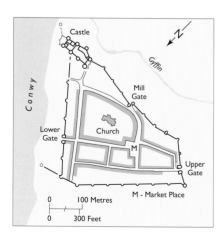

ambitious project than the 800 yards (734m) of wall surrounding the town of Caernarfon. Among the most intriguing features of Conwy's defences is the row of twelve privies west of the Mill Gate, a unique multiple sanitary arrangement built to serve the needs of the king's wardrobe, the royal secretariat which was located at Conwy in the mid-1280s.

In the late thirteenth and early fourteenth centuries, nine royal boroughs came into existence in Wales, either as new foundations or as existing settlements brought into the burghal fold. In addition, a similar number was established by seigneurial encouragement. By 1309, when the last of the creations — the borough of Bala — was founded, Wales had 109 settlements with at least some pretensions to borough status. Up to half of them contracted markedly, or achieved only stunted growth or totally failed. Trelleck, which may have been the largest town in Wales in 1300, shrunk when its industrial importance to the Clare family came to an end following the death of the last Clare earl of Gloucester at Bannockburn in 1314. At New Radnor, a 25-acre (10ha) settlement was laid out in the late thirteenth century, though not all its original plots have ever been occupied. Cefnllys, established by the Mortimer family in Maelienydd, has long been totally abandoned, as has the borough of Newton at Dinefwr.

Of the successful towns, the great majority were situated in the southern coastlands; the Edwardian boroughs were small, for the magnificence of their fortifications bore little relationship to their size (Caernarfon initially had merely 70 burgages or urban plots, and Conwy 112). Cardiff, with its 421 burgages,

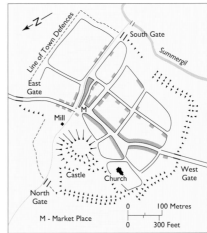

New Radnor was a planted town probably first laid out in the late thirteenth century. Its initial growth was rapid, with up to 189 burgesses or townsmen recorded in 1304. The plan of the borough shows the extent of early ambitions, but today the modern town is less densely developed than its medieval predecessor. The urban fringe remains essentially rural (© Crown: Royal Commission on the Ancient and Historical Monuments of Wales, DI2009_0182).

was among the larger of the Welsh towns of the High Middle Ages; by 1300 it had spilled out beyond the confines of its defences and spawned the extramural settlement of Crockherbtown. Similar growth occurred in other towns, Abergavenny, Carmarthen, Haverfordwest and Pembroke among them. Street alignments emerged that would still dominate the townscapes of the twenty-first century. The wide central street of Carmarthen marks the site of the medieval cattle market, and comparable features may be seen at Brecon, Welshpool, Monmouth and elsewhere. Monmouth can also boast one of the most attractive of Wales's medieval buildings — the fortified bridge erected across the river Monnow in the late thirteenth century. Other surviving defences added in the period 1170–1348 to Welsh towns of Anglo-Norman provenance include the walls and gatehouse at Chepstow, the south gatehouse at Kidwelly, and the walls of Tenby; indeed, so proud are the citizens of Tenby of their town's defences that in 1989 they founded the Walled Towns Friendship Circle, which had by 2009 a worldwide membership of 152 towns. The town's Five Arches, described by Augustus John as 'a piece of cheese gnawed by rats', is the Circle's logo.

While the town walls of Chepstow, and even more so those of Conwy and Caernarfon, are impressive, they are overshadowed by the splendours of the castles that are associated with them. Wales's thirteenth-century castles are its greatest architectural monuments, and the fact that the country's most distinguished buildings are the product of conquest and immigration is a paradox commented upon by the eighteenth-century topographical writer, Thomas Pennant, who described the Edwardian castle at Caernarfon as 'the most magnificent badge of our subjection'. Some of the most appealing fortifications — Castell y Bere, Dinas Brân, Dolforwyn and Dolwyddelan among them — were built by the Welsh princes; Llywelyn ap Gruffudd's decision to build Dolforwyn Castle was a particular defiant act for it was a direct challenge to the royal castle at Montgomery. Yet, it has to be acknowledged that the great majority of the most elaborate castles were erected under the auspices of the English king or of those of his barons who held marcher lordships.

Among the baronial castles are Pembroke, with its imposing round tower (about 1204) — one of the earliest of its kind in Britain — Chepstow and Kidwelly, with their superb spur buttresses, the magnificently sited castles of

Wales's thirteenth-century castles are perhaps its greatest architectural monuments. Some of the most appealing were those fortifications raised by the native Welsh princes, including Castell y Bere in the magnificent landscape north-east of Tywyn.

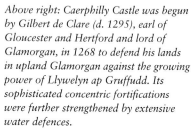

Llansteffan, Cilgerran and Carreg Cennen (the last originally a Welsh castle but rebuilt by the Giffard family), and Grosmont, Skenfrith, and White, the 'Three Castles' of northern Monmouthshire in their delightfully verdant settings. Even more outstanding is Caerphilly; work on the castle, which is among the largest in Europe, began in 1268. With its water defences, its fortified dam and its island fortress, it is one of the earliest and most elaborate examples of a concentric fortification. Almost equally remarkable is Denbigh (1282–1311), where the great gatehouse with its three octagonal towers is a masterpiece of military architecture.

It is possible that the Denbigh gatehouse was designed by James of St George who was the Master of the King's Works and the organizing hand behind many of Edward I's Welsh castles. Edward ordered the construction *de novo* of seven castles in Wales and the rebuilding or enlargement of several others. Of the seven, Flint has a fortified keep or freestanding donjon, a concept which was outmoded by the late thirteenth century. Four of the castles — Aberystwyth, Rhuddlan, Harlech and Beaumaris — are concentric fortifications in the tradition of Caerphilly; indeed Beaumaris, built on a level and therefore unconstricted site, is the epitome of symmetric perfection despite never being finished. At Conwy and Caernarfon, where castle and town walls are superbly integrated, concentricity was abandoned in favour of massive curtain walls and monumental gateways. Conwy, considered by Goronwy Edwards to be 'incomparably the most magnificent of Edward I's Welsh castles', consists of two adjoining wards each flanked by a barbican. Its inner ward contains the royal palace built for King Edward and Queen Eleanor, royal rooms of a quality unsurpassed in Britain of the High Middle Ages. The layout at Caernarfon is not dissimilar to that of Conwy; Caernarfon's distinction lies in its magnitude. Some 580 feet (180m) in length, it is nearly 200 feet (60m) longer than Conwy. Caernarfon stands out, too, in its echoes of Rome and Constantinople — deliberate expressions of its imperial role.

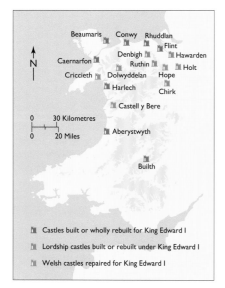

Above: Castle building during the Edwardian campaigns in Wales in the late thirteenth century.

Right: Harlech was one of the entirely new castles established in north Wales by King Edward I at the end of the thirteenth century. Begun in 1283 and virtually complete by 1289, the formidable stronghold was later captured by Owain Glyndŵr, probably in 1404. It served as the residence of his court and family until it was retaken by Prince Henry, the future King Henry V, in 1409.

Opposite: The west door of the church of the Cistercian abbey at Strata Florida dates from around 1200 and is an unparalleled composition in the late Romanesque style. The superb artistry of the doorway reflects the fact that the abbey enjoyed the patronage of the Lord Rhys and succeeding princes of Deheubarth. In the thirteenth century, its monks were important custodians of Welsh historical and cultural traditions.

Edward I's Welsh castles represented an expenditure of almost £100,000, well over twice the king's regular annual income. In addition, his father and grandfather spent thousands of pounds on castles in Wales, as did the leading lords of the March. The High Middle Ages saw an equivalent if not a greater expenditure on monastic buildings, those of the Cistercians in particular. Most of the surviving Welsh Cistercian abbey churches were built between 1170 and 1230. As at Margam they offer evidence of the simplicity favoured by the early Cistercians and of the evolution of ecclesiastical architecture from Romanesque to early Gothic. An intriguing interpretation of the late Romanesque style can be seen at the west door of Strata Florida Abbey church. The arch, which once enclosed the door, has no capitals; instead, its shafts are linked by ribbon-like bands that terminate in scrolls reminiscent of shepherds' crooks. Equally intriguing was the scale originally planned for the rather stark abbey church at Cwmhir. The intention was to provide the church with a fourteen-bay nave, five bays more than there are in the nave of Canterbury Cathedral.

Some Cistercian abbey churches were rebuilt in a far more elaborate style indicating that in the history of religious austerity, nothing fails like success. Among them were Tintern (about 1269–1301) and Neath (about 1280–1330), where the influence of the Decorated Gothic style early employed at Westminster Abbey is apparent. Of the churches of other monastic orders, the most impressive thirteenth-century work is that of the Benedictines at Brecon, where the chancel is a superb example of early Gothic. In addition, Brecon has Wales's only substantial remains of a medieval friary — the Dominican house now incorporated within the buildings of Christ College.

The cathedral at St Asaph was extensively damaged after the troops of King Edward I put it to the torch in 1282. The reconstruction of the church seems to have begun two years later and culminated with the completion of the tower in 1392 (© Crown Copyright (2009) Visit Wales).

The present cathedral church at St Davids was commenced under Bishop Peter de Leia (1176–98). The nave is a superb example of late Anglo-Norman Romanesque architecture.

The High Middle Ages also saw extensive building by the secular wing of the Church. All four of the ancient cathedrals of Wales contain important evidence of the architecture of the period. Work on the magnificent nave of St Davids, one of the last great Romanesque churches to be built in Britain, began about 1182 during the episcopate of Peter de Leia (1176–98). In addition, the bishops of St Davids were avid builders of great houses — the hall at Llawhaden, the palace at Lamphey and the bishop's palace at St Davids, described by Glanmor Williams as 'the most beautiful building [erected] in Wales in the Middle Ages'. Above all, the years 1170 to 1348 were a period of intense construction of parish churches. Of the hundreds of churches built in Wales in those years, some of the remoter ones, such as Rhulen in Radnorshire, are so unassuming that it is difficult to assign them to any particular style. In the wealthier parts of Wales, churches with sturdy towers proliferated; that at Cheriton in Gower is among the most attractive. Town churches were particularly subject to the church rebuilding boom of the late Middle Ages, but work from the period 1170–1348 may be found in particular at St Mary's, Haverfordwest.

The growth of towns and the rebuilding of churches are an indication of the growing prosperity of Wales by the late thirteenth century. There was an expansion in trade, landward and seaward, and the mineral resources of Wales — lead in Flintshire and iron and coal in the south — were being increasingly exploited. The wool produced by the flocks of the uplands, which had originally been exported as fleeces, began to be processed in Wales, and by 1350 the country had at least seventy-five fulling mills. These developments tended to undermine the rigid social divisions of earlier centuries, a change assisted by the decline in the number of manors worked by bond labour, at least in the regions which until 1282 constituted *Pura Wallia*. The tax records of 1292–93 show that in Merioneth freemen outnumbered bondmen by four to one, and by then absolute villeinage had almost disappeared from most of central and south-west Wales. By the early fourteenth century, demesne farming was being abandoned in

Marchia Wallie also; this further blurred the distinction between the free and the unfree, a development which had an impact upon settlement patterns.

Even greater was the impact of the growth of population. By 1300, Wales had at least 300,000 inhabitants. The free population of *Pura Wallia* could be remarkably prolific. The land of Iorwerth ap Cadwgan, who flourished in the 1220s, was by 1313 shared among twenty-seven of his descendants. Chronic overcrowding of the original descendants' lands could be avoided by carving out new holdings — the motivation for much of the assarting. By 1334, the descendants of Edryd ap Marchudd, who originated in Abergele, had fifteen settlements extending from Betws-y-coed to Bodelwyddan. The inhabitants of *Marchia Wallie* could also be prolific. By the early fourteenth century, the tenant families of upland Hay held less than 2 acres (0.8ha) of arable land apiece, and similar patterns of rural overpopulation could be found in the lordships of Monmouth and Brecon. Population growth was aided by the colonists attracted to Wales in the wake of the Edwardian conquest. At least 20,000 acres (8,000ha) of the Vale of Clwyd were cleared of their Welsh proprietors, and around the royal boroughs further clearances provided land for the immigrant burgesses. Many of the incomers came from areas with strong traditions of arable agriculture and they boosted the proportion of land in Wales subject to the plough.

The prosperity apparent in Wales by 1300 was precarious. Population growth had driven families to settle on poorer land and thus communities were being pushed to the margins of cultivable soil. Imbalance between arable and livestock husbandry could lead to serious problems of soil exhaustion. Animal diseases such as the sheep scab epidemic of 1291 could drive entire communities into the abyss. There is evidence by the early fourteenth century that the period of favourable climate which had begun around 1080 was coming to an end. Appalling weather between 1315 and 1318 caused a great famine across Europe. The Hundred Years' War began in 1337 and led to heavy taxation and the collapse of the currency. And there was worse to come.

The bishop's palace at St Davids was almost entirely rebuilt in the Decorated style of Gothic architecture by Bishop Henry de Gower (1328–47). The bishop, who probably had family links to the Gower Peninsula, had been educated at Oxford and in his early career had become familiar with the latest architectural trends in England. Architectural details in the palace point to the employment of master craftsmen from the Bristol area in its construction.

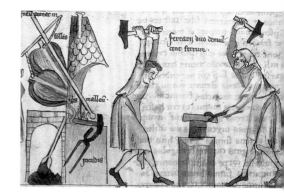

The growth of towns and a thriving market economy led to an increase in the exploitation of mineral resources in Wales. This manuscript illustration shows smiths of the High Middle Ages at work at a forge (© Board of The British Library, Sloane Ms. 3983, f. 5).

THE LATER MIDDLE AGES

THE MAKING OF WALES 1348–1536

In Wales, as in the rest of Europe, the later Middle Ages were ushered in by the Black Death. Carried by the fleas of the black rat, bubonic and pneumonic plague killed at least a third of the inhabitants of the Old World between 1347 and 1370. Twenty-five million people died in Europe alone; the pestilence was at its worst between 1347 and 1350, but it struck again and again, particularly in 1361 and 1369. The cataclysm may not have been as severe in Wales as elsewhere, for the death toll was highest in large towns and in thickly populated lowland districts. Nevertheless, the plague had a profound effect upon the country's settlement pattern and social organization. The number of inhabitants — probably in decline since the 1310s — slumped; indeed, it was to take at least 250 years before the population of Wales would again be as large as it had been at the opening of that decade.

The implications of demographic decline were far-reaching. Borough plantation became a thing of the past and existing towns contracted. As population pressure eased, there was a retreat from the more marginal lands, the inhabitants of which had dwelt in scattered settlements rather than in villages. Wales does not have deserted villages in numbers or size comparable with the Midlands of England, where villages were abandoned in their

Opposite: Raglan Castle in Monmouthshire is far and away the most elaborate fortified complex built in Wales in the fifteenth century. Begun by William ap Thomas (d. 1445), its construction continued under his son, William Herbert (d. 1469), who became earl of Pembroke in 1468. The Yellow Tower of Gwent, the top of which can be glimpsed in the centre distance of this view, was a self-contained fortress in its own right. Two large courtyards housed the chambers and lodgings commensurate with the status of a family of rank.

The Black Death may not have been as severe in Wales as elsewhere in Europe. Nevertheless, scenes like this, from a contemporary manuscript depicting the impact of the plague on Tournai (Belgium) in 1349, must have been familiar across the country, particularly in urban areas and the more densely populated lowlands (Bibliothèque Royale de Belgique, Ms. 13076–7, f. 24v/akg-images/VISIOARS).

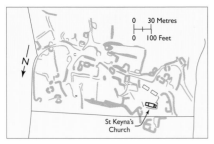

One of the consequences of a changing economy and a demographic decline was the shrinkage and depopulation of villages. Wales does not have the number of examples comparable with parts of England, but they do exist. This aerial view of Runston, near Chepstow, shows an isolated chapel surrounded by the remains of its village. The plan shows the extent of the former village earthworks (Photograph © Crown: Royal Commission on the Ancient and Historical Monuments of Wales, 94/CS/0463).

hundreds. Nevertheless, deserted villages have been identified in parts of the Welsh lowlands — in the neighbourhood of Barry and Flemingston in the Vale of Glamorgan, for example, and at Eglwys Gymyn near Laugharne and Runston near Chepstow. The exodus from them was not as sudden as was once believed; Runston still had a few inhabitants as late as the eighteenth century.

As villages of unfree tenants became depopulated by disease and migration, the scattered strips of villein holdings began to be reorganized into consolidated farms. Similar developments occurred in the lands of the free population as death from pestilence slowed down the division of property among numerous male heirs and as the land of a man dying without heirs escheated to his lord. Ambitious members of Welsh gentry families were anxious to be released from what they considered to be the restrictions of traditional Welsh tenure; they wished to hold land according to English law, thus permitting them to accumulate property and to bequeath it to a single heir. The contraction in the labour force gave the final quietus to the direct farming of demesne land and as a result many lords of the March came to have only a tenuous connection with their Welsh territories. This created a vacuum which the emerging Welsh gentry were eager to fill.

The Black Death greatly aided the process whereby social division based on legal rank was yielding to social division based upon wealth. Implicit in the change was the replacement of the holdings of the free and the unfree by a pattern of landed estates, and the creation of a society consisting of a few wealthy proprietors, a multitude of property-less tenants and an underclass of pauperized cottagers. This was the society which eventually came into being over the greater part of Wales, a development which had a profound impact upon the appearance of the country.

Throughout Europe, the authorities, lay and clerical, reacted to the crisis of the late fourteenth century by subjecting the mass of the population to ruthlessly exploitative lordship. Resentment of exploitation and of the curtailing of ancient liberties was a European-wide phenomenon. In Wales, it had an extra dimension, arising from the animosity of a conquered people towards its foreign lords, an animosity which found expression in the severe unrest of the 1340s, the hopes in the 1370s of deliverance through Owain Lawgoch (d. 1378), great-nephew of Llywelyn ap Gruffudd, and, above all, in that astonishing insurgence, the revolt of Owain Glyndŵr (1400–10).

The devastation wrought during the Glyndŵr revolt swept away any amelioration that the Welsh economy might have undergone since the Black Death. Both sides were involved in depredation, for while Glyndŵr was accused of 'bringing all things to waste', the English king was said to have 'proclaimed "havoc" of the whole of Wales'. At least forty towns suffered severely; Cardiff took centuries to recover, and such were the ravages visited upon Nefyn that it never regained its earlier prosperity.

The cathedrals of Bangor and St Asaph were partially destroyed, as were scores of parish churches. Royal troops razed the friary at Llanfaes, burial place of Joan, wife of Llywelyn ap Iorwerth, and at Strata Florida the abbey buildings became a barracks and the church a stable. So despoiled was the Cistercian monastery at Margam that it was said that the monks

were obliged to roam like vagabonds. Mills were destroyed, houses and crops burnt and the huge communal fines imposed upon the rebellious Welsh pauperized entire communities.

The Glyndŵr revolt led to a renewed interest in fortification. In 1414, the burgesses of Beaumaris were given permission to surround their town with walls; in the following year, walls were built to protect the eastern suburbs of Carmarthen and at much the same time Ruthin and Kidwelly were girded with defensive ditches. Most of the castles of the Principality were in the hands of the Crown. As the fifteenth century advanced that became true of many of the castles of the March, and some of them also underwent a degree of strengthening and repair. More extensive building occurred at those castles occupied permanently or intermittently by their owners. The Beauchamp lords of Glamorgan constructed a range of buildings along the western curtain wall at Cardiff in the 1430s, and in the late fifteenth century the Stradlings built a south range at St Donat's Castle. In the 1490s Rhys ap Thomas (d. 1525) remodelled much of the castles of Carew and Weobley, and, somewhat later, the lords of Chirk added a south range to their castle. In addition, there were more modest fortified buildings — tower houses such as those at Angle, Broncoed, Talgarth and Scethrog, although some of these may date originally from the fourteenth century.

Far and away the most elaborate fortified complex built in Wales — indeed, built in Britain — in the fifteenth century was the castle at Raglan. The Yellow or Great Tower, a self-contained fortress in its own right, and the south gate were built between about 1435 and 1445 by Sir William ap Thomas (d. 1445). The buildings around the two great courts, erected in the 1460s, were the work of his son, William Herbert (d. 1469), one of the first Welshmen to adopt a permanent surname. Although the courtyard buildings, especially those on the north side, were extensively remodelled by Herbert's great-great-grandson, William, third earl of Worcester (d. 1589), in the late sixteenth century, Raglan still retains the essential shape it had when William

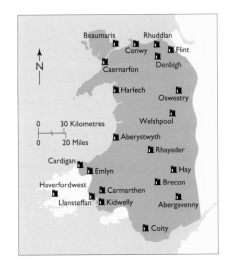

The regions subject to Owain Glyndŵr at the height of the Welsh revolt in 1404–05. Major castles subjected to Welsh siege are also shown.

The well-preserved early sixteenth-century mansion at Llancaiach Fawr, near Gelligaer, incorporates defensive features that clearly indicate considerable anxiety about security on the part of its builder. It is, however, unusual, for by that date most Welsh house builders were content with unfortified residences.

Herbert was executed in 1469. With its delightful pastoral setting, its great bulk, its superb machicolations and its ingenious gateway defences, Raglan is perhaps the most fascinating of all the medieval buildings of Wales. Among its features are gunloops and gun embrasures, for the castle was built at a time when the use of gunpowder was becoming increasingly widespread.

The gunloops and gun embrasures were located in positions which rendered them ineffectual, for the elaborate scale of the defences at Raglan was motivated more by ostentation than by military considerations. Furthermore, the chief intention of the building work at some of the older castles, such as Cardiff, Chirk and Carew, was to add to domestic comfort rather than to the fortifications. Some early Tudor houses — in particular Llancaiach Fawr near Gelligaer — have fascinating defensive features, but Welsh house builders were increasingly content with non-fortified dwellings. While there are 400 tower houses in County Limerick and hundreds in Cumberland and Northumberland, there are less than a score in the whole of Wales.

The confidence, which allowed the fortress mentality to be abandoned, had profound implications for the making of Wales, for it meant the emergence of a landscape dotted with mansions rather than castles, and with towns free from restrictive defences. It also meant, as Peter Smith has put it, that 'the distinction between a military caste, safe behind battlements, and a peasant class, living in undefended cottages, started to fade, and the mainstream of domestic architecture began to flow in quite another direction, in the direction of buildings undistorted by the necessities of war'.

In northern and eastern Wales, the dominant late medieval type was the hall-house described by Peter Smith as 'a great lofty room, its timbers disappearing into the darkness of a roof blackened by the smoke from an open hearth and ventilated by draughts from glassless windows'. Among the most interesting of Wales's fifteenth-century hall-houses are Bryndraenog in Radnorshire, with its magnificent cruck trusses tree-ring dated to 1436, Great House, Newchurch, also in Radnorshire, built in 1450, which has the widest cruck hall in Wales at 28 feet (8.6m), and Cochwillan near Bethesda, with its splendid hammer-beam roof. But of all the medieval houses of Wales undoubtedly the most appealing is Tretower,

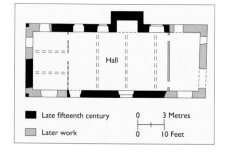

■ Late fifteenth century	0 3 Metres
□ Later work	0 10 Feet

The ground plan of Cochwillan shows how the hall dominated the entire house (After Smith 1988).

Opposite: In northern and eastern Wales, the dominant type of late medieval dwelling was the hall-house. Cochwillan near Bethesda, with its hammer-beam wooden roof, is seen as a grand finale of the upper-class hall. The house was probably built by Gwilym ap Gruffudd (d. 1500) who was appointed high sheriff of Caernarvonshire by King Henry VII.

Tretower Court, near Crickhowell, is undoubtedly the most appealing medieval house surviving in Wales. It was built by the Yorkist supporter, Sir Roger Vaughan, in the years before his death in 1471. The plan shows the full extent of the house.

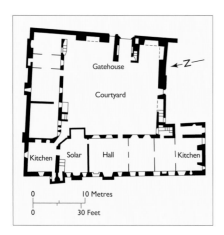

the hall-house built for Sir Roger Vaughan (d. 1471) between about 1450 and 1470 in the enchanting valley of the Rhiangoll.

These houses were all gentry dwellings of substantial proportions. More significant as an indicator of prosperity are the smaller dwellings of less exalted members of society. The fifteenth century was the first in which significant numbers of people had the means to acquire durable houses. The construction of such dwellings for at least some people below the gentry level indicates the emergence, by about 1450, of a yeoman class. These buildings are particularly numerous in the north-east. Perhaps the most intriguing of them is Tŷ Mawr, Castle Caereinion, which, until its true character was recognized by Peter Smith in 1971, appeared to be a dilapidated agricultural range. The ruin was, in fact, a brick-encased hall-house built of timber cut down in 1460. Splendidly restored, the Royal Institution of Chartered Surveyors hailed it as the 'building of the year' in 2000. Very few surviving houses pre-date Tŷ Mawr; the earliest so far identified is Hafodygarreg, near Erwood, which has been tree-ring dated to 1402.

Most of the yeomen's dwellings built in north-eastern and central Wales were timber-framed buildings; indeed, three quarters of the Welsh houses surviving from before the 1530s are of half-timbered construction. Their walls were prefabricated by skilled carpenters on an almost assembly-line system which brought a reasonable dwelling within reach of a large number of people.

Although Wales seems rich in stone, little of it is of high building quality, for the country lacks anything comparable with the great oolitic belt which crosses England. Thus, in the later Middle Ages, and for centuries to come, the carpenter much outshone the mason, and the whole of Wales north-east of a line from Machynlleth to Newport was the domain of the half-timbered building — a far more extensive region than surviving buildings would suggest.

This was as true of the towns as of the countryside. From Beaumaris to Monmouth, the recovering towns of late fifteenth-century Wales sparkled with timber-framed houses, and would continue to do so until the early nineteenth century. Now, as Peter Smith sadly observes, only Ruthin remains. 'It should', he declares, 'be scrupulously preserved as a national monument, as our best reminder of a departed urban gaiety before it was effaced by the dull reign of stone and stucco'. Since Smith wrote (1975), Nantclwyd House, a splendid mid-fifteenth-century urban hall-house, has been beautifully restored and opened to the public.

Dwellings of the standard built for yeoman families were beyond the means of the mass of the population. The great majority of the buildings erected in Wales between the fifteenth and eighteenth centuries were impermanent dwellings. A variety of building materials was used, particularly clom — a mixture of clay, horsehair and cow dung — although houses were also built of turf, timber and stone. No such houses built in the Wales of the late Middle Ages have survived intact, but signs of their existence — sometimes stone footings, often earth platforms, and frequently the grassy humps which covered them after they had been abandoned — are among the most plentiful indications of human settlement visible in upland Wales.

The hall-houses of the gentry and the dwellings of the yeomen provide evidence of the revival of the Welsh economy by the later fifteenth century. Literary sources, in particular the very distinguished body of Welsh poetry produced in the century after 1450, are further evidence, for a society close to destitution is not one that can maintain the servants of the muse through the long years of their apprenticeship and provide them with the hospitality they crave.

Proof of the rising prosperity is the increasing activity of the ports. Carmarthen, recognized as a staple port in 1326, was probably the most

Tŷ Mawr, Castle Caereinion, was thought to be nothing more than a dilapidated farm building until 1971, when it was discovered to be a late medieval aisled hall-house that had later been encased in brick. Dendrochronological (tree-ring) dating carried out during conservation has shown that the timber used in its construction was felled in 1460 (© Elisabeth Ingram).

Nantclwyd House, Ruthin, is a striking reminder of the many fine timber-framed buildings that once existed in Welsh towns. Built in the mid-fifteenth century as a hall-house, it was much altered in succeeding centuries. Now open to the public after restoration, its long history is interpreted for visitors in a series of period rooms (© Gareth Parry 2007).

Right: Aberconwy House, built in 1420, lies a short distance from Conwy's quay and suggests returning prosperity after the turmoil of Owain Glyndŵr's uprising. Probably a merchant's house, it is likely that the ground floor served as a shop or storehouse, while the upper floors provided domestic accommodation.

The church of St Nefydd and St Mary at Llannefydd is perhaps the most attractive of the double-nave churches characteristic of the Vale of Clwyd. Virtually all these churches were constructed in the Perpendicular style of Gothic architecture in the fifteenth and early sixteenth centuries (Clwyd-Powys Archaeological Trust).

important of them, but others, especially Chepstow, Tenby, Swansea, Caernarfon and Beaumaris, were handling increasing numbers of ships. Aberconwy House, a jettied town house with ground-floor shop or store, was built in 1420 near the quay and illustrates the early recovery of Conwy following the convulsions of the Glyndŵr rebellion. Thomas White (d. 1482), who ensured Henry Tudor's safe departure from Tenby, was one of the town's merchants, and a particularly prosperous one to judge by his tomb in St Mary's Church. The most intriguing evidence of the activity of a late medieval Welsh port is the ship discovered in the river Usk at Newport in 2002. Although partially damaged, the ship, 84 feet (25m) long, retains the shape of its hull, a fact which makes it one of the most exciting maritime discoveries of recent years. Datable to the mid-fifteenth century, it was carrying a cargo from Portugal; it may have anchored in the Usk for emergency repairs, but there are those who argue that late medieval Newport was wholly capable of dealing with the cargoes of such large ships.

The Church also shared in the recovery, as the remarkable boom in church building in the late fifteenth and early sixteenth centuries testifies. Again the north-east led the way. Indeed, so extensive was the building and rebuilding in the Perpendicular style that much of the evidence of the region's earlier medieval churches has been lost. Ecclesiastical and domestic architecture developed in tandem. Fine timber roofs were the glory of hall-houses as they were of churches, and what was a hall-house with its step to the dais but a secular version of the church with its step to the altar? Among the delights of the north-east are the double-nave churches so characteristic of the Vale of Clwyd. Abergele is the largest of them, but

Llannefydd, with its light and spacious feel, is perhaps the most attractive. The additional nave was probably built to accommodate an increasing population, but it may represent the desire to provide space in which to honour the burgeoning cult of the Virgin Mary. The enlargement of churches provided walls that could be covered with murals. Almost all Wales's late medieval murals were painted over following the Protestant Reformation, but recent restoration work has uncovered some splendid images — those at Llangattock Lingoed in Monmouthshire, for example, or at Llancarfan in the Vale of Glamorgan, covered by no less than twenty-two layers of whitewash, and in St Teilo's Church in the Llwchwr Valley, a church re-erected at Wales's National History Museum at St Fagans, near Cardiff.

A portion of the well-preserved wall painting of the legend of St George recently discovered at the church of St Cadoc in Llancarfan in the Vale of Glamorgan. This exceptionally fine painting was executed in the fifteenth century.

Among the most attractive religious buildings erected in late medieval Wales is St Winifred's Well at Holywell, with its fine vaulting, its four-centred arches and its superb traceried screenwork — of which only fragments now remain. Pilgrimage to wells was a feature of the popular religious observance of the later Middle Ages, a practice which, in Wales, harked back to the delight of its Iron Age inhabitants in watery places. By 1500, the country had at least 500 wells which were venerated because of their saintly associations, a veneration that long survived the Protestant Reformation and which led in 1997 to the establishment of the Wellsprings Fellowship. St Winifred's Chapel at Holywell was completed in the first decade of the sixteenth century. It was built under the patronage of the Stanley family; the churches commissioned by the family include those at Gresford, Mold, Northop, Holt and Wrexham. Now known as the 'Stanley churches', these are Wales's finest group of Perpendicular churches. Among their splendours are their towers, that of Wrexham in particular. Gresford, with its wonderful harmony of design, its glorious roof and its magnificent east window, is the finest parish church in Wales.

The building and rebuilding of town churches, of which Wrexham and Mold are such fine examples, was much in vogue in the years 1450 to 1530. Other major projects include St John's, Cardiff and St Cybi's, Holyhead, as well as extensive rebuilding work such as the chancel at Presteigne, the nave at Welshpool, the tower at St Mary's, Brecon, the roof, porch and north aisle at Tenby and the clerestory at St Mary's, Haverfordwest. There was work also at the four cathedrals. Bangor and St Asaph were restored and remodelled; Llandaff was enhanced by the handsome Jasper Tower, traditionally ascribed to the patronage of Jasper Tudor (d. 1495), uncle of Henry VII; St Davids acquired the superb Perpendicular chapel of Bishop Vaughan (1509–22) and, in about 1538, it received its crowning glory, the oak ceiling of the nave, 'a work of almost Arabian gorgeousness'.

In this building activity, little resembling a Welsh style or styles is apparent. The Jasper Tower, St John's in Cardiff and a number of the handsome churches of southern Monmouthshire were in the tradition of the Somerset churches of which St Mary Magdalene, Taunton, is the exemplar; Gresford was modelled upon the Perpendicular churches of the Cheshire Plain, although in quality it surpasses all of them; the Wrexham tower was inspired by that pinnacled marvel, the tower of St Peter's, Gloucester; Holyhead and other north-west Wales churches such as Llaneilian and Clynnog-fawr were the work of incoming craftsmen, probably those imported to undertake the work at Bangor Cathedral.

Nevertheless, some of the less ambitious churches of Wales — the dignified, unadorned towers of Defynnog, Talgarth and Llanddowror, for example — do point to the existence of native craftsmen working in their own idiom. This is more pronounced among carpenters than among masons. Wales has only one church wholly built of timber — All Saints, Trelystan, splendidly situated on the slopes of the Long Mountain east of Welshpool. The country has, however, a wealth of timber bell turrets, porches, roofs, screens and lofts.

The screens and lofts are among the finest of all the creations of the makers of Wales. They are, stresses Glanmor Williams, the product of

Opposite: St Winifred's Well at Holywell in Flintshire is a remarkable structure, with stonework of the very highest quality. It was completed in the first years of the sixteenth century.

St Giles at Wrexham is one of the finest examples of town church rebuilding in the late fifteenth and early sixteenth centuries. The tower, probably by the master mason William Hort, is its greatest glory.

Above: The nave of the tiny parish church at Partrishow, north of Abergavenny. The carved wooden screen and rood loft of about 1500 far outshine the simple architectural detail of the remainder.

Right: This detail of the rood loft at Partrishow reveals the consummate skill of the carpenter who carved it. Most of the screens and other wooden furnishings in Welsh churches of the late Middle Ages would have been created by craftsmen working within 'a strongly defined native tradition of woodworking'. Regrettably, only a few precious examples of 'the flowing exuberance and vitality' of those artists survive.

'a strongly defined native tradition of woodworking', and he suggests that the carvers, confined, as they were, to 'a limited number of highly stylized themes and patterns', had close affinities with the Welsh poets, for 'in wood and in word, the flowing exuberance and vitality of the artist were enhanced rather than fettered by his strict adherence to the meticulous detail and the exacting classicism of his artistic conventions'. Traces of over 300 screens have been discovered in Wales. Only a few survive, and their destruction — particularly that of the most magnificent of them, the screen at Newtown — is one of the greatest blows suffered by the Welsh cultural heritage. Of those that do survive, probably the most appealing are the screens at Llanegryn, north of Tywyn, Llananno, north of Llandrindod, Llanfilo, near Brecon, and Partrishow, north of Abergavenny. Anyone seeing the screen at Partrishow, with its 'mysterious and charming silver patina', cannot but agree with Glanmor Williams that the traceries of a Welsh screen are 'as congenial an expression of Welsh medieval aesthetics as a *cywydd* or an *englyn*'.

Skill with timber underlines the central importance of woodlands in the economy of late medieval Wales. They were the source not only of building material but also of fuel for heating and cooking, timber for furniture, charcoal for smelting, tannin for the leather industry, ashes for the dyeing and soap industries, soles for clogs, staves for barrels and the means of making a host of household utensils; in addition they offered game, the pleasures of the chase, pannage for pigs and shelter for outlaws. Yet, by the early sixteenth century, only about 15 per cent of the surface of Wales was forested, a percentage no higher than that of the High Middle Ages. Thus it would seem that any reafforestation that had occurred as a result of the fourteenth-century contraction in population had been reversed by the renewal of assarting in the following century. Woodlands still abounded along the borderlands, but in Anglesey, Pembrokeshire, Cardiganshire and the Vale of Glamorgan, anything resembling a forest had long disappeared. This did not mean that the landscape in those regions was treeless, for everywhere there were copses and wooded slopes, almost all of them — in marked contrast to today — made up of indigenous species.

Thus, by dint of the labour of countless generations of the makers of Wales, the country was by the 1530s largely a cleared landscape. It was described in that decade by the topographer John Leland, and detailed information is also available in the great survey of Church property — *Valor Ecclesiasticus* — compiled in 1535. The picture that emerges is that of a pre-industrial society based upon peasant farming, but with some significant secondary economic activity also based in the main upon agriculture. Compared with today, Wales in the 1530s was a sparsely populated country. It had perhaps 270,000 people, fewer than it had had in 1300 and less than a tenth of the present population. About 15 per cent were town dwellers, compared with the vast majority today. Probably only five towns, Carmarthen, Brecon, Wrexham, Haverfordwest and Cardiff, had as many as 1,500 inhabitants, and in any case, town dwellers, with their cattle on the town lands and their backstreet sties and byres, were themselves half agriculturalists.

Carpenters, like the one depicted as Noah in this manuscript illustration of 1420–30, would have been familiar figures in late medieval Wales. Wood was essential in every sphere of life, and, although only about 15 per cent of Wales was forested by the early sixteenth century, woodlands were crucial to the country's economy (Bodleian Library, University of Oxford, Ms. Barlow 53 [R]).

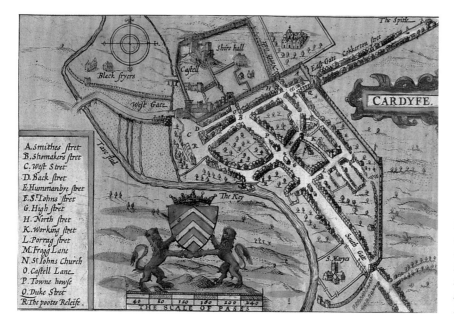

By the 1530s, Cardiff was probably one of only five towns in Wales with a population of around 1,500. The layout and size of the town were probably very similar to the arrangements mapped by John Speed in 1611 (By permission of The National Library of Wales).

The process of the enclosure of earlier open-field systems had begun in various parts of Wales by the late sixteenth century. By 1622, when this survey of the manor of Barry was made by Evans Mouse, virtually all the land in the Vale of Glamorgan had been enclosed (Glamorgan Record Office, DF/Manorial).

Opposite: The droving of cattle to England for fattening and sale became firmly established in late fifteenth-century Wales. A pattern of roads emerged based on the drovers' routes, and these were to have a marked influence on Welsh topography. This bridge at Pont-Scethin is located between Harlech and Dolgellau on the drovers' route to London (© Crown Copyright (2009) Visit Wales).

In many ways, the countryside did not look markedly different from the way it looks today. It had fewer enclosed fields and hedgerows. George Owen claimed in 1603 that gavelkind 'had made the whole countrie to remain… without hedges and enclosures', and Rice Merrick stated in 1578 that, two generations previously, cattle could run to the sea without hindrance from the main road crossing the Vale of Glamorgan. Yet Leland noted that fields had been enclosed in Anglesey, and it is now accepted that there was extensive construction of boundary hedges in medieval Wales. The country was less uniformly green than it was to be in the early twenty-first century, for corn was grown virtually everywhere. While corn produced 75 per cent of the tithe paid by the lowland parish of Newton Nottage, it accounted for 20 per cent even in the highland parish of Merthyr Tydfil, and the hills were dotted with barns and corn mills. Virtually all the corn was grown for home consumption, for it was Wales's pastoral, not its arable, farming which produced the country's surpluses.

Sheep and cattle were virtually the sole source of income in the countryside. In many ways, sheep were the most important form of livestock. It was their grazing which prevented the reafforestation of the uplands and, as the mountains became increasingly the domain of sheep, transhumance declined, for sheep, when not milked — and they rarely were in Wales — do not need tending daily. Although summer migration did not come to an end until about 1790, many *hafotai* had become independent farms by the early sixteenth century. Even more significant was the wealth produced by turning fleeces into cloth, for the cloth industry was a highly effective means of spreading wealth. The industry failed to prosper in the south-west, which helps to explain the scarcity of late medieval houses in that region. It flourished mightily in the north-east and was successful in the middle borderlands and the south-east, surely the key to the richness of those regions in early yeomen's dwellings.

Sheep produce fleeces, meat and leather. Cattle produce meat, leather, horn, milk, butter and cheese. Leather making, an important and underemphasized activity in pre-industrial Wales, made itself felt, olfactorily and otherwise, in all Welsh towns. Dairy products had a central role in the economy of lowland Wales, with Bristol drawing heavily on the output of the coastal south. The trade in beef cattle had a role almost everywhere. The droving of cattle to England for fattening and sale became well established in the late fifteenth century, and as a result emphasized a pattern of roads that would strongly influence Welsh topography and serve to emphasize west–east, at the expense of north–south, communications.

Cattle droving would continue to be a central feature of the Welsh economy until the creation of Wales's railway network, less than 150 years ago. It opened up vast areas of remote country, led to the establishment of scores of forges and taverns and was the chief ultimate source of the wealth which permitted Welsh landlords to build their mansions, lay out their parks and, in a myriad other ways, leave their impress upon the land of Wales.

FROM THE 'UNION' TO THE STUART RESTORATION

THE MAKING OF WALES 1536–1660

In the 1530s the English Parliament passed legislation which represented the culmination of developments which had been afoot in Wales for a quarter of a millennium. The legislation would provide a framework for the life of the Welsh people, in matters secular and religious, for the next quarter of a millennium. The legal and administrative assimilation of the country by the English state in 1536, and the religious changes initiated by Thomas Cromwell in 1533, culminating in the acceptance of the Thirty-Nine Articles in 1563, had an impact upon every aspect of Welsh life.

The Act of 1536 laid down that the county system established by Edward I in the Principality was to be extended to the March. Seven new counties came into existence and county administration was put into the hands of the Justices of the Peace, men drawn almost exclusively from the emerging gentry class. Wales was to have twenty-seven MPs, fourteen representing the counties and thirteen the boroughs.

Central to the assimilation was the abolition of any legal distinction between the Welsh and the English. This meant that the penal laws passed during the Glyndŵr revolt were nullified (though not formally repealed) and that the law of England would be the only law recognized by the courts of Wales. Thus, in the eyes of the law, the Welsh would henceforth be English. Yet, it would be equally valid to argue — as there was no longer any advantage in boasting of the condition of being English — that henceforth everyone living in Wales was Welsh, a principle which would be built upon in subsequent generations.

The Act of 1536 — modified by that of 1543 — served to define the land of Wales, for (despite the one-time anomalous position of Monmouthshire) Wales has, since the 1530s, been considered to be the territory contained within the thirteen counties. To demarcate the borders of Wales was irrelevant to the legislators of the 1530s, for their intention was to incorporate Wales into the English realm. Yet demarcate it they did. The border thus created did not follow the old line of Offa's Dyke, nor the eastern boundaries of the Welsh dioceses; it excluded districts such as Oswestry and Archenfield, where the Welsh language would continue to be spoken for centuries — districts it would not be wholly fanciful to consider as *Cambria irredenta*.

The reign of King Henry VIII (1509–47) saw the passage of legislation in 1536 and 1543 that marked the legal and administrative assimilation of Wales by the English state (The National Archives, PRO, E344/22).

Opposite: The great chamber in Plas Mawr, Conwy, built for Robert Wynn (d. 1598) between 1576 and 1585. Wynn was a younger son with few prospects and made his fortune serving Sir Philip Hoby, a gentleman of the royal household. In the house's plasterwork, Wynn mingled royal badges and monograms with heraldic emblems of the princes of Gwynedd from whom he claimed descent.

The Act of 1536 — again modified by that of 1543 — also served to
define territories within Wales. Although six of the counties of Wales —
Anglesey, Caernarvonshire, Merioneth, Flintshire, Cardiganshire and
Carmarthenshire — date back wholly or partly to the thirteenth century,
it was in 1536 that the counties became the primary definition of community
beyond the very local. Some of them — Denbighshire, for example —
hardly had much geographical coherence, but as they were the units for
the selection of MPs, the appointment of high sheriffs and, above all, the
judicial and administrative activities of the Justices of the Peace, they rapidly
became the focuses of intense loyalty. Cartographers — key figures in the
recording of the making of Wales — seized upon the counties as the natural
units to depict. Saxton mapped them all in 1579 and they were delineated,
each on a separate page, in five different atlases between 1611 and 1645.
The counties were also the units for the work of topographers and historians,
as the writings of Owen on Pembrokeshire and Merrick and Stradling on
Glamorgan testify.

The shiring of Wales meant the designation of thirteen county towns; some of them — Harlech in particular — hardly grew beyond villages, but others gained increased prosperity from their new status. Speed's atlas, published in 1611, contains sketches of shire halls at Cardiff and Caernarfon and mentions the shire hall at Denbigh. Undoubtedly other county halls existed, but no trace of them has survived. By the nineteenth century, nine of the original county towns had proved to be unsuitably located and other centres were chosen. Of the remaining four, the status of Cardiff as county town of Glamorgan was much disputed, but Caernarfon, Carmarthen and Brecon were never challenged as the capitals of their eponymous counties. Those three towns, together with Denbigh, were also designated the centres of the circuits of the Great Sessions of Wales, a system of courts which lasted until 1830. They were the capitals of the four corners of the country, and, in the hierarchy of Welsh towns, they were the ones with the fullest functions. However, to the extent that Wales as a whole had a capital, it lay beyond the country's border. That was Ludlow, the one-time *caput* of the marcher lordships of the Mortimer family and, from the late fifteenth century until 1689, the seat of the Council of Wales. With its magnificent castle, its splendid church and its delightful townscape, Ludlow cannot but arouse covetousness in a Welsh patriot.

The legislation of 1536 and 1543 greatly strengthened the position of the emerging class of Welsh gentry. The granting to the Welsh of full equality under the law meant that all careers were open to upper-class Welshmen. They were particularly attracted to the law; Old Gwernyfed in the Wye Valley was one of the numerous great houses built from the profits of that profession. Others prospered through trade and commerce, the source of the wealth which allowed Richard Clough to be such a prodigious builder. As JPs, high sheriffs and MPs, the leading gentry won recognition as the sovereigns of

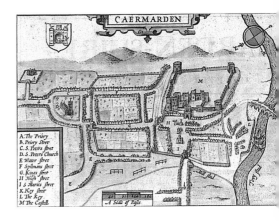

Carmarthen, whose status as the county town of Carmarthenshire was never challenged, was depicted in John Speed's atlas published in 1611 (By permission of The National Library of Wales).

Above: The 'new men' of the Tudor age in Wales were particularly attracted to the law. Old Gwernyfed in the Wye Valley — probably built for Sir David Williams, MP for Brecon — was one of the many great houses built with the profits of the profession.

From the late fifteenth century until 1689, the English border town of Ludlow was the seat of the Council of Wales. In this period, to the extent that Wales as a whole had a single capital, it lay here, beyond the country's border.

their countryside, and their neighbourhoods were enriched with the houses, parks, tombs and coats of arms created to vaunt their enhanced prestige.

The abolition in 1536 of the privileges of the marcher lords brought to an end the power once exercised by the holders of the castles of the conquistadors, thereby endowing the countryside with a more diffuse pattern of centres of power. The insistence upon the use of English law meant that partible inheritance, a practice already abandoned by many Welsh gentry families, was proscribed. Thus, the way was open for those intent upon estate building, an activity which ensured that over the subsequent three centuries Wales was a country dominated by a small caste of landed proprietors.

Religious changes aided the estate builders, for the suppression of the monasteries led to huge transfers of land. In landscape terms, the suppression was the most significant aspect of the Reformation. Carried out between 1536 and 1540, it meant the plunder of all the monasteries, nunneries and friaries and the ruination of buildings for which there was no obvious alternative religious use. Wales's Benedictine priory churches, largely urban in their setting, had been used by local parishioners as well as by the monks. They survived relatively well; indeed, all eight of them (nine if the nunnery at Usk is included) are still places of worship today. That is also the case at Margam, where the church of St Mary occupies part of the nave of the Cistercian abbey, and at Brecon, where the choir of the Dominican friary is the chapel of Christ College. Of the remaining forty or so religious houses in Wales, all fell into ruin and some disappeared altogether. A number of them were greatly dilapidated before the suppression; the Cistercian monastery of Strata Marcella, for example, was in a state of advanced disrepair by the early sixteenth century. Now nothing is visible above ground there, and the same is more or less true of the Cistercian houses of Grace Dieu, Maenan, Whitland and Llantarnam. Action has been taken to ensure that it will not also be true of Cwmhir, where what was left of the nave was in danger of being pilfered into obliteration.

The rest of the Cistercian abbeys, Tintern in particular, but also Basingwerk, Cymer, Neath, Strata Florida and Valle Crucis, survive as picturesque ruins. Monasteries of other orders — the Tironian at St Dogmaels, the Augustinian at Haverfordwest, Llanthony and Penmon, and the Premonstratensian at Talyllychau — have their ruins, but, with the exception of Brecon, the friaries have virtually disappeared; there is no more melancholy sight in Wales than the remnant of the Carmelite friary at Denbigh.

Thus was the country robbed of a great part of its architectural heritage. Something was salvaged; much of the arcading at Cwmhir was re-erected in the parish church at Llanidloes and the fine roof at Cilcain church may have come from Basingwerk Abbey. Yet the losses were immense. Although the walls of Tintern still stand to roof height, the place is but a shell. Although the west doorway at Strata Florida is still a thing of beauty, the upper Teifi Valley has been dispossessed of its great glory. Into this arena of despoliation stepped the gentry. The conventual buildings of some religious houses were adapted as homes of landowning families. Sir John Price took up residence at the prior's house at Brecon and turned the west side of the cloister into stables. Richard

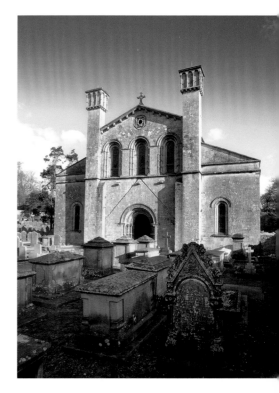

The suppression of the monasteries in 1536–40 occasioned the destruction of a great part of the country's architectural heritage. However, some former monastic churches were to survive, and, as at Margam, they continue to serve as places of worship today.

Opposite: After the suppression, it was far from uncommon for the conventual buildings of Welsh monasteries to be adapted as homes for gentry families. Sir Richard Williams acquired the Cistercian abbey at Neath soon after its suppression in 1539, and set in train the transformation of the late medieval abbot's lodging into a splendid Tudor house. The large opening in this view marks the position of a grand bay window that lit the long gallery. The house seems to have remained inhabited until at least the 1740s.

Margam was another former Cistercian abbey where a Tudor house was raised over earlier monastic buildings. The Mansel family had raised a 'faire and sumptious house' there by the late sixteenth century. The rambling mansion, depicted here in an anonymous painting of about 1700, was demolished in the late eighteenth century after the owner, Thomas Mansel Talbot, decided to move the family seat to Penrice Castle in Gower (Private Collection).

The Stedmans were another family that took advantage of the suppression of the monasteries. They erected a house on the south side of the cloister at Strata Florida Abbey. It is shown here in a 1741 engraving by Samuel and Nathaniel Buck (By permission of The National Library of Wales).

Williams at Neath and the Mansels at Margam commissioned the building of great houses within abbey precincts. The Carnes (a family which remained loyal to Roman Catholicism) formed a large house out of the conventual buildings at Ewenny; members of another Catholic family, the Turbervilles, were responsible for an elaborate house on the site of a remote grange of Neath Abbey at Sker and the Stedmans for a more modest dwelling on the site of the south side of the cloister at Strata Florida.

It was the land rather than the buildings of the Church which was the chief target of the avarice of the gentry. The religious houses owned between 10 and 15 per cent of the surface area of Wales, and thus the suppression involved a change in the ownership of hundreds of thousands of acres of Welsh land. Most of the monastic estates were purchased from the Crown at around twenty times the annual rent, although the royal favourite, Henry, earl of Worcester (d. 1549), heir to the Herberts of Raglan, obtained much of the possessions of Tintern for next to nothing. The sales did not lead to any great change in land management and use, for the monasteries had long abandoned direct farming and had leased their land to laymen, often members of the same families as those who obtained absolute ownership of it in the wake of the suppression. The land transfers greatly helped to confirm the power of the gentry as the dominant class in Wales, and much assisted their efforts to ensure that as much terrain as possible came under their unfettered control.

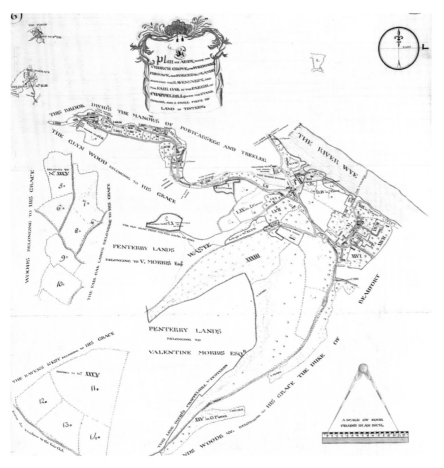

The suppression of the monasteries was accompanied by huge transfers of land from the Church to eager estate builders. The Monmouthshire estates of Tintern Abbey passed to Henry Somerset, earl of Worcester (d. 1549). His successors, as dukes of Beaufort, continued to hold the abbey site until 1901. The Beaufort estate around the immediate environs of the abbey was mapped in 1764 (By permission of The National Library of Wales, Badminton Maps, vol. 2, no. 6).

The religious houses possessed spiritual as well as temporal property. This consisted in the main of appropriated livings — the ownership of the tithes and endowments of parishes. At the suppression these livings also passed into the hands of the gentry, particularly in the dioceses of Llandaff and St Davids, where at least half the parishes came to have lay patrons. Some of the patrons delighted in their churches, seeing them as an adjunct of the estate and reserving parts of them for their family tombs. Thus at St Nicholas, Montgomery, the Herberts lie in the Lymore Transept and at Stackpole the owners of Stackpole Court lie in the Lort Chapel. In most cases, however, appropriation meant siphoning off ecclesiastical income, the basic cause of the poverty of the Welsh Church in subsequent centuries and of the abject condition of many of its places of worship. Lay pressure could result in the surrender of major sources of ecclesiastical income. Bishop Kitchin (1545–63) leased out in perpetuity the manor of Llandaff, once the source of a third of the episcopal income; Bishop Barlow (1536–48) was forced to surrender the manor of Lamphey — 'the Castel Gandolfo of the bishops of St Davids' — in a poor exchange for the rectory of Carew, and at St Asaph Sir John Salusbury robbed the diocese of extensive property by borrowing the chapter seal to prepare forged leases. The increasing dilapidation of the cathedrals of Wales — particularly that at Llandaff — was the consequence of such transactions and malpractices.

The palace at Lamphey was a favoured country residence of the bishops of St Davids and stood at the centre of a major estate. Nevertheless, lay pressure compelled Bishop Barlow (1536–48) to surrender the manor of Lamphey in an unfavourable exchange for the rectory of Carew.

Other aspects of the Reformation also served to reduce ecclesiastical income. Pilgrim offerings, profits from sales of candles and payments for Masses came to an end. The appearance of parish churches was drastically modified as images were removed, murals painted over, rood lofts mutilated, shrines destroyed and altars replaced by communion tables. The hatred of 'Romish' practices that led to such modifications reached its peak at St Davids, where Bishop Barlow wished to abandon the cathedral because of its remoteness and its association with saintly relics. He established the bishop's residence at Abergwili near Carmarthen and there is some evidence

The simple church of St Ellyw in Llanelieu, near Talgarth, gives a powerful impression of the impact that the Reformation had on the appearance of parish churches in Wales. Unusually, the tympanum above the screen has survived along with traces of its painted decoration and a ghostly outline of the now vanished rood (Alex Ramsey for the Friends of Friendless Churches).

that he ordered the removal of parts of the roof from the bishop's palace at St Davids, leaving the splendid building to the mercy of the elements — an act of breathtaking vandalism.

The generation before the 1530s had seen a boom in church building. It came to an end with the Reformation. This may be because enough churches had already been built — particularly as there would henceforth be more room in them as a result of the discontinuance of Roman Catholic practices — or because of the poverty of dioceses, or because lay philanthropy found other outlets. Whatever the reason, it is striking that, despite an increasing population, hardly any new churches were built in Wales in the century following the 1530s. There is one striking exception. In 1578, the Puritan-inclined Robert Dudley, earl of Leicester (d. 1588), began building a church near the castle at Denbigh. Had it been completed, it would have been the first Protestant church to have been built in Wales and one of the very earliest to have been built in the territories of the English Crown. Deliberately eschewing the 'Romish' Gothic, it has round arches and Tuscan columns and was designed not for ritual but for preaching. Work on it was abandoned in 1584; it is now a somewhat forlorn ruin, but it can be considered the forerunner of what would eventually be the quintessential Welsh place of worship — the Nonconformist chapel.

A significant, but often underestimated, consequence of the Reformation was the sanctioning of clerical marriage. Married priests had not been unknown in medieval Wales, for bardic patrons such as Dafydd ap Tomos of Faenor in Cardiganshire and Hywel ap Dai of Northop in Flintshire were prosperous clerics much given to uxoriousness. Yet in pre-Reformation Wales, a priest's wife and offspring were something of an anomaly and the endorsement of clerical marriage in 1549 was probably fundamental to the readiness of many a cleric to embrace Protestantism, for it meant respectability for his wife and legitimacy for his children. The change placed a heavy financial burden on the Church, as a celibate can be housed far more cheaply than a family man. It also had architectural implications, for the time would come when Wales would be dotted with rectories and vicarages, buildings frequently larger than the churches served by their occupants.

The Reformation, like the 'union' of Wales with England, was an aspect of that intensification of the sovereignty of the English Crown which was the essence of Tudor monarchy. Admittedly, the notion that the coming of the Tudors and the integration of Wales into the legal and administrative system of England meant that anarchy rapidly gave way to effective authority is highly misleading. Yet the growing efficiency of the machinery of government did mean that violence and disorder were coming under increasing control. The belief, already widespread in the late fifteenth century, that the state could provide security, became firmly accepted. Thus, the building of fortified dwellings was wholly abandoned, although as late as 1626 Thomas Morgan commissioned at Ruperra a non-defensible version of a castle complete with cylindrical angle towers. That properly defensible houses were no longer built is an indication not only of a more peaceable society, but also of an evolutionary tempo much faster than that of most of the rest of Europe.

The church begun by Robert Dudley, earl of Leicester, at Denbigh in 1578 is the one striking exception to the lack of major church building in Wales in the Elizabethan period.

Ruperra Castle was commissioned in 1626 by Sir Thomas Morgan. Although furnished with corner towers and crenellations, it was never intended to be a serious fortification. Rather, as John Newman remarked, it is 'an outstanding example of the nostalgia for the chivalric past felt in the early seventeenth century' (© Crown: Royal Commission on the Ancient and Historical Monuments of Wales, C2003/200/3).

Increasing security also helped to promote economic growth, which in turn facilitated a marked increase in population. The figures can only be tentative, but it would seem that the number of Wales's inhabitants rose from around 250,000 in 1530 to 360,000 in 1620. Economic growth did not result in the enhancement of the living standards of every section of the expanding population. The period saw dramatic inflation, with the price of ordinary goods rising at least fourfold. The purchasing power of the poorest sections of the community halved and the gulf between the social classes widened greatly. While yeomen were able to acquire increasingly commodious houses, and the richer gentry could dwell in palatial surroundings, the poor of the sixteenth and seventeenth centuries, like those of the later Middle Ages, had to be content with very modest houses. William Richards, writing in 1682, described them as 'dunghills shaped into cottages', but, as he was a satirist, the comment is perhaps unreliable. Evidence concerning the housing of the poor is very limited at least until the later decades of the eighteenth century, a marked contrast with the plentiful evidence concerning the houses of yeomen families. As the hundreds of such houses surviving testify, the years 1530 to 1640 were the era of the great rural rebuilding, particularly after about 1575 when open hall-houses began to be adapted, and new house types were built. Indeed, the great majority of the buildings that have survived from the three centuries 1500–1800 are the farmhouses occupied by the 'middling sort' of people. Cyril Fox and Lord Raglan surveyed 470 such houses in the old county of Monmouth and, since their work of 1954, many more houses have been identified. Yet the rebuilding was by no means a Wales-wide phenomenon. In the Vale of Meifod in northern Montgomeryshire, Peter Smith commented in 1975, 'every other house appears seventeenth century or earlier', whereas few signs of houses obviously older than 1660 have been discovered in the Vale of Aeron in mid-Cardiganshire. Increasing wealth permitted not only new houses to be built, but also existing houses to be progressively modified. The primary modification was the installation of a fireplace and chimney. Early fireplaces tended to be erected on the lateral wall or the gable end of the house. This was particularly the practice around Pembroke and St Davids, where the so-called Flemish chimneys, with their cylindrical or conical stacks, are so massive that it almost seems that the house has been added to the chimney rather than the chimney to the house. In the north-east and in central Wales, however, it became far more common to place the fireplace across the middle of the hall, either opposite the entry or backing upon the walkway leading from it.

The installation of a chimney had far-reaching implications. If placed on an internal partition wall, it divided the hall into two, thus bringing to an end the concept of a single room as the arena of all household activities. With smoke being drawn up the stack, less ventilation was needed, a development which coincided with a marked increase in the production of window glass. Although smallholders' houses in northern Glamorgan still lacked glass as late as 1820, the dwellings of almost all those with a modicum of wealth had glass windows by 1660, perhaps the greatest single improvement in the standard of living ever to have taken place. An open fireplace in the middle of the floor

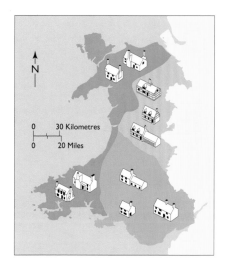

The years from 1530 to 1640 are recognized as a period of great rural rebuilding, with the storeyed house becoming common in most areas. This very simplified map shows the principal regional divisions in the style of houses in Wales. In the west, a style with chimneys on the outer wall predominated. In the eastern part of the country, chimneys were more common inside. In the north-east, these formed a lobby at the entrance, whereas, in the south-east, the fireplace backed on to the entry passage (After Smith, in Owen 1989).

Garn at Llanychâr in Pembrokeshire is a good early example of a house with a large fireplace in one of the lateral walls. Here it is a primary feature. The round chimney — a so-called Flemish chimney — is common in the region (© Crown: Royal Commission on the Ancient and Historical Monuments of Wales, C86007/3).

Opposite: Trewern Hall near Welshpool took on its essential form in 1610, though it may incorporate parts of an earlier building. It is one of the finest houses of its period surviving in Wales.

The four sketches and plans shown here attempt to simplify and summarize the development of the farmhouse in Wales from about 1500 to about 1680 (After Smith, in Owen 1989).

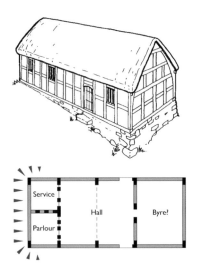

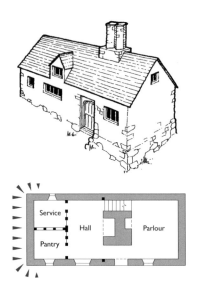

A half-timbered, single-storey hall-house of about 1500, sited on a hill. There is no formal fireplace, with a hearth probably sited in the floor at the centre of the hall.

A hall-house rebuilt as a storeyed house about 1560. A fireplace and chimney replace the earlier gable vent arrangement, and the walls are of stone.

needs high headroom for the smoke to disperse, but a house with a chimney can accommodate an upper floor. The consequent doubling of floor space meant that members of even modest families could have bedrooms. Many dwellings which now have chimneys, two storeys and partitions are the result of imposing a new arrangement upon an open hall; however, in some areas, newly built houses, complete with chimneys and two storeys, were being erected by the late sixteenth century.

The hall-houses had a strong regional distribution, but in the areas where they were common — in north and east Wales — they were built both for the gentry and for less affluent families. Regional differences were intensified in the house types which succeeded the hall-house, with social distinctions expressed in relative size and sophistication of construction. The house was a focus of an economic unit, and the relationship of house to farm buildings varied from region to region. In the less favoured areas of the south and west, the longhouse, in which the homestead and cow-house are linked by internal access, was a common building type. Of those that survive, some have medieval origins, but almost all of them have been extensively modified, in particular through closing the access between the house and beast-house. It is likely also that the outer rooms of some medieval hall-houses — Tŷ Mawr, Castle Caereinion, for example — had once housed cattle, but that these were converted into parlours in more prosperous days. Even where there was no direct access between them, the attachment of house to farm buildings tended to be associated with pastoral farming, and, often, with lower status. In contrast, on prosperous farms, free-standing farm buildings could vie in quality with hall-houses, as the splendid barn erected at Gellilyfdy in Flintshire in 1586 amply testifies.

While yeomen clung to the two- or three-bay hall-house, the richer families were more ambitious, building wings, mullioned windows, stairwells and elaborate chimney stacks, a style which reached its climax at Pentrehobyn near Mold, a substantial house in the sub-medieval tradition completed in the early seventeenth century. Decades earlier, however, a new style was intruding, for, in the later sixteenth century, at least in the progressive parts of Britain, the classical architecture of the south of Europe was, as Peter Smith has put it, beginning to displace the organic architecture of the north. The Renaissance house brought a revolution in basic plan. There was a novel concern for symmetry; the outward appearance of a building became a prime consideration, with elaborate attention given to the front façade — itself a new concept, for the notion that a house had a front and a back was alien to medieval thinking. A rational analysis of the functional requirements of the interior led to the study of the proportions of the main rooms, to ensure independent access to each of them, and to the construction of grand staircases. As houses came to have parlours, dining rooms and libraries, the hall shrank to a mere vestibule. As the designs of grander houses became more ambitious, it became the work of architects rather than craftsmen, a factor which contributed to the undermining of the vigour of regional building styles; nevertheless, a strong vernacular tradition persisted where the building of more modest houses was concerned.

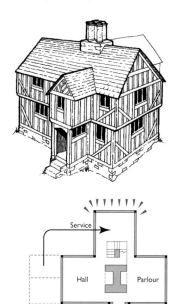

Left: In 1600, Richard Basset added a 'tower of the orders' to the fourteenth-century manor house at Old Beaupre in the Vale of Glamorgan.

Of the half-timbered houses of the borderland, this example could date to about 1630. It might be considered an early Renaissance house, with a cruciform or cross-shaped plan and a porch to the front.

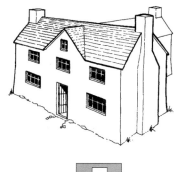

By about 1680, early centrally planned houses had begun to appear.

Wales's earliest Renaissance house was Bachegraig in the Vale of Clwyd, completed for Richard Clough three years before his death in 1570, and now sadly demolished. Inspired by the Flemish Renaissance, it was a cube surmounted by a pyramid roof with two tiers of dormers and crowned by a cupola. At much the same time Clough built Plas Clough near Denbigh, a less innovative building but one which — with its stepped gables — also drew inspiration from the Low Countries. Both houses contained extensive work in brick, which — apart from some of the vaulting at Raglan Castle — had not been used in Wales since Roman times. On occasion, Renaissance features were grafted on to older buildings, most spectacularly at Old Beaupre in the Vale of Glamorgan where in 1600 a 'tower of the orders' was added to a fourteenth-century manor house. In addition to Bachegraig and Plas Clough, Welsh houses built under the influence of Renaissance ideas include St Fagans

(about 1590), Plas Mawr in Conwy (1576–85), Plas Teg near Hope (1610), Brynkinalt near Chirk (1612) and Treowen near Monmouth (1627).

In most of these buildings, however, pre-Renaissance elements were still a major factor in design, for the full implications of the Renaissance style were not completely absorbed until the later seventeenth century. Plas Mawr is particularly rich in plaster ceilings, an indication of Renaissance liking for surface ornament, as opposed to the exposed, finely carved roofs preferred by earlier generations; Plas Mawr has these too, but they were hidden by plasterwork as soon as they were completed. A wealth of plasterwork may also be found in the Long Gallery constructed at Powis Castle in the 1590s. Other castles remodelled at least partly in a Renaissance idiom include Carew, where Sir John Perrot (d. 1592) built a suite of five great rooms in the 1580s, and Raglan, where between 1549 and 1646 the earls of Worcester were vigorous builders.

Raglan was not only enriched with additional buildings. It was also enhanced by one of the finest gardens ever constructed in Wales. By the death of the fifth earl in 1646, there were three long, walled terraces and a large lake with a water parterre adjoining the castle; in addition, there were summer houses, a bowling green, orchards, hopyards, walks and a wealth of statuary. The structure of the garden is still apparent, as are elements of sixteenth- and seventeenth-century pleasure grounds at St Donat's, Chirk, Llantrithyd Place and Haroldston. At Troy House near Monmouth the gateway of the walled garden survives, as do the pillars of the entrance to the formal gardens at Old Gwernyfed and the walls of the garden enclosures at Bryn Iorcyn. Among the most intriguing gardens of the period is that at Aberglasney, where the 'cloister garden' with its parapet walk on three sides is believed to have been built for the Rudd family in the early seventeenth century.

Some enthusiastic gardeners imported non-indigenous trees to beautify their grounds. Chief among them were the horse chestnut, introduced in the sixteenth century, and the sycamore, which was well established in Wales by

Opposite: Plas Teg near Hope in Flintshire, built in 1610 by the 'wise, mild, temperate' Sir John Trevor (d. 1630), is among the most memorable houses in Wales. It is one of several great houses of the period which ushered in the new spirit of the Renaissance.

Above: The 'cloister garden' at Aberglasney, which is believed to have been built for the Rudd family in the early seventeenth century.

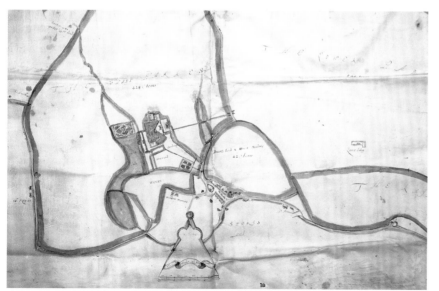

Raglan Castle was converted into a veritable palace in the late sixteenth century by William Somerset, third earl of Worcester (d. 1589). Edward, the fourth earl (d. 1628), inherited his father's sophisticated gardens, and went on to add further refinements. These splendid Renaissance gardens, with pools, terraces and parterres, were mapped in 1652 (By permission of The National Library of Wales, Badminton Map 1).

The Rodney Pillar was erected on the Breidden in 1781. The 'gentlemen of Montgomery' subscribed to raise this monument to Admiral Sir George Rodney (d. 1792), but it also stands as a memorial to the Royal Navy's debt to the woodlands of Montgomeryshire.

A limekiln at Parc le Breos, Gower. Limekilns became an increasingly common feature of the countryside as agricultural improvers sought to enhance productivity through the addition of lime to sweeten the soil (© Crown: Royal Commission on the Ancient and Historical Monuments of Wales, DS2007_286_003).

1660. Thomas Bowen of Trefloyne near Tenby was planting North American conifers in the 1590s and, in the mid-seventeenth century, Thomas Hanmer (1612–78) of Bettisfield was noting his plantations of cypresses, cedars and other exotica. Few if any new species of ornamental plants had been deliberately introduced into Wales since the Roman era; with the activities of Bowen, Hanmer and others, a process began which would go far to transform the appearance of large areas of Wales.

The domination of woodland Wales by non-indigenous trees belonged, however, to the future. In the early seventeenth century, there was every indication that the Wales of the future would have no woodland at all. By then, the proportion of the country that was forested had declined to below 10 per cent, although the construction of hedges with their hedgerow trees — as many perhaps as 3 per acre (6 per ha) — gave the landscape a more wooded appearance than the percentage would suggest. Deforestation was caused partly by the decline in the popularity of the chase; there were seventeen known deer parks in sixteenth-century Glamorgan but only three survived into the following century. In addition, many of the great oaks of the borders were felled for shipbuilding; the Rodney Pillar on the Breidden, erected in 1781, was a belated recognition of the navy's debt to the woodlands of Montgomeryshire.

Industry, too, took its toll of the forests. Although a well-managed woodland can yield timber for charcoal in perpetuity, not all industrialists were concerned to husband the resources of nature. At Talyfan in Glamorgan, a forest was given over to grazing by sheep in 1596 after the timber had been cut down for smelting, and laments from the Cynon Valley indicate the bitterness aroused by ruthless tree felling there.

But it was above all the needs of agriculture which were causing the contraction of the woodlands. The poet Thomas Churchyard praised the Welsh in 1587, for 'They tear up trees and take the roots away… And plough the ground where sturdy oaks did stand'. There was in sixteenth-century Wales, with its rising population, a lust for assarted land. Landlords sought to intensify ownership rights and increase production through large-scale enclosure. Although strip cultivation survived in parts of Cardiganshire, Pembrokeshire, Denbighshire and Glamorgan, almost the whole of lowland Wales had been enclosed by 1640, and thus the enclosure movement which was to loom so large in the English Midlands in the eighteenth century had no Welsh equivalent. Among the gentry, there was a growing interest in improved farming methods, an interest reflected in the limekilns which increasingly dotted the landscape. In the uplands, there was much encroachment of the waste and surreptitious enclosure of hill grazing land. The flight from the marginal land which followed the demographic crisis of the fourteenth century was being reversed. Between 1530 and 1620, the population of upland parishes increased up to four times more rapidly than did that of lowland parishes, where land available for colonization was in short supply.

Part of the population rise in some upland parishes was the result of their incipient industrialization. The hundreds of craters visible today on Halkyn Mountain are the work of eighteenth- and nineteenth-century lead miners, but they overlie similar work undertaken by miners centuries earlier. Other industrial activities were also modifying the landscape. The south Wales coalfield contains a number of bell pits, many of which were dug in the sixteenth and seventeenth centuries. They are shallow shafts sunk vertically down to mineral deposits and when no longer being worked they fill up to leave funnel-shaped depressions. As Leland noted in the 1530s, slate quarrying was being undertaken in extensive areas of Caernarvonshire, Merioneth and Denbighshire, and he also described lead mining in Cardiganshire, Montgomeryshire and Flintshire.

Industrialization was afoot in the lowlands too. In the neighbourhood of Swansea, a port which exported 3,000 tons of coal a year by 1607, mining was transforming an entire landscape, and in the same region the smelting of Cornish copper ores was beginning to cause long-term pollution problems. The most appealing evidence of industrialization in early modern Wales comes from the tributaries of the Wye at Tintern, where a wide variety of industries — wire making in particular — had been established by the late sixteenth century in a landscape of unsurpassed beauty.

Such industries absorbed some of the surplus rural population, but the usual escape from the overpopulated countryside was to migrate to the nearest town. As most rural areas were ethnically Welsh, the influx meant that the towns of Wales were, by the early seventeenth century, largely Welsh in speech. Similar developments occurred in rural areas; in the Vale

Mining of the rich mineral veins on Halkyn Mountain, Flintshire, which contain ores of lead, zinc and copper, may have begun in the Bronze Age and continued until the 1970s. However, the mountain's pock-marked terrain is largely the creation of eighteenth- and nineteenth-century lead miners who dug shallow bell pits along the veins (© Crown: Royal Commission on the Ancient and Historical Monuments of Wales, DI2007_0696).

of Glamorgan, where the indigenous population had been swamped by in-migration following the Norman Conquest, migration from the uplands meant that by 1600 the ethnic balance was being reversed. The influx into the towns was a cause of grave concern; in 1603, for example, the Corporation of Swansea expressed its dismay over the town's burgeoning urban proletariat. Although some towns, Llandovery for example, suffered severely because they were no longer the *caput* of a marcher lordship, many doubled in population between 1530 and 1660. Wrexham, with over 3,000 inhabitants, was probably the largest town in Wales by the mid-seventeenth century, but Carmarthen and Brecon were not far behind.

Of the surviving buildings of urban Wales in the period 1530–1660, incomparably the most impressive is Plas Mawr, Conwy. More in keeping with the scale of the Welsh townscape, however, are the half-timbered houses of Ruthin and Beaumaris and the corbelled stone buildings of Tenby and Pembroke. Presteigne can boast the Radnorshire Arms Hotel, while Llantwit Major has the Swan Inn and a charming town hall. The shire hall at Denbigh, mentioned by Speed, was remodelled in 1780, but much of the original work of 1572 is still apparent. Llanidloes has perhaps the most attractive of all of Wales's early civic buildings — the half-timbered market hall built around 1600. Thirteen endowed grammar schools were established in Wales between 1541 and 1616; some of the original buildings survive at Ruthin (1574) and there are slight remains at Llanrwst (1610). Riverside towns were eager to acquire stone bridges. Handsome structures had been built across the Dee at Holt and Llangollen around 1500. Other surviving bridges of the sixteenth and early seventeenth centuries include those over the Usk at Brecon and Crickhowell, the Wye at Monmouth and the Conwy

The late sixteenth- or early seventeenth-century bridge across the Usk at Crickhowell is particularly graceful. Riverside towns of this period were eager to improve communications with the construction of such stone bridges.

at Llanrwst. The last, frequently but not certainly attributed to Inigo Jones, is particularly graceful, as is that at Crickhowell, with its segmented arches, its cutwaters and its refuges.

The prosperity of which the urban expansion was a symptom was faltering by the 1620s. Following the poor harvests of 1622–24, death from starvation became commonplace and in 1636–37 the plague returned, as it did again in 1639. Population growth slowed down and then went into reverse, particularly in the 1640s when the Civil War added to the woes caused by nature. The economic dislocation, the looting, the gratuitous cruelty — particularly of the royalist forces — and the spread of disease which resulted from the war were far more grievous than the deaths in battle. The war had implications for the landscape also. New defences were constructed, such as the bulwarks at Carmarthen, the redoubt at Caerphilly, the reinforcements to the curtain wall at Chepstow Castle and the artillery bastions at Raglan. In the course of the war, fine houses such as Mathafarn and Caergai were destroyed and several towns, Wrexham in particular,

Right: As a consequence of the Civil War, the decision of the triumphant parliamentarians to render castles useless as fortifications was a great blow to the Welsh architectural heritage. Two sides of the Great Tower at Raglan were brought crashing down following the siege of 1646.

Below: An illustration of 1650 showing a mortar in use. Artillery was extensively used during the Civil War to shatter castle walls, and traces still remain in the landscape of bulwarks and bastions thrown up to accommodate siege guns.

suffered greatly. Iconoclastic attacks by Puritans on churches have probably been exaggerated, but parliamentary soldiers were said to have melted down the organ pipes at Wrexham to make bullets, and the depredations at Llandaff Cathedral were not made good for centuries.

The greatest blow to the Welsh architectural heritage was the decision of the triumphant parliamentarians to render all castles useless as fortifications. Raglan, the seat of the first marquess of Worcester, Charles I's most ardent supporter, was attacked with crowbars and pickaxes and the great hexagonal tower was undermined, causing two of its sides to collapse. The castles at Aberystwyth and Newcastle Emlyn were blown up, as was the barbican at Pembroke. The great castles of north Wales were unroofed; their glass, lead and timber were sold and their staircases were removed, though the decision utterly to demolish the town walls and castle at Caernarfon was not carried out.

Among the activities of the parliamentarians was the sequestration of the landed possessions of their opponents and of the Church, a policy which could have led to even more sweeping changes in the pattern of landholding than those which had followed the suppression of the monasteries. Yet as Cromwell was not vengeful, and as his regime hardly survived him, the Welsh gentry and the Welsh Church did not suffer any large-scale, permanent confiscations. Only one leading Cromwellian — Philip Jones (d. 1674) — built up a substantial estate. His descendants still live at Fonmon Castle, which is claimed to be Wales's oldest continuously inhabited dwelling. Thus the Civil War and the Interregnum, though momentous happenings, did little to interrupt the estate-building activities of the Welsh gentry, activities which allowed them wholly to dominate the life of Wales in the century after 1660.

As a close friend of Cromwell, Philip Jones (d. 1674) became a dominant force in south Wales politics in the 1650s. He amassed a considerable estate and with it acquired Fonmon Castle near Barry. A medieval castle, it was extended in the late seventeenth century and remodelled in the eighteenth century (© Billy Stock/Photolibrary Wales).

FROM THE STUART RESTORATION TO THE INDUSTRIAL REVOLUTION

THE MAKING OF WALES 1660–1780

In 1660, the king and the court, the bishops and the House of Lords were all restored. Yet, although the Restoration appeared to be the triumph of institutions with medieval origins, the true beneficiaries were the greater landowners and the leading figures in the City of London. Henceforth, the king would only be able to rule with the consent of the members of the House of Commons, and they were selected almost exclusively to serve the interests of the landowning elite. In their localities, estate owners were largely free from the interference of the central government and were not seriously threatened by the classes beneath them; for several generations no other class would be able to compete with them in wealth, status and power. In the decades following the Restoration, almost all the landed families adopted strict settlement, a legal arrangement whereby the head of the family, generation after generation, inherited the estate in its entirety.

Marriage alliances were the chief factor in ensuring that large estates expanded and that their number contracted. The phenomenon was most marked in the history of the Williams Wynn family of Wynnstay, which, through a series of marriages, united seven estates, thereby creating a landed agglomeration which would eventually embrace some 150,000 acres (60,000ha). The process depended to a large degree upon the emergence of a single heiress, usually the result of the premature death of all her siblings. That could suggest that she came from sickly stock, the explanation, perhaps, of the demographic crisis so marked in Welsh gentry families by 1700 — although the drinking habits of husbands were also probably a factor. As estate accumulation progressed, Welsh heiresses were sufficiently wealthy to attract suitors from beyond Offa's Dyke, a central factor in the Anglicization of the ruling class of Wales.

As estates grew in size, the Welsh ruling class contracted to a few dozen families at most, a development reflected in the repetition of the same names in the lists of Welsh parliamentary representatives. The concentration of land in the hands of the few meant that many houses which had been the seats of gentry families came to have less exalted occupants. The status of the houses at Llwydiarth and Plas-y-Ward, centres of estates absorbed into that of Wynnstay, was much demoted. The larger the estate, the more ambitious the building plans of its owner. In the decades after 1660, resident Welsh

Sir Watkin Williams Wynn and his mother, Frances, née Shakerly, in a portrait by Joshua Reynolds painted around 1768–69. Frances was one of the women who helped the Williams Wynn family assemble their enormous estate. She purchased the Mathafarn and Rhiwsaeson estates on her son's behalf in 1752 (©Tate, London 2009, N05750).

Opposite: The handsome little border town of Montgomery, with its town hall of 1748, is one of the most delightful Georgian architectural feasts in Wales (© Crown Copyright (2009) Visit Wales).

Built for Sir William Morgan (d. 1680), Tredegar House near Newport is the most attractive house erected in Wales in the late seventeenth century. The gardens and parkland which surround the house were also first established during Sir William's time.

landowners could construct houses on a scale previously confined to court officials such as John Trevor (d. 1630) of Plas Teg.

The most attractive building erected in Wales in the late seventeenth century was Tredegar House near Newport. Completed by 1680, its appeal lies in its superb symmetry, its lavish ornamentation and its warm brickwork. The pace of building quickened in the eighteenth century, particularly in the north-east, where in the 1720s the country houses of Leeswood, Emral, Soughton and Pickhill were completed, all of them in the baroque tradition. Pickhill Hall, in particular, followed the general contemporary practice of concealing the roof behind a parapet, as did Nanteos, the mansion built near Aberystwyth in 1739. Parapets were also part of the splendid façade of Coldbrook House near Abergavenny (about 1750), of the more severe but excellently proportioned façade at Ynysmaengwyn near Tywyn (1758) — both, sadly, demolished — and of the remodelled front at Taliaris near Llandeilo (about 1780). By then, the revolution in domestic architecture ushered in by the Renaissance was fully appreciated, a development aided by the regular visits of Welsh gentry to Bath and Dublin, and, in the case of the wealthier of them, to the font of the Renaissance in Italy. Building in stone was much assisted by the growing use of explosives in quarries, the reason, perhaps, for the retreat from most of Wales of the tradition of building

Left: Around 1720–60, the baroque architectural style entered its rococo phase across much of Europe, though in Britain this found little favour. Examples of playful, scrolled plasterwork do exist, and there is some notable ironwork, such as the superb gates at Chirk Castle made by the Davies family of ironsmiths (© The National Trust).

Above: A further charming interpretation of the rococo style can be found in a series of carved funerary tablets set up in churches around the Black Mountains between about 1720 and 1840 by Thomas Brute and his descendants. This tablet, erected to the memory of Ann Griffiths who died in 1804, was carved by John Brute and can be seen at Partrishow church, north of Abergavenny.

half-timbered mansions. The tradition lasted longest in Montgomeryshire, but even there it was being abandoned; Plas Newydd, near Carno, erected in 1704, was probably the last half-timbered gentry house to be built in Wales. Brick was used at Tredegar House, Pickhill Hall and Coldbrook House, but, if not burnt at the site as they were at Coldbrook, bricks were more expensive than stone. There are no recorded examples of pre-eighteenth-century brick buildings in south-west or north-west Wales. Elsewhere, building in brick was a foible of the rich. That was to be the case until economies in production came to outweigh the costs of distribution, a situation which did not arise until the development of the canal and railway networks.

In many parts of Europe in the eighteenth century, the baroque style was entering its rococo phase, marked by elegance and a love for fantastic and asymmetrical decoration. It found little favour in Britain, although Fonmon Castle has a delightful rococo library. It did, however, appeal to one family of artists, as the superb work of the Davies family of ironsmiths testifies. The gates at Chirk, Leeswood and Erddig are among Wales's greatest treasures; with their whimsical inventiveness, manifested above all at Chirk, they are among Europe's most distinguished examples of late baroque art. A more naïve, but highly attractive interpretation of rococo can be seen in the tablets carved between about 1720 and 1840 by Thomas Brute and members of his

The Italianate terraces at Powis Castle near Welshpool are part of one of the most important historic gardens in Wales. Their architect was the Dutch-born William Winde (d. 1722), who was known to be at the castle in 1697 (© Crown Copyright (2009) Visit Wales).

family; a feature of the churches around the Black Mountains, their unabashed joviality makes for very cheerful funerary monuments.

The Davies gates are evidence of the desire of landowners to beautify their grounds as well as their houses. Further evidence comes from garden making, an activity much practised by the gentry in the century after 1660. The most magnificent of their efforts are the terraced gardens at Powis Castle, probably laid out in the 1690s and restored in the twentieth century. Other surviving gardens of broadly the same period include the formal walled enclosures and canal at Erddig near Wrexham, the terraces at Llangedwyn Hall south of Chirk and the yew-hedged garden at Llanmihangel Place in the Vale of Glamorgan. Some of the country's finest erstwhile gardens, such as those at Llannerch and Bettisfield, can now only be traced through forlorn earthworks, overgrown walls and neglected plantations, but a number of handsome avenues survive — lime at Mostyn and Soughton, oak at Tredegar House, sweet chestnut at Llanfihangel Court north of Abergavenny and Scots pine at Llangibby Castle north of Newport. Garden buildings — orangeries, gazebos, summer houses — proliferated, the most magnificent of them being the orangery at Margam; some 330 feet (100m) in length, it is the largest orangery in Britain. The practice of adorning pleasure grounds with buildings reached its climax at Wynnstay, where 'Capability' Brown (1716–83), the leading eighteenth-century landscape architect, designed buildings and pleasure grounds. Before Brown's arrival at Wynnstay around 1777, the park there had been bisected by a straight avenue, 1.25 miles (2km) long. It was something of an anachronism, for, by the 1770s, fashionable landscape architects were inveighing against straight lines. The idea that pleasure grounds should be formal, thus contrasting with nature, was being abandoned in favour of the notion that they should be an enhancement of nature, rich in fine clumps of trees, meandering drives, gurgling brooks and sinuous lakes. As nature was ceasing to be a threat, it could surround the house, and the world outside could be separated from the pleasure grounds not by a wall but by a ha-ha.

Gnoll near Neath, where winding paths, cascades and an artificial cave were constructed in the 1740s, is among the earliest of the parks of Wales to be landscaped in the 'Romantic' manner. More magnificent was Piercefield near Chepstow, where the woodland path, now part of the Wye Valley Walk, offered superb views of the Lancaut (Llancewydd) Peninsula and the great bend in the river. 'Capability' Brown's disciple, William Emes, was active in the 1760s at Chirk, where he obliterated all formal features, and in the 1770s at Baron Hill, where his plantations framed the view of Snowdon across the Menai Strait. Park making could involve a major rearrangement of the landscape, with the creation of knolls and escarpments, the diversion of roads, the relocation of farms or even of entire villages and the transformation of valleys through damming — work carried out with great panache at Stackpole, west of Tenby. Such activities are proof of the virtually untrammelled power of the greater landlords, and were to be carried out with even more vigour in the half century after 1780.

Landowners were eager to beautify their grounds as well as their houses, and there were numerous examples of extensive garden making across Wales from the century or so after 1660. Garden buildings were to proliferate; this orangery at Margam, built in 1786–90, is a late, but magnificent, example (© Crown Copyright (2009) Visit Wales).

Below: The park at Gnoll, near Neath, was one of the earliest in Wales to be landscaped in the 'Romantic' manner. This striking informal cascade, the winding course of which skilfully imitates nature, was created for Herbert Mackworth in the 1740s (© Neil Turner/Photolibrary Wales).

Below left: Piercefield, on the edge of the Wye Valley near Chepstow, was laid out in the later eighteenth century. It is one of the most successful dramatic parkland landscapes of the era. This plan of the grounds was published in 1801.

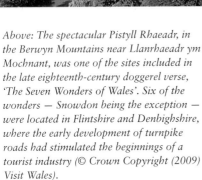

Above: The spectacular Pistyll Rhaeadr, in the Berwyn Mountains near Llanrhaeadr ym Mochnant, was one of the sites included in the late eighteenth-century doggerel verse, 'The Seven Wonders of Wales'. Six of the wonders — Snowdon being the exception — were located in Flintshire and Denbighshire, where the early development of turnpike roads had stimulated the beginnings of a tourist industry (© Crown Copyright (2009) Visit Wales).

Above right: Paul Sandby's Dolbadarn Castle and the Valley of Llyn Peris, *which he painted around 1764, is an excellent example of the tendency of many Romantic painters to exaggerate landscapes in order to celebrate their ruggedness (© Birmingham Museums and Art Gallery, 1953p370).*

The laying out of parks was an aspect of the Romantic movement — that revolution in sensibility which transformed attitudes towards the landscape. In 1700 sensitive travellers pulled down the blinds of their coach lest they should be pained by the barbarity of mountainous scenery; little more than fifty years later aesthetes were glorying in the wild, the sublime and the Picturesque. Thus, Wales was 'discovered', and by the 1770s the beginnings of a tourist industry could be discerned, an industry which would come to dominate large areas of Wales. Mountains changed from supernatural eyesores to natural phenomena, to become eventually marketable commodities.

The north-east, where by 1760 there were five turnpike companies with roads linking the region to the transport system of England, was the first part of Wales to be 'discovered'. In the doggerel, 'The Seven Wonders of Wales', written in the late eighteenth century, all the 'wonders', except for Snowdon, were in the counties of Flint and Denbigh. The north-east was also the home of Thomas Pennant (d. 1798), whose *A Tour in Wales* (1778, 1781) was central to the growth among the English intelligentsia of the belief that Wales was intellectually interesting. Appreciation of landscape was fostered by the poets; John Dyer's innovative topographical poem 'Grongar Hill', completed in the 1720s, celebrated the glories of the Tywi Valley. William Gilpin's account of his 1770 travels in the Wye Valley did much to foster the cult of the Picturesque as did the writings of Uvedale Price, who commissioned a piece of Romantic fantasy on the seafront at Aberystwyth — a building which would be incorporated into what became the University College of Wales.

Painters promoted the notion of the ideal landscape, with mountain, lake and ruin in splendid asymmetry, images pioneered by Poussin and Claude and continued by the Welsh painter, Richard Wilson (d. 1782). The work of many a Romantic painter — that of Paul Sandby (d. 1809), for example — did not provide an accurate portrayal, for there was a tendency to exaggerate landcapes in order to celebrate their ruggedness. Indeed, it would be necessary to wait until the age of the photograph before wholly dispassionate images would be available. Nevertheless, workaday topographical artists such as the brothers Buck provided credible delineations of mansions and urban and rural scenes, and their work became well known through reproduction as aquatints and copper engravings. Equally significant was the work of cartographers. Ogilby's strip road maps (1675), Collins's coastal charts (1693), Lewis Morris's *Plans of Harbours…* (1748) the atlases of Bowen, Kitchin and others, and, above all, the great mass of unpublished estate maps, are fundamental sources for the study of the changing landscape of Wales.

The townscape was changing too, and the eighteenth is the earliest century from which significant quantities of the buildings of urban Wales survive. Welsh towns were still very small; in the mid-eighteenth century, about 15 per cent of the population was urban, a proportion only marginally higher than that of the High Middle Ages. The number of towns with more than 1,500 inhabitants probably did not exceed a dozen, for the chief urban centres of the various regions of Wales lay outside the country, at Bristol, Hereford, Shrewsbury, Chester and Dublin. Most of the towns of Wales existed primarily to serve the agricultural communities surrounding them, although industry was helping to swell the populations of Swansea and Wrexham, and to make towns of hitherto inconsiderable villages, as at Holywell and Pontypool. With their mouldering castles and collapsing walls and gates, many Welsh towns could appear to be in an advanced state of dilapidation; with their piles of dung and excrement, tanning yards, rotting vegetables and carcasses, and absence of drains and pavements they could be highly insalubrious. Yet grossly insanitary neighbourhoods could lie cheek by jowl with commodious and immaculate housing, for the contrast between rich and poor was more stark in the towns than in the countryside.

The commodious houses belonged in the main to professional men, for the eighteenth century saw a marked expansion in middle-class vocations. Lawyers, doctors, merchants, land agents, salaried government officers and

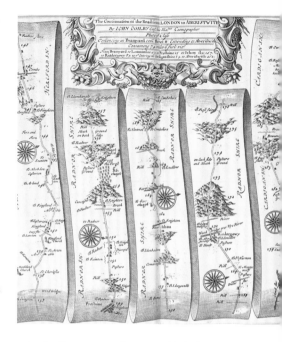

John Ogilby's strip road maps, published in his Britannia of 1675, are one of the sources of our knowledge of the appearance of Wales in the late seventeenth century (© Board of The British Library, Maps. C.7.e.8).

In the mid- to late eighteenth century, Swansea was one of the few towns in Wales with more than 1,500 inhabitants. It is estimated that its population around 1760 was about 3,000. This engraving of the castle and town was published by the brothers Samuel and Nathaniel Buck in 1741 (By permission of The National Library of Wales).

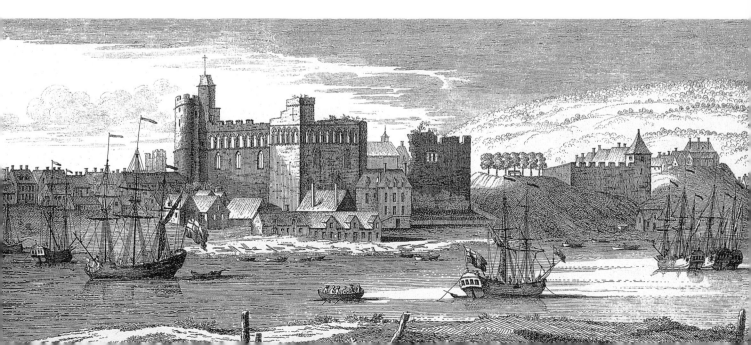

master mariners rose in numbers and status. They built town houses, as did the landed gentry in local capitals such as Brecon and Carmarthen. In those towns, which later expanded vastly, almost all such houses and many early public buildings have been swept away. It is therefore those towns that stagnated, or enjoyed only modest growth, which offer evidence of eighteenth-century urban architecture. Monmouth has a delightful town hall (1724), Pembroke has several attractive eighteenth-century hotels and Ruthin has a fascinating county gaol (1775). Abergavenny, Brecon, Cowbridge, Carmarthen, Tenby, Haverfordwest, Welshpool, Llanfyllin, Denbigh, Conwy and Beaumaris all have handsome streets of the period, although some eighteenth-century frontages are now concealed behind later façades. Above all, there is Montgomery, where the town hall of 1748 nestles in a mesh of streets rich in eighteenth-century cornices, doorcases, fanlights, gables, dormer windows, octagonal-fronted bows and a wealth of other undisturbed delights.

By the eighteenth century, Renaissance ideals had filtered down to local builders. Middle-class houses gradually began to display scaled-down aspects of the classical idiom, with central doorways, symmetrically placed windows and emphasized quoins and keystones. Sash windows came to replace casements in all but the smallest houses. They became a hallmark of the buildings erected in the territories of the British Crown, a contrast with the casement windows preferred in most of mainland Europe. A sash window is a tall oblong opening with the glazing pattern broken by a dominant horizontal bar; a casement window is usually a wide oblong opening with a dominant vertical bar. The difference goes far to explain why the impact of a Welsh or an English street scene differs from that made by a street scene in France or Germany.

By the eighteenth century, the urge to build was expressing itself almost totally in secular terms. In the High Middle Ages, up to half the investment in building was motivated by religion, but in the century after 1660 the proportion was very small indeed. The Salusburys commissioned a private chapel at Rug in 1637, as did the Wynns at Gwydir Uchaf in 1673, buildings

An engraving from about 1750 of Monmouth's town hall, which was designed by an otherwise unknown Bristol architect named Fisher. Its baroque style, which was inspired by the buildings of Sir Christopher Wren, was already rather old-fashioned at the time of its construction in 1724. Extensive alterations in 1829–30 included the addition of courtrooms. John Frost and some of his fellow Chartist insurrectionists were tried here (By permission of The National Library of Wales, Welsh Landscape Collection).

In 1774 Parliament passed prison reform acts after John Howard (d. 1790) and others exposed the unsanitary conditions and inhumane practices that were widespread in British gaols. Ruthin Gaol, which was built to the design of Joseph Turner in 1775, was evidently an early response to these demands for improved conditions. It was extended and rebuilt in the following century, and remained in use as a prison until 1916 (© Ruthin Gaol).

Opposite: The Wynn family chapel at Gwydir Uchaf near Llanrwst is a rare example of an Anglican place of worship retaining elements of seventeenth-century High Church liturgical arrangements.

Many churches in Wales fell into decay in the eighteenth century, and none more so than Llandaff Cathedral. Much of the structure became ruinous, with roofs collapsing. In 1750, a classical temple was erected in the choir and nave, though all traces of this are now gone. John Wood's temple can be seen in this engraving of 1846 (© National Museum of Wales).

prized as rare examples of Anglican places of worship retaining the liturgical arrangements of seventeenth-century High Churchmanship. Such activity was unusual, for less than a dozen churches were built in Wales between 1660 and 1770. The finest of them is St Deiniol, Worthenbury, south-east of Wrexham (1736–39), with its semicircular apse and its rococo plasterwork. Some ruinous churches — St Myllin, Llanfyllin, for example, and St Mary's, Monmouth — were rebuilt, but many were left to decay further, thus bequeathing problems to the church reformers of the nineteenth century. Llandaff Cathedral became a ruin; the south-west tower collapsed and the roof of the nave fell in, and all that was done was to erect in 1750 a classical temple within the ruins — 'a much more serious piece of architecture', as John Newman has put it, 'than later critics imagined'. Landowners preferred to spend on funerary monuments — sophisticated memorials such as that to the Myddletons at St Mary's, Chirk, or to Maurice Jones at Llanrhaeadr-yng-Nghinmeirch.

While the Anglicans were building few places of worship, Christians of other traditions were launching a remarkable building campaign. The Toleration Act of 1689 permitted Protestant Trinitarian Dissenters to worship freely, provided they licensed their meeting houses. Some of the founders of Welsh Dissent had built places of worship — the remains of that of Wales's earliest Baptist congregation (1649) may be seen at Ilston in Gower — but, during the era of persecution, services were generally held in the open air or even in caves. After 1689, purpose-built chapels could be erected. Some congregations did not choose, or did not have the resources, to do so. Private houses remained the centres of many Dissenting churches, and other congregations met in outbuildings; until 1749, the Independents of Llanbrynmair worshipped at a lean-to conventicle on the farm of Tŷ Mawr. In more prosperous areas — Abergavenny and Llanwenarth, for example — the opportunity to build a chapel was immediately seized. The investment in construction was not great; a chapel usually cost between £60 and £100, although £252 was spent on Trosnant Baptist chapel, built near Pontypool in 1779.

The simplest of the early meeting houses were those of the Quakers. Dolobran, south of Llanfyllin, where all the fittings have been carried off to Philadelphia, was built in 1700 by the Lloyd family, founders of Lloyds Bank; it is movingly austere, as is The Pales, east of Llandrindod. Among the Independents and the Baptists, with their emphasis upon preaching, meeting houses were designed to ensure that the largest possible number were able to hear the preacher. Where Nonconformity flourished, chapels were almost invariably rebuilt and thus, even in the heartlands of early Dissent, the chapels tend to be nineteenth-century structures. The earliest chapels are most numerous in regions such as Radnorshire, where the population and the Dissenting tradition stagnated. Early chapels were usually oblong boxes, with the one or two entrances on the long wall and the pulpit on the opposite long wall. Maesyronnen, west of Hay, a cruck-roofed building converted into a chapel at the end of the 1690s, is the earliest surviving example, and it is there, above all, that the quintessence of early Welsh Nonconformity may be experienced.

In the mid-eighteenth century, those rejecting the Anglican parish church were few. They included the Roman Catholics, to whom the Toleration Act of 1689 did not apply. They were obliged to seek to disguise their building schemes; thus, the Jones family of Llanarth, east of Abergavenny, commissioned a Roman Catholic chapel that had the outward appearance of an orangery. The number of Wales's Roman Catholics would increase markedly in the nineteenth century, particularly in the wake of Irish migration.

The increase in the number of Protestant Nonconformists would be vastly greater, partly because of the success of the Methodist Revival. Welsh Methodism, which took a Calvinist form in contrast with the Arminian tendencies of the Wesleyanism of England, originally aimed at revitalizing the established Church. Its leaders had no intention of creating a new denomination, or, initially at least, of building meeting houses. Yet, the Calvinistic Methodists became a denomination in 1811 and long before that they found that they needed their own places of worship. In 1742, seven years after the conversion of Howel Harris (1714–73), the most dynamic of the leaders of the Revival, the members of the congregation at Groeswen near Caerphilly built themselves a meeting house. It was Wales's first Methodist place of worship, but its congregation defected to the Independents in 1745. The second to be built — that at Aberthin near Cowbridge — remained in the possession of the Methodists. A low, whitewashed building with a long-wall entrance flanked by two windows, it was the first-fruit of a building programme which, over the following 150 years, would endow Wales with hundreds of Methodist chapels. In style, the great majority of later chapels derive, however distantly, from the Renaissance hall-nave. Ironically, Howel Harris himself

In 1696–97, the Independents converted an early cruck-roofed building at Maesyronnen, near Hay on Wye, to serve as a chapel. The building is utterly simple in appearance and is the place to experience the quintessence of early Welsh Nonconformity (© Country Life).

The oldest surviving Methodist place of worship in Wales can be found at Aberthin near Cowbridge. The first chapel was built in 1749 and was replaced in 1780 by the building which now serves as the village hall.

As the eighteenth century progressed, settlement on marginal mountainous land became more extensive. High-altitude holdings became independent farms, with vast lengths of drystone walls constructed across the landscape, as here in Dyffryn Ardudwy.

preferred a different tradition; the Gothick premises he built for his 'commune' at Trefeca were broadly contemporary with the celebrated use of that style by Horace Walpole at Strawberry Hill in London.

Dissent and Methodism found their most ardent supporters among the 'middling sort of people', the substantial farmers of the countryside and the aspiring lower middle class of the towns. The growing allegiance to such religious movements indicates that the membership of those social groupings was increasing, evidence that the economy of Wales was becoming more prosperous and diversified. That economy could sustain more people, although many of the additional mouths were inadequately fed. It would seem that Wales's inhabitants increased in number from 360,000 in 1620 to perhaps 500,000 by 1770. The increase was not a smooth upward progress. A run of bad harvests in the 1690s — the era of the 'Little Ice Age' — resulted in a severe crisis of subsistence; child deaths at Wrexham trebled and local dearth in the hill country of Montgomeryshire scythed down the more vulnerable. Smallpox became virulent, carrying off up to a quarter of the population of Penmachno in 1705–06; other diseases, too, were lethal, the typhus epidemic of 1727–31 causing great mortality. Yet the evidence of the parish registers — admittedly flawed — suggests that in most years after about 1710, births exceeded deaths by a significant margin, and that the excess became more marked after 1750; indeed, it would seem that between 1750 and 1780 the Welsh population was increasing at the rate of 2.75 per cent per decade.

The increase had a marked impact upon the landscape. Settlement on marginal mountainous land, apparent before 1660, became more extensive as the eighteenth century advanced. Transhumance, a long-declining practice, became extinct as high-altitude holdings became independent farms. Vast lengths of drystone walls were constructed; a feature of much of the Welsh uplands, they represent, perhaps, the most laborious activity ever undertaken by the makers of Wales. Much of the land brought into cultivation was the waste land of Crown manors, for usurping the property of the Crown was one of the primary undertakings of eighteenth-century Welsh landowners. Many areas were enclosed through informal agreement. In 1760, however, unenclosed land north of Welshpool became the subject of an enclosure act; by 1780 another five acts had been passed, but, in that year, a quarter of the land of Wales was still unenclosed, for the great boom in enclosure acts occurred in the following three decades. While legislators were changing the pattern of ownership in the uplands, it was the peasantry who were the main agents in changing their appearance. There was a widely but erroneously held belief that anyone who could build in one night a cottage on the waste became the owner of it. Thus the *tai unnos* and other squatter cottages constructed by the homeless and the destitute became necklaces around the boundaries of the *ffriddoedd* (the unenclosed upland grazing lands). Penrhos at Maenclochog, an enlarged version of an original *tŷ unnos* has been restored and is open to the public by arrangement. The impact upon the landscape of the activity of the squatters aroused widespread comment. On the slopes of the Brecon Beacons, for example, 'it seemed as if an Irish estate had been transferred and filled in as a patchwork among the Welsh mountains'.

In the lowlands too the rising population and the increasing pace of economic development were modifying the landscape. Progressive landowners were eager to reorganize their holdings. The arable strips inherited from

The squatters who built cottages on the margins of the unenclosed uplands in eighteenth-century Wales would have had to rely on whatever building materials were to hand. This old house, which was recorded near Strata Florida in 1888, gives a striking impression of the rough, but often ingenious, construction methods that must have characterized such humble dwellings (Cambrian Archaeological Association).

The tai unnos (one-night cottages) were, by their very nature, hastily built and often insubstantial structures, and none survives in its original state. Many, abandoned, have simply vanished from the landscape, while others have been remodelled and enlarged by successive owners. Penrhos, near Maenclochog in Pembrokeshire, began as a tŷ unnos, but has been transformed into a small, but sturdy, cottage (Scolton Manor, Pembrokeshire County Museum).

Progressive landlords of the eighteenth century were eager to reorganize their holdings. Small fields with meandering hedges was the landscape characteristic of lowland Wales. This fieldscape with hedgerows is in the Tywi Valley of Carmarthenshire. Dryslwyn Castle stands on the promontory in the centre.

medieval forms of tenure still existed, as the numerous references to quillets indicate, but the urge to create consolidated farms and to construct hedges was great. The landscape characteristic of lowland Wales — small fields with meandering hedges — was emerging, a marked contrast with the 'new' landscape of Midland England, with its large fields and straight hedges. Crooked hedges were preferred, for they were believed to provide better shelter for cattle. Fields could be very small indeed; in Carmarthenshire, it was not unusual for there to be fifteen to twenty on a farm of 50 to 60 acres (20 to 24ha), and hedges could constitute up to 10 per cent of the area of a holding.

As early as the 1730s, some Welsh landowners were practising crop rotation and planting clover, hops, potatoes and turnips, thus adding new elements to the rural scene. The more progressive among them were anxious to have firmer control over the activities of their tenants. 'Every field will be kept to the culture I dictate', declared the enthusiastic improver Philip Yorke (d. 1804), the owner of the Erddig estate. This often involved the replacement of the traditional life leases with annual leases, a change with implications for rural housing. With life leaseholders, the farmhouse and its outbuildings were generally the responsibility of the tenant, who built and repaired in the tradition of the locality. With annual leases, they were the responsibility of the landowner, who might introduce new building practices and materials. Yet too much should not be claimed. The linking of estate with estate had led to an increase in the number of absentee landlords, many of whom had only a tenuous relationship with their tenants; the tenants themselves, profoundly conservative and lacking in capital, were often deeply resistant to any pressures for change.

With the quickening of economic growth, the proportion of the inhabitants of Wales not wholly dependent upon agriculture for their livelihood increased. The woollen industry moved into its proto-industrial phase. By the 1770s, there were fifteen fulling mills around Dolgellau and, on many farms, outbuildings were adapted as *tai gwŷdd* (loom houses). More significant as an indicator of the future was the growth in the mining and metallurgical industries. In 1693, legal action over the lead mine at Esgair Hir in Cardiganshire led to the recognition that base metal ores were the property of the owners of the land from which they were extracted, a decision central to the readiness of landowners to encourage mining. Cardiganshire, where in the 1750s 2,000 lead miners were tunnelling and creating spoil heaps, was, declared Lewis Morris, 'the richest country I ever saw'. Lead mining had its periods of prosperity in Flintshire too, where coal mining and copper smelting also flourished. Dr Johnson, visiting Holywell in 1774, counted nineteen different works within 2 miles (3.2km) of St Winifred's Well; indeed, so varied were the early enterprises at Holywell that the Greenfield Valley below the town is a veritable open-air museum of industrial archaeology. Neath was even more important as a centre for smelting non-ferrous ores, and there in the 1710s the progressive entrepreneur, Humphrey Mackworth (d. 1727), built the first tramways in Wales, an activity which would absorb much of the energies of industrialists in subsequent decades. Neath, however, was to yield first place to Swansea; by the 1750s, Swansea was the source of half the copper smelted in Britain, much to the distress of those who would have preferred their town to earn a genteel reputation as a spa and watering place. Smelting poisoned the land around the works; successful reclamation schemes were launched in the 1960s, but they made little provision for the retention of historic copper-smelting plants. The White Rock Industrial Archaeology Park does, however, contain some evidence of the eighteenth-century works. River quays of the 1770s also survive and slag shaped into bricks is much in evidence in buildings around Swansea.

Initially, at least, iron smelting did not expand as rapidly as did the smelting of other ores. Abraham Darby had discovered in 1709 that iron

The Greenfield Valley, near Holywell, Flintshire, was a thriving industrial area when Dr Johnson visited in 1774. He counted nineteen different works within 2 miles (3.2km) of St Winifred's Well. Many of the surviving remains have been preserved and interpreted for visitors.

By the 1750s, Swansea had become a major centre for the smelting of non-ferrous ores. The lower part of the Swansea Valley was the source of half the copper smelted in Britain, and the area was to retain its importance in this respect for over a century. This engraving of 1810 shows the Hafod copper works on the Tawe (© National Museum of Wales).

could be smelted with coked coal, but as charcoal was preferred, at least until the mid-eighteenth century, iron making continued to be located sporadically and close to sources of coppice wood. Among the most interesting of such furnaces is the Dyfi Furnace built around 1755 and powered by the flow of the river Einion, a structure splendidly restored by Cadw.

Dyfi Furnace had been abandoned by 1810, for by then smelting using charcoal could no longer compete with smelting using coke. Indeed, long before 1810, ironmasters at Bersham, near Wrexham, at Pontypool, and, above all, at Merthyr Tydfil had established coke-using furnaces, enterprises which would transform large tracts of Wales. The impact upon the landscape of mid-eighteenth-century iron making may best be appreciated at Bersham, where the Clywedog Valley is rich in industrial monuments.

The growth of smelting with coke meant that coal mining, which had originally been an independent industry concerned largely with exports, became, for a period at least, subordinate to metalworking, and served mainly a home market. Mackworth was one of the coal industry's pioneers; his workings at Neath were not the traditional shallow holes, for he had mines up to 360 feet (110m) deep, with engines to raise coal and water from the base of the shafts. Increasing demand and improving techniques caused coal production in Wales to increase from 220,000 tons in 1750 to 760,000 tons in 1775. Although the proportion of the output exported declined, its tonnage did not. Swansea exported 8,694 tons of coal in 1710 and 64,502 tons in 1780.

The increasing pace of economic activity was both a cause and a result of improved transport. Before the coming of the turnpike trusts in the mid-eighteenth century, the roads of Wales were uniformly appalling. A traveller in Monmouthshire drowned in a pothole in the 1690s; it must have been of considerable depth, for he was on horseback at the time. The five bills relating to turnpikes in the north-east passed by 1760 had, by 1780, been supplemented by thirty-five acts relating to all the regions of Wales.

Opposite: Dyfi Furnace was built around 1755 as a charcoal-fuelled blast furnace. It had been abandoned by 1810, by which time smelting with coke had become well established. It was later converted into a sawmill.

The growing use of coke to smelt iron in the eighteenth century stimulated the development of coal mining in south Wales. At the Mackworth workings at Neath, engines were used to raise coal from shafts that had been sunk up to 360 feet (110m) deep. This print shows a mine near Neath in the closing years of the eighteenth century (By permission of The National Library of Wales, PB02533).

The turnpike companies of the eighteenth century built new roads and improved existing ones. They recouped their expenditure through levying tolls. Toll houses were to become a new feature of the landscape. This example survives at Abergavenny.

The expanding road network of the eighteenth century led to an increased demand for bridges. In 1756, William Edwards succeeded in spanning the Taff at Pontypridd with a single-arched bridge — the widest stone arch in Europe at the time. It was to feature in many engravings, as in this example by S. Alken from an original by J. Smith (© National Museum of Wales).

Opposite: The construction of lighthouses was one reflection of the expansion of seaborne trade in the late eighteenth century. Point of Ayr lighthouse, designed by Joseph Turner, was first built in 1777.

The turnpike companies built new roads or improved existing ones, recouping their expenditure through levying tolls. Road building had wide-ranging landscape implications. The post road to Holyhead was improved in the 1770s, opening up much wild country and leading to the erection of coaching inns and toll houses. Cernioge, high on the Denbigh Moors, was a well-known posting house, and there are attractive toll houses at Pentrefoelas, Llangollen and Chirk. Better roads encouraged tourism and led to the rise of spas and watering places. By the 1750s, Llandrindod had a hundred-bed hotel with in-house shops, ballrooms, concert rooms and billiard rooms. Turnpike companies were obliged in 1773 to erect milestones, and those that survive are a delightful feature of the landscape.

The expanding road network increased the demand for bridges. In mid-Wales, the Usk, the Wye and the Severn were all repeatedly and handsomely bridged, work which perhaps can be best appreciated at Llandrinio, where in 1775 the Severn was spanned by a three-arched bridge of yellow sandstone. The most remarkable bridge of eighteenth-century Wales is at Pontypridd, where in 1756 William Edwards, a stonemason of Eglwysilan, succeeded in spanning the Taff with a single arch; 140 feet (42.7m) across, it was at the time the widest stone arch in Europe and was much featured in paintings and engravings. Edwards built at least another seven bridges; that at Dolauhirion, north of Llandovery, is virtually in its original state and it has all the grace of its prototype at Pontypridd.

There was investment in water as well as land transport, for the expansion of seaborne trade was one of the leading features of the eighteenth-century Welsh economy. Mackworth constructed a small dock at Neath in about 1720. By 1780, the navigable 3 miles (4.8km) of the river Tawe were lined with wharfs, coal banks and quays, and Swansea was much agitated by the need to deepen the river and to remove the bar at its mouth. The town quay at Cardiff was rebuilt in 1760 and similar work was being undertaken along the Dee estuary at Flint, Greenfield, Mostyn and Ffynnongroyw. There was activity at Holyhead, Beaumaris, Bangor, Barmouth, Cardigan and Haverfordwest, with the construction of warehouses and the lengthening and strengthening of quays. Lighthouses were built on the Skerries (1717) — a hugely profitable venture which gave a degree of security to the growing number of ships sailing to Liverpool — on Flatholm (1737) and at Point of Ayr (1777), but perhaps the most intriguing constructions produced by the expanding sea trade were the watchtowers built along the north Wales coast to give warning of pirate raids.

Yet, as with agricultural improvements, too much should not be claimed. In 1780, Welsh ports were still almost wholly underdeveloped and the country's roads still grossly inadequate. Despite increasing industrial development, those employed in agriculture were the majority in almost all the hundreds of Wales. Although mining in particular had greatly changed the appearance of some localities, those localities were small islands in an overwhelmingly rural environment. But this situation was not destined to endure, for, in the decades after 1780, the activities of the makers of Wales brought about a transformation on a wholly unprecedented scale.

THE FIRST INDUSTRIAL ERA

THE MAKING OF WALES 1780–1850

The decades between 1780 and 1850 were pre-eminently the era of the remaking of Wales. In seventy years, the population more than doubled from about 530,000 to 1,189,000, and the proportion employed in agriculture declined to a third. The islands of industry perceptible in 1780 became linked up to create industrial belts, particularly in an arc along the upper rim of the south Wales coalfield. By 1851, there were eighteen towns in Wales with populations of more than 5,000, a figure not reached by any of the towns of Wales in 1780. The largest of them was Merthyr Tydfil, the home of 46,378 people by 1851, a year when the town had an output of iron equivalent to a quarter of that of the entire United States of America. It was at Merthyr, above all, that the new Wales in the making was most apparent. Merthyr, and the rest of the industrial communities straddling the northern boundaries of Glamorgan and Monmouthshire, developed as centres for the manufacture of pig iron, an industry which was becoming dominated by a few leviathans. In the early eighteenth century, Wales's largest iron manufactory, that of the Hanbury family at Pontypool, produced 400 tons of iron a year; in the 1840s Dowlais, then the largest of Merthyr's four major iron companies, was producing 75,000 tons a year.

Opposite: Blaenavon was one of the new south Wales communities created through the iron industry. The earliest blast furnaces here were built in 1788–89, and in ten years were employing 350 people. The houses of Engine Row, to the right of this view, were built around 1788, and were probably intended to attract key workers.

Merthyr Tydfil was the greatest iron town of Wales, and had become the home of 46,378 people by 1851. There were four major iron companies; this painting of 1840 by G. Childs shows the furnace top area at the Dowlais works (© National Museum of Wales).

The Crawshay 'feudal stronghold' of Cyfarthfa Castle (1825) was sited to overlook the family's ironworks (© Crown Copyright (2009) Visit Wales).

The belt of earlier industrial development, stretching from Llanelli to Neath, had a more varied industrial base, which included the manufacture of tinplate and of an increasingly wide range of non-ferrous metals. At its heart was the lower Swansea Valley, which long dominated the world copper trade. The region transformed by the copper industry has been described in what must be the fullest study ever published on an industrial landscape: Stephen Hughes's *Copperopolis* (2000).

The scale of industrial development, and the size of its units of production, went far to determine the nature of the communities brought into existence to serve the growing enterprises. In much of industrial south Wales, an equal, if not more important factor, was the upland location of the centres of iron making. Merthyr is 750 feet (230m) above sea level, while Beaufort and Brynmawr are at altitudes exceeding 1,300 feet (400m). The early industrial communities sprang up in areas which were previously virtually uninhabited, and could not therefore draw upon pre-industrial civic and architectural traditions. Housing, urban amenities and transport facilities had to conform to the contours of a mountainous terrain, thus giving rise to a townscape unique in character.

Early industrialists were proud of their undertakings and liked to have them in full view. Thus Cyfarthfa Castle (1825), a chunky, crenellated pile, overlooked the works of the Crawshay family, and at Dowlais, Penydarren,

The twelve cottages at Forge Row, Cwmavon, were built about 1804 to accommodate workers employed at nearby Varteg forge. The row was restored by the British Historic Buildings Trust in 1987–88.

Nantyglo and elsewhere the owner's grand house offered a prospect of his works. Although workers in Merthyr and elsewhere were generally far better housed than were rural labourers, the dwellings of the industrial working class contrasted painfully with those of the ironmasters. By the later nineteenth century, when most of the hillside terraces so characteristic of the south Wales coalfield were built, by-laws and public health considerations had ensured that some basic standards were observed. In the period 1780 to 1850, however, lack of regulation and the need to house a growing influx of workers quickly and cheaply meant the large-scale construction of dwellings which were lamentably inadequate. Most of them have now been swept away, but until recently they survived in large numbers, especially in Merthyr Tydfil and in other towns on the coalfield's northern rim.

The most primitive were the one-room-and-loft dwellings such as those at Bunkers Row, built at Blaenavon in about 1789 and demolished in 1972. From 1810 to 1825 the Crawshays favoured a three-roomed house, with the extra room at the back covered by a 'catslide' roof — the layout of the Rhyd-y-car row rebuilt at the National History Museum at St Fagans. Another early terrace, at Forge Row, Cwmavon, has been restored by the British Historic Buildings Trust. The steep hillsides of the coalfield offered sites for 'dual' rows, one built over another, as occurred at Nantyglo about 1794. The lower houses were of one storey, built 'back-to-earth' and entered

The Triangle at Pentrebach, Merthyr Tydfil, was built between 1839 and 1844 by the Plymouth Ironworks to house its workers. The layout was determined mainly by the boundaries of the land available. The houses were well built and had four rooms. They were typical in design for their date, but were above average size, perhaps to reward workers who had not taken part in the Chartist uprising of 1839. There were no internal services; privies, each shared by up to ten households, were built over a stream behind the row (© National Museum of Wales).

from the downhill side; the two-storey upper houses had their doors at ground level on the uphill side.

Some industrialists were more ambitious in their housing schemes. Examples of the more spacious houses built for skilled workers may be seen at Engine Row, Blaenavon (1788). Butetown (Y Drenewydd), built about 1804 by the Rhymney Iron Company on land owned by the Bute estate, and now admirably refurbished, has fine symmetrical façades and overhanging roofs; a scaled-down version of Butetown — Chapel Row at Blaenavon — was demolished in the 1970s, a fate which also overtook the remarkable Triangle built in the 1840s by the Plymouth Iron Company at Pentrebach. By the 1840s, however, workers' houses were generally built in streets lined on both sides by uniform two-storey houses. That arrangement was far superior to the infilling of courts, a pattern of building which had led in Swansea to the construction of almost a thousand miniscule courtyard dwellings of a highly unsalubrious character.

Essential to the prosperity of the upland ironworks was an effective way of conveying their output to the ports. The matter was addressed between 1790 and 1812 when a number of canals were built, including the four linking the hill country with the ports of Swansea, Neath, Cardiff and Newport. Canal building was a major enterprise; aqueducts, tunnels, feeders and bridges had to be constructed and fifty-one locks were needed on the 25-mile (40km) canal linking Merthyr with Cardiff. The canals of the coalfield have suffered many indignities; made redundant by the coming of railways, their vulnerability to subsidence, their lack of links with a wider network and their numerous locks have caused them to be largely abandoned, although attractive stretches of the Neath Canal have been restored, and the fine series of locks on the Monmouthshire Canal north of Newport remains an impressive monument to the canal makers of Wales.

Canal construction went hand in hand with the building of tramroads — the horse-worked railways of the pre-locomotion age. Although expenditure

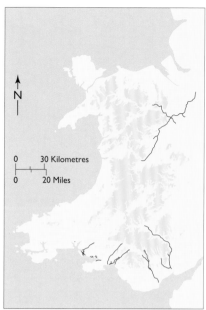

Above: Canals built in Wales by about 1840.

Above left: The fourteen locks of the Cefn Flight on the Monmouthshire Canal north of Newport were completed in 1799. The flight, which rises 167 feet (51m) over 0.5 mile (0.81km), remains an impressive monument to the canal builders of Wales. This photograph of 1896 shows part of the flight (© The Francis Frith Collection).

on canals was greater, tramroad building was a more widespread activity; about 1,000 miles (1,600km) of tramroads were built to serve the ironworks of the south Wales coalfield, compared with 160 miles (256km) of canals. The most ambitious of the tramroads was the 25-mile (40km) Sirhowy Tramroad (1805) linking Tredegar with Newport. More than £40,000 was spent on its construction, and so central was it to the prosperity of the Monmouthshire coalfield that, in its early decades, it yielded a dividend of over 30 per cent.

Of the ironworks themselves, twentieth-century clearance schemes have obliterated much of what once remained of major works constructed before 1850. Some of the iron towns — Merthyr in particular — were long negligent towards their industrial heritage. The most appealing location of the iron industry in Wales was the Clydach Gorge, north of Brynmawr, described by John Newman as 'a remarkable relict landscape…in a setting of great natural beauty'. On the site of the Neath Abbey Ironworks, there are two superb furnaces of 1793, among the tallest masonry furnaces ever constructed. A remarkably intact bank of coke ovens survives at Ebbw Vale, and Tondu has a range of seven stone-built iron-ore calcining kilns and up to a hundred coking kilns.

By far the most significant site is Blaenavon, where the main enterprise was resited in the 1850s and where the original works have been superbly conserved. The site includes the houses in Stack Square and Engine Row, the cast house and forge, the five blast furnaces, the calcining kilns and a magnificent water-balance tower. On the neighbouring mountains are fascinating examples of 'hushing' — the releasing of water to scour out surface seams of coal and iron ore. To the north lay the forges of Garnddyrys, linked to Blaenavon by a 1.5-mile (2.5km) tunnel; opened in about 1815, it was the longest tunnel on any tramroad of its era. Garnddyrys, with its leering mass of slag, is a hugely evocative place. The Blaenavon complex was linked to the Brecknock and Abergavenny Canal by Hill's Tramroad (1818), an

Two superb furnaces of 1793 — among the tallest masonry examples ever constructed — survive at the site of the Neath Abbey Ironworks.

incline where stone sleepers and grooves cut by hauling ropes are still visible. The Blaenavon industrial landscape includes Big Pit, which is now the National Coal Museum, and Forgeside, where Gilchrist and Thomas discovered the 'basic method' of using phosphoric ores to produce bulk steel. The significance of the landscape was recognized in 2000, when it became a World Heritage Site.

In the presentation of the visible remains of the first industrial era, the most encouraging development in recent years is the fact that Merthyr has come to appreciate the significance of its industrial heritage. The engine house at Ynysfach (1836) has been admirably restored, and work has begun on the restoration of the remains of Cyfarthfa Ironworks of the Crawshay family, where six of the seven blast furnaces are still intact. Treforest offers an even more impressive example of the activities of that family; there, the rolling mill, smithy and tinning house (1834–35) provide unrivalled evidence of the tinplate industry of early nineteenth-century Wales.

The industrialization of south Wales led to a host of unique developments, especially those related to the early history of railways. The world's first documented railway passenger service was that provided by the Oystermouth Railway at Swansea in 1807. The earliest known iron railway bridge (which had a combined use as an aqueduct) is Pontycafnau at Merthyr Tydfil, designed in 1793 by Watkin George. The first ever use of a steam locomotive to haul a load on a railway was made on the Penydarren Tramroad near Merthyr by Richard Trevithick in 1804.

Trevithick's experiment was the harbinger of the age of the locomotive. Wales's first standard-gauge railway designed to be operated by steam locomotives was that from Llanelli to Pontarddulais, opened in 1839. It was followed in 1841 by the Taff Vale Railway linking Merthyr with Cardiff, the venture which inaugurated the south Wales coalfield's second industrial era. In the following nine years, at least twenty bills relating to railway development within the coalfield were passed, and by 1850 the implications of locomotion, for society, for the economy, and for the landscape, were apparent.

Opposite: The landscape around Blaenavon has been shaped by centuries of industrial activity. In the foreground of this aerial view is Pwll-du Quarry, which supplied limestone to kilns at Llanfoist. The quarry was served by a branch of Hill's Tramroad, which can be traced snaking below the now empty reservoir built to power the quarry's water-balance lift. In the distance, Keeper's Pond can be seen to the left. It was created in the early nineteenth century to hold water for the forge at Garnddyrys to the north. To the right, are the black spoil heaps left from opencast coal mining during the Second World War. At the top of the picture is the town of Blaenavon. The historical importance of this landscape was recognized by its designation as a World Heritage Site in 2000 (© Crown: Royal Commission on the Ancient and Historical Monuments of Wales, 99-CS-0381).

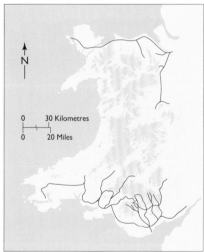

Above: Railways built in Wales between 1839 and 1860.

Isambard Kingdom Brunel's Taff Vale Railway opened in 1841 and linked Merthyr and Cardiff. Merthyr-born artist, Penry Williams, painted this watercolour of the viaduct that carried the railway over the river Taff at Goitre-coed (© Ironbridge Gorge Museum Trust).

Before the advent of locomotion, the ports of south-west and north-west Wales were busier than were those serving the southern coalfield. In 1835, 275 ships were registered at Cardigan, the highest figure in Wales apart from Beaumaris. However, by the end of the 1830s, the ports of rural Wales were rapidly being outclassed. In 1839, Cardiff acquired the West Bute Dock, acclaimed on its opening as the largest masonry dock in the world; financed solely by the marquess of Bute, its construction was central to the eventual emergence of Cardiff as the largest urban centre in Wales. The Town Dock at Newport was opened in 1842 and, before the end of the 1840s, floating harbours and improved wharfs had been constructed at Swansea, Neath, Llanelli and Burry Port.

So far, the industrial impact of the economic growth of the period 1780–1850 has been considered solely in the context of the south Wales coalfield — and justifiably so, for the economy of which Merthyr was the crucible grew until it sustained well over half the population of Wales. But, in many respects, economic growth had a more spectacular impact upon the landscape in other parts of Wales. The canals of the south Wales coalfield, although more significant economically, did not have the visual appeal of

Telford and Jessop's ten-arch aqueduct of 1796–1801 at Chirk was built for the Ellesmere Canal. The viaduct by Henry Robertson was erected almost fifty years later, in 1846–48, for the Shrewsbury and Chester Railway. Together they present a spectacle of almost Roman grandeur.

other Welsh canals, in particular the Brecknock and Abergavenny Canal (1797–1800, 1811–12), the navigable feeder of the Ellesmere Canal, starting at Llandysilio near Llangollen (1808), and the Montgomeryshire Canal (1819). The Ellesmere Canal includes two marvels — Telford and Jessop's aqueducts at Chirk and Pontcysyllte. The latter, 'the stream in the sky', is the most astounding achievement of the canal age; an iron trough, 1,007 feet (307m) long, 126 feet (38m) above the ground and held up by nineteen piers, it was hailed by Sir Walter Scott as 'the finest work of art I have ever seen'. Telford was also the engineer of the schemes to improve the coast route between Chester and Bangor and to reconstruct the Holyhead road. As part of the former work, he designed the Conwy Suspension Bridge (1826), which, with its crenellated towers, superbly complements the castle. As part of the latter, he was responsible for the Menai Bridge (1819–26); its elegance and unprecedented span of 585 feet (178m) won such fame that, in distant Russia, the poet Pushkin sang its praises.

Other features, too, prove that industry could leave as visible a mark on other parts of Wales as it did on the south Wales coalfield. The scarred landscape at Minera, the astonishing number of craters dug by lead miners on Halkyn Mountain, the massive bleach works at Lleweni, the extensive lead mines of Cwmsymlog and Cwmystwyth, the numerous small woollen mills of the Teifi Valley and the brick pits at Buckley all testify to the quickening pace of economic growth. The excavation of the great hole at the Penrhyn slate quarry — the largest single excavation in the world until the 1980s — was well under way by 1850, as was the creation of the vast caverns at Blaenau Ffestiniog. Of all the memorials to nineteenth-century Welsh industry, the most spectacular is in Anglesey. Copper-ore mining on Parys Mountain south of Amlwch was at its height between 1790 and 1815 when up to 15,000 tons of gunpowder a year was detonated there. The result is a stupendous gulch, its sides aglow with orange and yellow tints.

As in the south Wales coalfield, so also elsewhere in Wales, expanding industry created a demand for cheaply and rapidly built dwellings. In the north and west too, much of the industry was located in the upland districts, at altitudes of between 650 and 820 feet (200 and 250m) on Halkyn Mountain, at Minera and at Blaenau Ffestiniog, and up to 1,300 feet (400m) in the lead-mining districts of Cardiganshire and Montgomeryshire. Penybryn, a row of single-storeyed cottages built in the Ystwyth Valley in about 1835, was typical of the housing of the upland lead miners. In the slate-quarrying towns, housing could be appallingly congested; an example is John Street, Bethesda. But as the quarrying districts had a strong tradition of combining slate working with farming, many of those employed in the quarries lived in the agro-industrial dispersed settlements which are such a feature of upland Caernarvonshire Those whose smallholdings were more distant lived during the week near their place of employment in barracks, such as those at the Dinorwic Quarry.

Among the most interesting of the surviving examples of early nineteenth-century Welsh industrial housing are the weavers' houses built in the woollen towns of Montgomeryshire. Often three or four storeys high, the ground and

The Conwy suspension bridge, opened in 1826, was designed by Thomas Telford (d. 1834) as part of a general scheme to improve the coast route between Chester and Bangor.

The enormous gulch on Parys Mountain, Anglesey, is the most stupendous of all the memorials to nineteenth-century Welsh industry.

In the textile-working towns of mid-Wales, many rows of houses were surmounted by open workshop floors or 'factory rooms'. The Newtown Textile Museum is located in what was once six back-to-back cottages topped by large weaving rooms on the two upper floors.

This farmstead near Aberdaron, with its rubble walls and slate roof, is characteristic of Llŷn smallholdings.

usually the first floors formed the dwellings which were frequently built back-to-back. The upper floor or floors were unpartitioned 'factory rooms' containing hand-worked looms. Scores of such buildings were erected at Newtown and Llanidloes between about 1820 and 1850; the Newtown Textile Museum is accommodated in a group of them, and the town's chief weaving quarter — Penygloddfa — is a conservation area.

The growth of industry, though revolutionary in its scale and its implications, was not sufficient, initially at least, to absorb the ever growing population. Between 1780 and 1820, squatting on upland waste land reached epidemic proportions and the multiplicity of tiny peasant holdings nearly drove the rural Welsh into the abyss that overwhelmed the Irish. A typical squatter settlement was that at Trefenter on Mynydd Bach in Cardiganshire, where by the 1840s there were forty smallholdings on some 160 acres (65ha). Squatters' homes were constructed from whatever was at hand, as were the rest of the dwellings of the rural poor. In south-west Wales, they sometimes had mud or clom walls, a form of building believed by later generations to be impermanent and a mark of shameful poverty, although modern ecologists consider them to be splendidly organic, and, with proper maintenance, very durable. Thatched and brightly painted they existed in their thousands in Cardiganshire and Carmarthenshire as late as the first decade of the twentieth century. In Pembrokeshire, where local slate was available, slate roofs were, by the early nineteenth century, ousting thatched roofs; the high winds of the most exposed parts of the county led to the grouting of the roofs with lime mortar, a distinctive feature of the cottages of the coastal west.

In much of the north, cottages were built of rubble, sometimes using stones of gigantic size. Along the borderland timber-framed construction, abandoned by the gentry, continued among the peasantry at least until the

early decades of the nineteenth century. In some areas, however, light frames covered with weatherboard were coming into fashion. Cottages progressively acquired fireplaces, glass windows, parlours, stairs, upper floors, dormer windows and additional service rooms, an evolution which exactly mirrored that of the yeomen's houses two or three centuries earlier.

Squatting was both a cause and a consequence of the enclosure movement, which also reached its climax between 1780 and 1820, a period when Parliament passed 106 bills relating to enclosures in Wales. Some of them — those relating to the marshes at Saltney, Malltraeth and Morfa Rhuddlan, for example — led to the drainage of low-lying and potentially fertile land. Most of the bills were, however, concerned with high moorland, and the aim of their promoters was not the improvement of agriculture but rather the intensification of landlord rights. The most ambitious of the acts were those passed in 1808 and 1815 dealing with the 40,000-acre (16,000ha) Great Forest of Brecon. It was blatant class legislation, for it deprived commoners of over half the grazing land to which they had previously had access and gave rich pickings to a few speculators. Scottish lowlanders leased much of the land allotted to the Crown, and their homesteads, sheltered by belts of conifers, are still features of the landscape. Enclosure led to the building of further vast lengths of drystone wall. In some areas, however, hedges were preferred, planted with quickthorn, or, occasionally, as in parts of Cardiganshire, with laburnum.

Enclosures were a major feature in the continuing growth in the size of the leading landed estates. Other factors — especially indebtedness among the smaller squires and the effect of partible inheritance practised by many yeomen farmers — also assisted the process. The Cardiff Castle estate of the Bute family increased in size by 25 per cent between 1790 and 1815, a period when vast sheep walks were added to the estates of Golden Grove, Faenol and Trawsgoed. The long war with France (1792–1802, 1803–15) led to higher prices for agricultural produce, thus permitting landlords to demand higher rents. The more fortunately placed among them could also benefit from the royalties and other profits yielded by industry. The increasing wealth of the landed elite was reflected in their building operations. Some of the new mansions remained faithful to the sober, harmonious traditions of the eighteenth century. This was particularly true of the work of John Nash, who, during his stay in Carmarthen (1785–96), was responsible for some remarkable small country houses, Llanerchaeron in Cardiganshire and Ffynone in Pembrokeshire pre-eminent among them.

Yet, the growing architectural eclecticism of the nineteenth century meant that Wales, by 1850, had been endowed with country houses in a bewildering variety of styles. Romanesque was employed at Penrhyn, Gothic at Margam, Tudor at Stanage, Jacobean at Llanrhaeadr Hall, Greek at Clytha House, Islamic at Garth, and Dutch at Clyro Court. As Thomas Hopper put it: 'It is an architect's business to understand all the styles and to be prejudiced in favour of none'. Hopper's work at Penrhyn Castle (1820–37) is the most prodigious fruit of the building boom in large country houses. Financed by the profits of the Penrhyn quarries, the castle, 625 feet (190m) long, has a vast

John Nash rebuilt the seventeenth-century house at Llanerchaeron for Colonel William Lewis in 1793–95. Given to the National Trust in 1990, it was restored and opened to the public in 2004 (© NTPL/Andrew Butler).

The staircase in the prospect tower of the spectacular Tudor Gothic mansion at Margam, which was constructed for Christopher Rice Mansel Talbot in 1830–35 (© Stephen Radford).

Thomas Hopper's gloriously Romanesque Penrhyn Castle of 1820–37 was financed by the profits of the Penrhyn slate quarries. By 1850, Wales had been endowed with additional country houses built in a bewildering range of styles.

keep, a grand staircase and a great hall, all awash with blind arcading, ribs and bosses, chevrons and billets. Although faithful in the main to the Romanesque, Penrhyn has some fourteenth-century features and much Arab-style ornament, for the historicism prized by later architects was not always apparent in the work of the early nineteenth century. Although Clytha House (about 1838) is learnedly Ionic, Margam (1830) is Gothick rather than Gothic, and the style employed at Garth (1809–15) was a very free interpretation of the traditions of the Moguls. Even stranger is Gwrych Castle near Abergele (1816–53); as much a gigantic folly as a dwelling house, its mixture of styles and its medley of towers and curtain walls surely make it Wales's most astonishing architectural agglomeration.

In the period 1780 to 1850, the landowners of Wales were even more prodigal in their landscaping activities than they had been in the mid-eighteenth century. The most extensive activities were those of Thomas Johnes (d. 1816) at Hafod in the Ystwyth Valley. Between 1790 and 1811, he financed a vast programme of afforestation; walks and bridges led to vantage points, and his estate was embellished with a cavern, pools, obelisks, fountains, summer houses and gazebos. Johnes had links with Stanage Park near Knighton, where between 1803 and 1809 Humphry Repton (1752–1818) designed scenic drives and lakes and directed a large-scale scheme of afforestation. The cult of the Picturesque reached its extreme form at Llangollen, where the servants of the Ladies of Plas Newydd adorned a ravine with rustic steps and bridges, cascades and pools and banks of moss and ferns. More ambitious were the plans carried out at the behest of William Paxton at Middleton Hall above the Tywi Valley; there, an extensive landscape was transformed by an elaborate scheme of water management, producing waterfalls, pools, bridges, weirs and bathing buildings. Paxton's commission provided the setting for the National Botanic Garden of Wales, opened in 2000.

Paxton also ordered the building of Paxton's Tower, a splendid folly overlooking the Tywi Valley. Folly building was a characteristic activity of the age of the Picturesque. Ruined castles and abbeys were considered to be primarily follies, and William Gilpin (d. 1804) suggested in 1782 that Tintern Abbey could be made more delightfully irregular by the judicious use of a mallet. Grottoes, decorated with shells, were a favourite form of folly and examples survive at Talacre in Flintshire, at Cilwendeg in Pembrokeshire and at Pontypool Park. The usual folly, however, was a tower, often with pretensions to being a memorial. Wales's largest is Clytha Castle (1790), but there are other interesting examples including the Ivy Tower at Gnoll (about 1780), the Anglesey Column at Llanfair Pwllgwyngyll (1817), the Bryncir Tower (1821) north of Porthmadog and the Tŵr y Dderi (1824) north of Lampeter. The oddest of Wales's follies is the Jubilee Tower erected in 1810 on the summit of the Clwydian Range; now in ruins, it was the earliest Egyptian-style monument to be built in Britain. Some apparent follies had other purposes; the two towers built by the Bailey brothers at Nantyglo in 1816 were intended to cow the workers and to offer a place of refuge to loyal employees of the hated ironmasters.

Major landscaping and garden making continued to appeal to the landowners of Wales in the period 1780–1850. The cult of the Picturesque was at its height, and there are few finer examples of its expression than the garden of the 'Ladies of Llangollen' at Plas Newydd. Among the features were these rustic steps illustrated in a nineteenth-century watercolour.

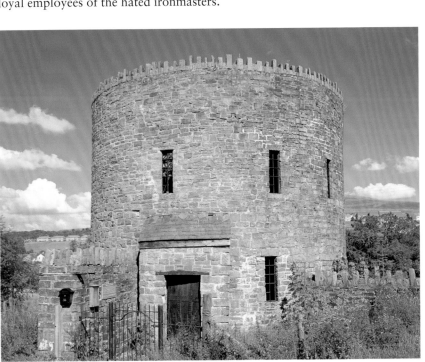

One of the round towers at Nantyglo, built by the Bailey brothers in 1816 as a place of refuge for the ironmasters' loyal employees in the event of industrial unrest (© Crown Copyright (2009) Visit Wales).

Opposite: It was not uncommon for some estate owners of the first industrial era to create entire villages, and even towns. Aberaeron was created by the Gwynne family. The plan below shows the two principal phases in the layout of the town, pre- and post-1840 (Plan after Hilling 1976; photograph © Crown Copyright (2009) Visit Wales).

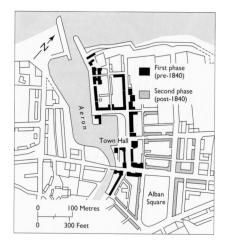

Established as a naval dockyard, Pembroke Dock was the largest planned town created in Wales between 1780 and 1850. Laid out as a grid, the town contains some attractive features. In the foreground of this view is the star-shaped Defensible Barracks built in 1844–45 to protect the town and dockyard (© Crown: The Royal Commission on the Ancient and Historical Monuments of Wales, 95-CS-1077).

Some landowners went further and created entire villages, and even towns. Marford near Wrexham, built between 1803 and 1815, is Wales's most charming estate village; there are others at Merthyr Mawr, Berriew and Llandegai. A more ambitious project was the industrial village of Morriston, begun by the Morris family in 1768 and completed in 1815; it had a gridiron pattern of streets with a church at the main intersection, and the Morrises also commissioned high-rise accommodation, the first block of flats in Wales. Two other landowners' projects had a less industrial setting. The Gwynne family initiated the creation of the town of Aberaeron with its harmonious, stuccoed streets, and W. A. Madocks (d. 1828) ordered the laying out of the equally harmonious Tremadog. By commissioning the sea wall which led to the draining of much of the estuary of the Glaslyn, Madocks was responsible for one of the most ambitious land reclamation schemes of the nineteenth century. His hope that the town he founded — Porthmadog — would become a major maritime centre had echoes in ambitions of members of the Greville family, the founders of the town of Milford Haven. Between 1780 and 1809, three parallel streets were built above the Haven and the Grevilles sought to make the town a major centre of whaling, shipbuilding and the transatlantic trade.

The largest planned town created in Wales between 1780 and 1850 owed nothing to the enterprise of landowners. That town is Pembroke Dock; a naval dockyard was established there in 1814, giving rise to a community twice as large as that of neighbouring Pembroke. Laid out as a grid, Pembroke Dock contains some fascinating buildings, including the Defensible Barracks, completed in 1845 — the last fortification in Europe built in accordance with the ideas of Sébastien Vauban — and the garrison chapel, claimed to be the sole Georgian classical church surviving in Wales.

Side by side with the creation of new towns and the burgeoning of industrial settlements was the expansion of the older market towns of Wales, almost all of which at least doubled in size between 1780 and 1850. They also became safer and more salubrious, for, by the 1840s, paving, draining, lighting and policing were growing concerns of the civic authorities. While country houses were increasingly eclectic in style, town houses generally remained faithful to the scaled-down Georgian tradition. Much of the townscape created in Wales between 1780 and 1850 survives, and is often loosely described as 'Regency'. Among the highlights are Laura Place at Aberystwyth, Victoria Place at Haverfordwest, the Bulwark at Brecon, Llanfyllin's High Street, Welshpool's Salop Road, and the greater part of the towns of Tenby and Beaumaris. Other styles tended to be chosen for public buildings — neo-Tudor, for example, at Mold's county hall (1834), and at Flint's town hall (1840). Among the most distinguished public buildings erected in Wales in the first half of the nineteenth century was the town hall at Bridgend (1843); impressively and austerely Doric, its demolition in 1971 was a sad act of philistinism. Equally Doric, but less austere, is the old shire hall at Brecon (1842), now the Brecknock Museum, while the Royal Institution at Swansea (1841) is in the rather more elegant Ionic. The North Wales Mental Hospital at Denbigh (1848) is grandly Jacobean, a style used

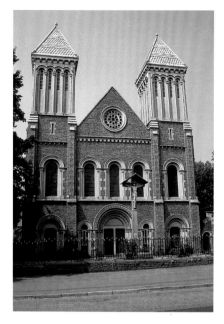

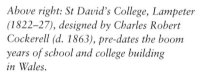

Above right: St David's College, Lampeter (1822–27), designed by Charles Robert Cockerell (d. 1863), pre-dates the boom years of school and college building in Wales.

Above: The wealth of the south Wales coalfield financed a number of churches of interest including St Mary's in Cardiff's Butetown. Its design is an interesting exercise in Romanesque, coupled with Byzantine details.

more modestly in the town's former Bluecoat School (1847). Other public buildings of the period include the shire hall at Presteigne (1829); within the hall were the judge's lodgings, splendidly restored and opened to the public in 1997. Forty-five workhouses had been built in Wales by 1850; some of them — that at Llanfyllin (1848) for example — have a certain charm. The massive House of Industry at Forden (1795), capable of housing a thousand inmates, was, as a contemporary put it, 'a splendid receptacle of misery'. In 1850, Wales's boom years of school and college building had not dawned, but by then the country did have some not unattractive educational buildings, in particular Cockerell's work at Lampeter (1822–27), Ginell's at Llandovery (1848) and Prichard's at Cowbridge (1849–52).

The buildings at Lampeter and elsewhere were the product of the revival of the Church of England in Wales. By the 1850s, the Established Church was beginning to face up to the challenge represented by a growing and increasingly redistributed industrial population, although it was in the succeeding decades that the Anglican Church's building movement took off. Parliament's belief that the teachings of the Established Church were the antidote to the rebelliousness of the working classes led to government grants for church building. Some 'Commissioners' Churches' were erected in Wales, generally uninspired buildings typified by those at Buckley (1822), Glyntaff (1837), and Bagillt (1839). The growth of market towns led to the construction of churches such as St David's, Newtown (1847), built in a neo-Gothic mode unmindful of medieval proprieties. The wealth of the south Wales coalfield financed some churches of interest — St David's, Rhymney (1843), for example, the last neo-classical church to be built in Wales, and St Mary's, Cardiff (1845), an interesting exercise in Romanesque with Byzantine details. The Oxford Movement led to a deeper knowledge of medieval architecture, particularly that of the twelfth and thirteenth centuries, considered to be quintessentially the age of faith. The church at Llangorwen near Aberystwyth (1841) — the first church to be built in Wales since the Protestant Reformation to have a stone altar — is an early product of the movement, as is the delightful ensemble of church, school and master's house at Llangasty-Talyllyn on the banks of Llangorse Lake (1848–50).

But the first half of the nineteenth century was above all the period of the building of Nonconformist places of worship. Between 1800 and 1850 a new chapel was being opened in Wales on average every eight days, and many hundreds more were to be built in the following six decades. According to the Religious Census of 1851, chapel accommodation in Wales was sufficient to seat 50 per cent of the population, and in several districts, particularly in the rural north, the number of seats exceeded the number of inhabitants. Some of the chapels represented a departure from the oblong box tradition — Peniel, Tremadog (1811), for example, with its Tuscan columned portico, and Capel y Groes (1838), the octagonal chapel at Margam. Of those of a more traditional design, the simpler remained faithful to the practice of having the opening and the pulpit on the long walls. That was the layout of Capel Cymer (1834), one

This charming group of church, school and master's house at Llangasty-Talyllyn overlooking Llangorse Lake was built in 1848–50. The patron was Robert Raikes, who was influenced by the liturgical and architectural ideals of the contemporary Oxford Movement.

of the earliest chapels to be built in the Rhondda. Some chapels — Ramoth, Cowbridge (1828), for example — were square in plan and crowned by a pyramid roof, but the style increasingly favoured was the oblong with the opening in the gable façade. The early nineteenth-century façades were very simple and restrained. As Peter Sager put it: 'If religion is based on the Word, never have God's houses been so parsimonious in their language'.

The simplicity is deceptive. In much of urban Wales, the chapels offered the only evidence of anything approaching deliberately conceived architecture, and as Nonconformists were not concerned to ensure that their places of worship had an eastern alignment, their buildings fitted into the street scene better than did those of more ritualistic denominations. Although the only design elements in the façade were the relationship between doors and windows, the emphasis given to the pediment, and the placing, or otherwise, of an inscribed plaque, the variety offered by such an apparently restricted range of options was surprisingly large; so much so, that of the thousands of gable-façade chapels built in Wales, not one is an exact replica of another.

The years 1780 to 1850 were not only the era of the radical remaking of Wales; they were also a period when the landforms of Wales and their underlying geology became the subject of increasingly informed study. Considering its relatively small area, the country has a remarkable variety of rocks; it was also easily accessible to the pioneers of the study of geology, factors which explain why four geological systems were given universally accepted names with Welsh associations. Carboniferous rock, formed between 354 and 298 million years ago, was a term adopted in 1822 as a result of the study of the strata of the south Wales coalfield; the term Cambrian rock (543m–490m) was adopted in 1835, as was Silurian rock (443m–417m); the term Ordovician rock (490m–443m) followed in 1879. Furthermore, Welsh place-names — Arenig, Llandeilo and Tremadog among them — have achieved geological immortality. Equally intriguing are mineral names, including anglesite (after Anglesey), cymrite (after Cymru) and namuwite (after the National Museum of Wales).

The study of Wales's landforms and geology developed hand in hand with the provision of an increasingly detailed record of the appearance of the Welsh landscape. The work of topographical artists, pioneered in the mid-eighteenth century by the Buck brothers, became vastly more plentiful; there can hardly have been a scene in Wales not drawn by the prolific Henry Gastineau (d. 1876). Landscape and seascape painters proliferated; Cyfarthfa Castle Museum at Merthyr has important depictions of the iron industry and the Glynn Vivian Gallery at Swansea houses fascinating paintings of the town's docks and shipping. Swansea has an honoured place in the history of photography, soon to become by far the most important medium in which to record the making of Wales. Calvert Jones, a close associate of Henry Fox Talbot, was the town's rector, and in March 1841 Jones was responsible for what is probably the earliest example of photography in Wales — the beautiful daguerreotype of Margam Abbey now in the National Library at Aberystwyth. Topographical dictionaries of Wales were published — that of Carlisle (1811) and of Lewis (1833) — and in 1846 the first issue of

Between 1800 and 1850, a new chapel in Wales was being opened on average every eight days. The Ramoth Independent Chapel of 1828 at Cowbridge was by no means exceptional, though its square plan crowned with a pyramid roof was not to retain great favour. The building is now the United Free Church.

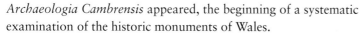

Left: Wales played a central role in the development of the science of geology. The country's remarkable variety of rocks and fossils provided ample material for study by the discipline's pioneers and four of the universally accepted names for geological systems have Welsh associations — Carboniferous, Cambrian, Silurian and Ordovician. The results of the early study of Wales's geology were embodied in William Smith's groundbreaking geological map of Britain, first published in 1815. The Welsh portion of the map is shown here (IPR113-11C British Geological Survey © NERC 2009. All rights reserved).

Above: Calvert Jones's beautiful daguerreotype of Margam Abbey. Taken on 9 March 1841, this is probably the earliest example of photography in Wales and the only daguerreotype by Calvert Jones known to have survived (By permission of The National Library of Wales, PG00726).

Archaeologia Cambrensis appeared, the beginning of a systematic examination of the historic monuments of Wales.

Above all, the late eighteenth and early nineteenth centuries were the pioneer years of the Ordnance Survey, founded in 1791. The first task of the mapmakers was the creation of a system of triangulation which would allow a close survey of the entire kingdom from accurately located points. The triangulation of Wales was carried out between 1800 and 1820, when issues such as the exact height of Snowdon were settled. By the mid-nineteenth century inch-to-a-mile maps covering almost the whole of the country had been published and by then the preparation of the 25-inch-to-a-mile maps was well advanced. Among the many merits of the Ordnance Survey maps is the fact that they provide a published record of thousands upon thousands of place-names, for one of the chief aspects of the making of a country is the way in which its inhabitants mark their land with names. Almost as important as a source are the tithe maps and apportionments prepared in the 1830s and 1840s, for they contain thousands of field-names as well as offering an almost complete record of the ownership and the use made of the land of Wales in the mid-nineteenth century. Accumulation of such knowledge would accelerate in subsequent periods, thus allowing the activities of the more recent makers of Wales to be documented with an unprecedented fullness.

THE SECOND INDUSTRIAL ERA

THE MAKING OF WALES 1850–1914

The remaking of Wales, apparent between 1780 and 1850, was consolidated between 1850 and 1914 — so much so indeed that Wales, perhaps to a greater extent than any other part of the United Kingdom is, in visual terms, a Victorian and Edwardian country. At least half its houses, the majority of its civic buildings and many of its churches and chapels are a legacy of the later nineteenth and early twentieth centuries.

By 1914, the Welsh economy was heavily dependent upon extractive industries, and the landmarks created by those industries dominated much of urban Wales. Above all, the coal industry of south Wales grew with extraordinary speed, fuelling steam engines and shipping around the world. As coal extraction took over from iron making as the chief industry of the south Wales valleys, the pitheads with their winding towers became the defining symbol of Welsh industrialization. Made of lattice steel and supported by elegant support struts and delicate arched trusses, they were structures of distinction, but they now survive only where coal production has been replaced by mining museums. Among other significant structures built to serve the coal industry were Penallta Colliery, north of Caerphilly (1909), and the complex at the Navigation Colliery at Crumlin (1911).

Evidence of other industries includes the neo-Gothic limekilns at Llandybie (1858), the fascinating ruins of lead mining at Bryntail, south of the Clywedog reservoir, a warehouse at Cardiff's East Bute Dock (1861) — a building whose functional integrity is more characteristic of the twentieth than of the nineteenth century — and the Boiler Factory at Queensferry (1905), hailed by Nikolaus Pevsner as 'the most advanced British building of its date'.

In the transformation of the landscape, industrial buildings were perhaps less significant than industrial refuse. By the early twentieth century, Wales was pre-eminently a land of tips. The most dramatic was the Great Tip above Merthyr, the accumulated spoil of Dowlais's mining and iron-working operations, but the largest was that at Bargoed, a huge, squat mountain. Another scarred landscape created by the industrialization of the south Wales coalfield is the vast limestone quarry at Trefil, north of Tredegar.

Other Welsh industries were even more prodigal producers of spoil heaps. Every ton of slate created nine tons of waste, much of which still lies around Bethesda, Llanberis, Corris and Blaenau Ffestiniog. Quarrying had a greater

The complex at Navigation Colliery, Crumlin, was built between 1907 and 1911 by Partridge, Jones and Company. It was a show pit of the period, with high-quality brick buildings and modern machinery.

Opposite: Iron and coal were by no means the only nineteenth-century industries to scar the landscape of Wales. The creation of the great hole at the Penrhyn slate quarry, near Bethesda, was well under way by 1850 (© Crown: The Royal Commission on the Ancient and Historical Monuments of Wales, AP_2006_1624).

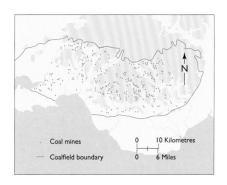

Coal mines in Glamorgan in 1913.

Between the 1840s and the 1880s there were almost two hundred lead mines in Cardiganshire, and zinc mines in the region were also flourishing. Virtually nothing grows on the spoil heaps which are contaminated with toxic residues, resulting in barren, but eerily beautiful landscapes, like that shown here at Cwmystwyth.

impact upon the landscape than had coal mining. Until the advent of large-scale opencast mining, coal workings were out of sight. With the exception of Blaenau Ffestiniog, with its massive slate mines, slate working was a surface activity. Above Llanberis, the giant steps carved out of the slopes of Elidir are breathtaking, and that is even more true of the deep amphitheatre at Penrhyn, near Bethesda. Almost as impressive are the workings on the north face of Yr Eifl, once a major source of granite setts. Lead and copper working produced more noxious waste. Nothing grows on the spoil heaps of the lead mines of Cardiganshire, Montgomeryshire and Flintshire, and by the early twentieth century copper smelting had wreaked havoc in the lower Swansea Valley.

Railways and docks vied with industry in transforming the landscape. The railways built in southern Wales in the 1850s bear the imprint of Isambard Kingdom Brunel, perhaps the greatest railway engineer of all time. It was he who designed the South Wales Railway, the Taff Vale Railway and the Vale of Neath Railway. Among those of his works that survive are the substructure of the tubular suspension bridge at Chepstow, the viaducts at Goitre-coed, Pontypridd and Llwchwr, and the dock at Briton Ferry. He sought to ensure that the main port serving ships sailing from Britain to southern Ireland should be at Neyland, where a splendid statue of him, complete with his high top hat, was unveiled in 1999.

Between 1850 and 1870, around 1,400 miles (2,250km) of railways were constructed in Wales, a figure which had at least trebled by 1914. A high proportion of the lines was built to serve the south Wales coalfield, where rivalry between companies produced a particularly dense network of

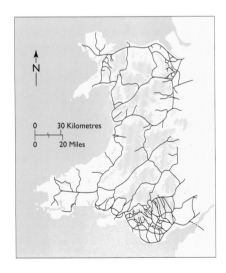

N

0   30 Kilometres

0   20 Miles

The railway network of Wales by 1914.

railways. Where a railway followed a valley, as did those of the pioneer companies of the coalfield, its construction offered few complications, although the gorge at Merthyr Vale was hard pressed to contain two railway lines, a road, a canal and a tramroad, as well as the river Taff. Cross-valley lines, involving cuttings, embankments and viaducts, had a far greater visual impact and represented a more difficult engineering challenge. The Crumlin Viaduct (1857), a 1,650 feet (503m) crossing of the river Ebbw supported on innovative iron trusses — sadly demolished in 1965 — was considered to be one of the engineering wonders of the later nineteenth century. Britain's most ambitious railway venture of the late nineteenth century was the Severn Tunnel; 4.5 miles (7km) in length, it was for more than a century the longest undersea tunnel in the world. Completed in 1886, its enormous engine houses at Portskewett, constructed to accommodate the pumps that remove 20 million gallons (91 million litres) of water a day from the tunnel, are a remarkable addition to the Welsh landscape.

Railways could have a striking impact elsewhere in Wales, especially when they intruded into areas hitherto almost totally undeveloped — for example, Talerddig, with its dramatic cutting, the Mawddach Estuary with its appealing wooden viaduct, and the Blaenau Ffestiniog–Bala railway with its sixteen viaducts and fifty-seven bridges. Some of Wales's most impressive railway structures were on lines serving routes already pioneered by canal and road builders. Thus, Robertson's viaduct at Chirk is cheek by jowl with Telford and Jessop's aqueduct, and Stephenson's railway bridges across the river Conwy and the Menai Strait complement Telford's masterpieces. The quarrying areas came to be served by a number of narrow-gauge railways, including that from Porthmadog to Blaenau Ffestiniog; opened in 1836 as a gravity and horse railway, it became in 1865 the first narrow-gauge railway in Britain to use locomotion to haul passengers as well as freight. Those of

The Crumlin railway viaduct built by T. W. Kennard in 1857 was considered to be one of the engineering wonders of the later nineteenth century (© National Museum of Wales).

The second half of the nineteenth century was the great age of railway building in Wales. A high proportion of the lines was built in the south Wales coalfield, but elsewhere the new railways could be a striking feature in the landscape. In the foreground of this aerial view of the Menai Strait is the Britannia Bridge of 1845–50, designed by Robert Stephenson (d. 1859). It complements Thomas Telford's suspension road bridge of 1819–26 in the distance.

The funicular tramway at Llandudno opened in 1902 to take visitors up the Great Orme (© Crown Copyright (2009) Visit Wales).

Newport's transporter bridge of 1906, a rare form of river crossing, was designed by F. Arnodin (© Crown Copyright (2009) Visit Wales).

the narrow-gauge railways that survive are among the most attractive features of the landscape. Among them are the funicular railways at Aberystwyth (1896) and Llandudno (1902), and Britain's sole rack and pinion railway — the 4.7 mile (7.5km) Snowdon Mountain Railway, opened in 1896.

The Welsh railway system, with its lack of major termini, was not endowed with magnificent stations. Some Welsh stations do, however, have considerable merit, especially the Italianate buildings serving the Chester and Holyhead Railway. That railway hugged the coast and thus had a marked impact upon the physiognomy of the northern coastal towns. At Colwyn Bay and Abergele, access to the seashore involves crossing the railway; at Flint, the line brutally disturbs the town's medieval layout and at Conwy it impairs the majesty of the borough's southern defences. Elsewhere, Wrexham was mauled by railway building, for much of its ancient centre was obliterated. Like Abergele, Barmouth and Aberdyfi were severed from the sea, and Port Talbot suffered greatly from its bisection by the South Wales Railway. At Cardiff, the railway was carried across the town on an embankment; a barrier therefore separated the docklands from the rest of the town, an obstacle with profound sociological implications. Railway building at Cardiff involved the diversion of the Taff and the creation of Wales's most renowned piece of real estate — Cardiff Arms Park, the site of the Millennium Stadium. It also led to the laying out within the town of vast areas of railway sidings accommodating trucks of coal awaiting shipment.

Road transport saw few innovative developments between 1850 and 1914, although the transporter bridge at Newport (1906) is a very rare species of river crossing. (The world's oldest surviving transporter bridge — that completed at Bilbao in 1892 — has been granted World Heritage status,

Above: The massive basin of Cardiff's Queen Alexandra Dock was the largest masonry dock in the world when it opened in 1907 (© Crown: The Royal Commission on the Ancient and Historical Monuments of Wales, 95/CS/1943).

Above left: Stack Rock Fort was first erected in 1852 on an outcrop of rock in mid-channel at Milford Haven. It was remodelled in 1870 to accommodate more guns and a larger garrison (© Crown: The Royal Commission on the Ancient and Historical Monuments of Wales, 915507/08).

although it lacks the scale and the grace of the bridge at Newport.) Transport by sea, above all the huge increase in the export of coal, gave rise to massive constructions. Cardiff acquired five large docks, including the Queen Alexandra, hailed on its opening in 1907 as the largest masonry dock in the world. Large-scale dock building also took place at Newport, Barry and Swansea, and Penarth, Port Talbot, Briton Ferry and Llanelli were endowed with at least a dock apiece. Elsewhere, port development was less extensive, partly because the growth of the railway network led to the decline of ports such as Haverfordwest and Cardigan, once the centres of a lively coastal trade. Slate export led to some construction work at Caernarfon, Bangor and Porthmadog, but in the north-east Mostyn was the only place to retain the shipping traditions of the Dee estuary. The most dramatic of Wales's maritime structures were the great breakwaters built at Holyhead and Fishguard; work at Fishguard was especially laborious, for the cliff face at Goodwick was torn down to accommodate the harbour.

Dock and harbour building was financed, either by individuals such as the marquess of Bute or by limited liability concerns such as the Great Western Railway Company. However, one group of coastal constructions was built under the direction of the central government. Between 1848 and 1872, about a dozen forts were built to protect the Milford Haven Waterway from an anticipated attack by the French. Known as Palmerston's Follies because of their association with the premiership of Lord Palmerston (1855–58, 1859–65), their scale, their starkness and the beauty of their location make them an astonishing addition to the Welsh landscape. The largest is Scoveston Fort, west of Neyland (1861–68), the most dramatic is Stack Rock (1852, 1870), which is located in the middle of the waterway and the most intriguing is Thorn Island Fort (1852–54), which was a hotel, and may yet be one again. Fortifications were also built in Glamorgan — at Flatholm Island, Lavernock and Mumbles.

Of all the achievements of the makers of Wales between 1850 and 1914, the greatest was to house the population, which rose from 1,189,000 to 2,523,000. The achievement was particularly marked in the industrial areas,

where population increase could be phenomenal. Blaenau Ffestiniog's inhabitants doubled in number between 1851 and 1871; those of Mountain Ash trebled between 1871 and 1891, as did those of Mynyddislwyn between 1901 and 1911; above all, there was the Rhondda, where the population increased seventy-seven-fold — from 2,000 to 154,000 — between 1850 and 1914. The townscape of industrial Wales, particularly that of the south Wales coalfield, has been widely criticized. Although a few companies built planned industrial villages with community buildings and a symmetrical layout (that of the Tredegar Iron and Coal Company at Oakdale is the best example), there was much to criticize, in particular the monotony of the endless streets of terraced housing, the lack of public amenities and the instances of gross congestion — in 1914, the built-up areas of Tylorstown and Ferndale in the Rhondda Fach had a population density of 182 persons per acre (450 per ha).

Nevertheless, there were some positive aspects. Most of the urban development undertaken after 1850 was subject to by-laws which laid down the width of streets and the length of back gardens. As the century advanced, drainage, sewerage, pavements and lighting were progressively provided and, even in the most congested districts, the open mountainside was never far away. There was a strong tradition of owner occupation, and therefore neglect by landlords was less of a problem in the south Wales coalfield than it was in districts where the vast majority lived in rented property. Indeed, many informed commentators — H. S. Jevons, founder of the Welsh Housing Association, among them — considered that the south Wales miners were better accommodated than were those of the other major coalfields of Britain.

Most of the houses of the south Wales valleys were built of local stone, with Pennant Sandstone dominating the central belt. Brick surrounds, often painted, became increasingly a feature of doorways and windows, as at Elliotstown at Tredegar with its spectacular terraces. Other decoration of the façade was rare, although there are streets — at Llanelli, for example — rich in recessed arches, rusticated quoins and elaborate architraves. Parallel rows of double-fronted houses such as the Scotch Houses at Llwynypia (about 1865) had by the last quarter of the nineteenth century given way to two-sided streets with single-fronted houses. By then the typical coalfield house had evolved: three ground-floor rooms one behind the other, a passage-hall and three small bedrooms, a pattern repeated hundreds of thousands of times in the valleys of the south Wales coalfield, and prevalent too in the industrial areas of the north. There, particularly in the Wrexham area, houses were generally of brick, a building material which became cheaper and more abundant following the development in the 1850s of brick kilns capable of mass production.

Houses with a layout similar to those in the coalfield also dominated the townscape of the southern ports, as the mass of working-class houses at Newport, Cardiff and Swansea amply testifies. In the ports, however, the presence of a middle class created a demand for more elaborate dwellings, although they were often scaled-up versions of the coalfield house. Wales is very rich in Victorian middle-class housing. Earlier high-status houses tended to be near the town centre, but, as growth accelerated, there was a movement

Opposite: The terraces at Llwynypia were begun about 1865 to house the workers of the nearby colliery. The population of the Rhondda increased from just 2,000 in 1850 to 154,000 in 1914. During these years, housing the growing population was the greatest achievement of the makers of Wales (© Crown Copyright (2009) Visit Wales).

The eighty terraced houses of Stanleytown in the Rhondda were built in 1895 at a price of £166 each. The architect was T. R. Phillips of Pontypridd (© Crown Copyright (2009) Visit Wales).

Located near the eastern edge of the south Wales coalfield, the miners' village at Oakdale was a product of the garden village movement. It dates from 1909 to 1924, at the very end of the second industrial era (© Crown: The Royal Commission on the Ancient and Historical Monuments of Wales, 905541-03).

Above: The streets around Stow Hill in Newport provide a good example of a Victorian residential area. Indeed, many towns of Wales are rich in middle-class housing of this era.

Above right: The streets of Cardiff present a cornucopia of Victorian delights. Above all there is Cathedral Road, a long avenue with a superb unity of design, yet with a bewildering array of detail in doorways and windows.

to more salubrious locations, a phenomenon nicely illustrated at Swansea; in 1851, the most privileged groups lived around St Mary's Church and the Royal Institution, but by 1871 they had migrated to the lower slopes of Townhill. Swansea has some excellent Victorian residential areas — the handsome stucco villas of Belgrave Gardens, for example. So does Newport, where the streets around Stow Hill are particularly attractive, and earnest seekers may find distinction at Neath, Llanelli and even Port Talbot.

Above all, there is Cardiff, a cornucopia of Victorian delights. The differing layouts of the various districts of Cardiff depended upon whether they were in single or fragmented ownership — the former generally leading to a degree of conscious planning and uniformity in building design, and the latter to a miscellany of high-density houses. The largest landowner at Cardiff was the marquess of Bute; his agents favoured the erection of middle-class houses in dignified streets often enhanced by public gardens, an example followed by most of the rest of the town's major landowners. Cardiff, it was complained, was too well built, for it had a chronic lack of modest dwellings within the reach of the lower paid. The high quality of its residential areas may be appreciated in places such as Plasturton Avenue and particularly Cathedral Road, a long avenue with a superb unity of design, though hardly any building is an exact replica of its neighbour. The walls are of Pennant Sandstone, the mullions and transoms of Bath stone and the façades are enlivened with gables, finials, lozenges and blind arcades, together with doorways topped by arches bewildering in their variety. The adoption of the mechanical sawing of building stone — a feature of the quarries of the later nineteenth century — helps to explain the ubiquity of Bath stone in the coastal towns of south Wales, not only in middle-class houses but also in those of the artisan class; modest houses such as those of Clydach Street in Cardiff's Grangetown all have bay windows constructed of Bath stone.

Beyond the confines of the south Wales coalfield and its ports, Welsh urban centres during the Victorian and Edwardian eras had a somewhat mixed history. The towns which had once been Wales's most populous centres — Carmarthen, Haverfordwest, Brecon, Caernarfon, Denbigh and Welshpool — stagnated or even shrank. Seaside towns and spas experienced significant growth as trips and holidays became more common. The northern coastal resorts, easily accessible to the burgeoning population of Lancashire by rail, expanded tenfold, and the resorts of the south and west coasts and the spas of mid-Wales enjoyed considerable prosperity. The most imposing of the resorts is Llandudno, laid out by the Mostyn family in the 1850s with the intention of benefiting from the Chester and Holyhead Railway. With the fine sweep of its promenade, and flanked by the Great Orme and the Little Orme, Llandudno is perhaps the most handsome of all Welsh towns. It has a wealth of ornate cast-iron arcading and also a splendid pier, one of the nine built in Wales in the late nineteenth century. Of the spa towns, the most interesting by far is Llandrindod, a coherent architectural assemblage in cheerful brick and enhanced by fine hotels and pretty woodland pavilions.

Despite accelerating urbanization, the majority of the inhabitants of Wales in the mid-nineteenth century were still country dwellers. Although those directly involved in cultivating the land had become a minority, farming continued to be the largest single source of employment. With a growing urban market for agricultural produce and increasingly effective means of distributing it, the prospects for agriculture seemed bright. By the early 1870s, 27 per cent of the cultivated land of Wales was under cereal, green or root crops, compared with 10 per cent a century later. 'High farming' involved

Llandudno is the most handsome of all Welsh towns. The resort was laid out by the Mostyn family in the 1850s, to attract tourists brought in by the Chester and Holyhead Railway.

Gregynog, north of Newtown, has the appearance of a half-timbered mansion, though it is in fact built of concrete and dates from about 1860–70.

The Home Farm at Leighton Hall was laid out in the mid-nineteenth century by a wealthy Liverpool banker, John Naylor. He spent some £200,000 on the farm and estate, founded on his firm belief in the efficiency of 'model farming'. The scale of the vast farm buildings can be appreciated in this aerial view (© Crown: The Royal Commission on the Ancient and Historical Monuments of Wales, 93-CS-0747).

heavy investment in drainage, manuring and fencing. Fencing in particular led to the imposition of a new orderliness upon the countryside. It was an activity made quicker and cheaper because of the increasing availability of barbed wire; indeed, between 1850 and 1914, the erection of thousands of miles of barbed-wire fences probably did more than anything else to alter the appearance of the Welsh countryside.

Farmhouses and outbuildings were rebuilt, with excellent work being done by the Cawdor estate in Carmarthenshire and the Grosvenor estate in Flintshire. Much of the work on the Grosvenor estate was designed by John Douglas (1830–1911), the most interesting architect working in north-east Wales in the late nineteenth century. The Gregynog estate pioneered the use of concrete, and in the north-west the Newborough, Glynllifon and Penrhyn estates each had their signature style. The names of the designers of many of the most appealing farm buildings erected in the second half of that century are unknown; among such buildings is the almost Romanesque massiveness of the barn at Aberduhonw clearly visible from the A470 immediately south of Builth.

The increasing prosperity of agriculture enabled the long impoverished rural areas of the south-west to enjoy a degree of prosperity. That was in part attributable to the growth of the woollen industry. In 1880, there were over 200 woollen mills in the three south-western counties, twenty of them in the Drefach Felindre area of north Carmarthenshire; some of the factories were buildings of considerable distinction, especially Cambrian Mills (1902), which now houses the National Wool Museum.

The 'great rebuilding', experienced in the borderlands between 1530 and 1640, took place in the uplands of south-west Wales between 1840 and 1880. 'To travel from Welshpool to Aberystwyth', states Peter Smith, 'is to pass from a seventeenth-century to a nineteenth-century landscape'. The relative prosperity of those uplands was not destined to endure. With the onset of agricultural depression in the 1880s, rural depopulation accelerated, causing the population of many rural parishes to decline by 30 per cent and more between 1880 and 1914. Settlements on high-altitude marginal land were abandoned. As a result, districts such as the slopes of Pumlumon abound in the ruins of the dwellings of those whom the alternative of work in an industrial area caused to abandon the drudgery of seeking to wrest a livelihood from an inexorable environment.

The waxing and waning of income from agriculture was central to the ambitions of landowners. With the agricultural depression, the ability to build great houses and to manipulate the landscape became confined to those with non-agricultural sources of wealth. The greatest of the individual landscape manipulators of Victorian Wales was the Liverpool banker, John Naylor, who between 1849 and 1874 spent a fortune on Leighton Hall and its estate, situated across the Severn from Welshpool. The house, a Gothic extravaganza decorated to designs by Pugin, was surrounded by vast gardens, enhanced by a viaduct, cascades and exotic trees; among them were the largest plantations of Californian redwoods in Britain and the original of the Leyland cypress, named after Naylor's bank and now the great menace of suburbia. The features of the estate included a funicular railway, a network of piping to supply farms with liquid manure, a gasworks and channels to drive turbines and water-rams. It was Liverpool money too which permitted Henry Sandbach to build Hafodunos, east of the Conwy Valley. Completed in 1866 and surrounded by luxurious grounds, it was one of the most interesting of the country houses designed by George Gilbert Scott (1811–78). The house was severely damaged by fire in 2004.

The wealth of the south Wales valleys financed the building or the acquisition of a number of country houses. None of them was within the coalfield, for coal owners lacked the ironmasters' desire to have a daily prospect of their enterprises. The houses included several in the Vale of Glamorgan, Hean Castle near Tenby, Llanwern east of Newport, Plas Dinam near Llandinam and Gregynog north of Newtown. Plas Dinam (1874), designed by Eden Nesfield (1835–88), is an early example of the revival of the domestic building style of the Middle Ages, while Gregynog, although seemingly a superb half-timbered mansion, is in fact built of concrete. The most remarkable building enterprises financed by the coalfield's wealth were those of John, third marquess of Bute (1847–1900). Castell Coch, surely Wales's most delightful landmark, is a wonderful recreation of a thirteenth-century castle. Cardiff Castle represents the climax of the high

Cardiff Castle, designed for John, third marquess of Bute by William Burges, was the climax of the high Victorian dream. The spires and turrets of the exterior enhance the capital's skyline, and the interior is sumptuously decorated and brimming with imagery. This view shows the Banqueting Hall (© Cardiff Council).

Victorian dream; its turrets and spires are a splendid addition to Cardiff's skyline, and its interior has a sumptuous theatricality unmatched anywhere. The marquess's vast wealth permitted him not only to build, but also not to build. Cardiff's extensive open spaces, the city's greatest asset, survived unbuilt upon because their owner was rich enough not to be tempted by the wealth their exploitation could produce.

The slate industry had financed the building of Penrhyn Castle, but in the second half of the nineteenth century the quarry owners built little of distinction, apart perhaps from the interminable Faenol wall, once described as the longest folly in Europe. Anglesey's copper industry did bear architectural fruit, for the income from Parys Mountain was the ultimate source of the wealth that financed the building of Kinmel Park near Abergele. In terms of architectural history, Kinmel Park was perhaps the most important building erected in nineteenth-century Wales. Designed by Eden Nesfield and completed in the 1870s, it is in the so-called Queen Anne style which evolved into the neo-Georgian style so widely employed in the early twentieth century. In that evolution, Nesfield's work is of seminal importance.

Kinmel had a room set aside for ironing daily newspapers, but by the time the house was finished the ability to maintain a lifestyle on such a scale was becoming increasingly difficult. Admittedly, Dyffryn House in the Vale of Glamorgan was completed for John Cory in 1894 and J. A. Rolls commissioned work at his enormous mansion, The Hendre, as late as 1900; nevertheless, by the early twentieth century, families with the funds necessary to build large country houses and to maintain an extravagant lifestyle within them were becoming progressively rarer.

The attention of architects turned instead to medium-sized houses unattached to an estate and located as often as not in a suburb rather than in open country. Llanfairfechan boasts Bolnhurst (1899), the work of H. L. North (1871–1941), a perfect example of the 'Arts and Crafts' style. The most distinguished practitioner of the style was Charles Voysey (1857–1941) and his sole building in Wales is Tŷ Bronna (1903) on the Cardiff—St Fagans road. Interest in suburban 'country' houses went hand in hand with the *rus in urbe* movement, which enjoyed widespread support in the early twentieth century, giving rise to garden villages at Wrexham (1901), Rhiwbina (1912–13, 1920–23), Swansea (1913) and Barry (1915). Among the chief advocates of such villages was T. Alwyn Lloyd (1881–1960), who spent his entire career arguing the case for architecture which would enhance rather than deface the landscape. The most remarkable of the garden villages is that at Wyndham Park, Peterston-super-Ely; begun in 1909, its flat roofed houses are, wrote John Newman, 'a paradoxically early essay in the Modernistic'.

As country houses were scaled down, so also were gardens, and by the twentieth century the cottage-garden style pioneered by William Robinson and Gertrude Jekyll was widely popular. It represented a reaction against the bedding-plant layout much prized by Victorian gardeners. Wales once had many examples of the over-elaborate Victorian garden — at Baron Hill, for example, where scores of gardeners were in constant attendance — but as they were grotesquely labour-intensive, none of them has survived intact. Shrub and tree gardens have proved to be more durable. The most glorious of them is Bodnant, above the Conwy Valley; begun in 1874 by the Lancashire industrialist Henry Pochin, it is one of the wonders of the world. Vastly enriched by the introductions of plant hunters, Bodnant contains virtually every tree capable of flourishing in a temperate climate. Imported plants also featured in the splendid Japanese garden at Shirenewton east of Newport. Introductions, however, could have unfortunate consequences, for *Rhododendron ponticum* now infests large areas of upland Wales, and Japanese knotweed is a menace in wide areas.

The creation of ambitious private gardens continued into the early twentieth century; Dyffryn in the Vale of Glamorgan and Mounton, near Chepstow, are among the best examples. By then, however, large-scale gardening projects were being increasingly undertaken by public bodies rather than by private individuals. Roath Park at Cardiff was laid out in 1887 and municipal gardens were established at Newport, Aberdare, Neath and elsewhere. Landscape manipulation was also becoming far more of a public enterprise. The most scene-transforming activities were those of the water committees of major municipalities. Cardiff, Newport and Swansea constructed a series of reservoirs in the Brecon Beacons, some of them — Newport's at Talybont in particular — resulting in prospects of great beauty. Liverpool began damming the river Vyrnwy in 1881, Birmingham the Elan in

In 1912, Raymond Unwin prepared the first plans for an estate of 300 houses for the Cardiff Workers' Cooperative Garden Village Society Ltd. The earliest phase of the development at Rhiwbina was built in 1912–13 (Stewart Williams).

The development of the naturalistic Bodnant Garden in the Conwy Valley was begun by the Lancashire industrialist, Henry Pochin. The terraces were created between 1904 and 1914 for his grandson, Henry Duncan McLaren (d. 1953), who was to become the second Lord Aberconway (© Crown Copyright (2009) Visit Wales).

1893 and Birkenhead the Alwen in 1911. The Vyrnwy Dam was the first large masonry dam to be constructed in Britain and the reservoir's straining-tower is a remarkable castellated structure rich in machicolations. The four reservoirs constructed in the Elan Valley between 1893 and 1904 are Wales's best example of a major civil engineering project transforming the landscape.

The proliferation of public buildings also emphasized the fact that, as the nineteenth century advanced, ambitious architecture was largely being built in the public rather than in the private domain — the first time that that had been the case since the castle-building activities of King Edward I. The prosperous and money-orientated economy of Wales created a demand for shops, department stores and banks. The growth of industry and the export trade led to the erection of port offices and exchanges. Solidarity in the coalfield was expressed in workmen's institutes and leisure needs were served by libraries, theatres and public houses. Urban growth gave rise to town and market halls and, with the establishment of the county councils in 1889, county halls and offices were built. The rise of Welsh national consciousness had architectural implications, as did the late nineteenth-century boom in educational provision. The Anglican restoration and extension movement reached new heights and chapel construction continued unabated.

In the wake of these developments, Wales was endowed with new buildings, many mediocre but some of undoubted quality. In the older market towns, the most striking transformation was the commercialization of the main streets. Shops, whose windows had previously been glazed with small panes, sprouted plate-glass ground-floor frontages, a development which destroyed the harmony of many a street scene. In places such as High Street, Welshpool, or Lammas Street, Carmarthen, those seeking to understand the townscape should direct their gaze to the upper storeys and to the backs of the buildings. The major towns acquired vast department stores — Ben Evans at Swansea, for example, and David Morgan at Cardiff — and Newtown was endowed with the remarkable Royal Welsh Warehouse (1872), from which one of the world's earliest shopping-by-post enterprises operated. Cardiff's wide burgages, the result of centuries of retarded growth, permitted the construction of delightful shopping arcades; Castle Arcade (1887), with its galleried first floor and its oversailing top storey, is the most attractive. In the smaller towns, the most intrusive new buildings were the banks; in Great Darkgate Street, Aberystwyth, for example, Barclays (1877), National Westminster (1903) and Midland (1909) — built in company house styles — are on a scale wholly out of proportion with the rest of the street.

In the ports, banks could be even more monumental, as at Butetown or at Wind Street in Swansea. Swansea has some impressive port buildings, in particular the Harbour Trust Offices (1903) and the Exchange Buildings (1913–14). More imposing is the splendid port building at Barry (1898), with its beautifully symmetrical façade and its fine columned and pedimented bays. In Cardiff's docklands, where the Bute estate hoped a great commercial city would arise, there are several buildings of distinction, although the dignity of the original layout has been much undermined. Particularly delightful is the Pierhead Building (1896–97), an exercise in French Gothic carried out in brick

Work on damming the river Vyrnwy began in 1881 and the lake was filled seven years later to provide water for Liverpool. The straining tower of 1881–92 is a remarkable structure and an outstanding achievement of Victorian water engineering (© Phil Rees/ Photolibrary Wales).

Cardiff's Pierhead Building was constructed in 1896–97 to a design by William Frame, who had been an assistant to William Burges at Cardiff Castle and Castell Coch. Constructed in red brick and terracotta, French Gothic influences are apparent (© Crown Copyright (2009) Visit Wales).

Opposite: Cardiff's commercial centre was adorned in the late nineteenth century with a series of delightful shopping arcades. Castle Arcade, with its galleried first floor, was built in 1887.

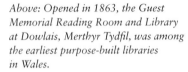

Above: Opened in 1863, the Guest Memorial Reading Room and Library at Dowlais, Merthyr Tydfil, was among the earliest purpose-built libraries in Wales.

Above right: Blaenavon Workmen's Institute was opened in 1895. The workmen of Blaenavon had formed a committee in 1882 to establish an institute and agreed to contribute a halfpenny a week from their wages. Of the total cost of £10,000, 90 per cent was raised by the workmen. The institute was designed by E. A. Lansdowne of Newport.

and terracotta. The most grandiose is the Coal Exchange (1884–88); its pompous exterior offers little suggestion of the glories of the interior, where the main hall, reconstructed in 1911–12, is richly elaborate.

Within the coalfield, the most striking buildings, apart from the chapels, were the workmen's institutes. The largest building ever erected in the south Wales valleys must surely be the institute at Abercynon (1904), demolished in 1995, and a close rival is the Park and Dare Institute at Treorchy (1895, 1913), happily still standing. Of all the institutes of the coalfield, the most attractive is that at Blaenavon (1893–94). Libraries played a role not dissimilar to that of institutes. The Guest Memorial Library at Dowlais (1863), reputedly designed by Charles Barry, was among the earliest purpose-built libraries in Wales. Others followed, including the rather ponderous Cardiff Central Library (1882, 1896), the neo-Tudor Gladstone Memorial Library at Hawarden (1902), the art nouveau Free Library at Newtown (1902) and the many Carnegie libraries, among them excellent examples at Cathays in Cardiff and at Wrexham.

Theatres, another aspect of the architecture of recreation, have had a more chequered history. At Swansea, where several theatres were built in the Victorian and Edwardian eras, only the Grand (1897) survives more or less intact. At Cardiff, with its less distinguished theatrical history, the sole intact theatre of those eras is the Arts and Crafts baroque New Theatre (1905–06), although the neo-Gothic façade of the Prince of Wales Theatre (1878) survives as the frontage of a public house. Aberystwyth can boast the fine Coliseum Theatre (1904), now the Ceredigion Museum, but the most appealing theatre built in Wales was Adelina Patti's miniature version of Bayreuth, erected in 1890 at Craig-y-nos in the upper Tawe Valley. Public houses and hotels were at least equal to theatres as centres of recreation. Urban Wales is rich in fine nineteenth-century and early twentieth-century pubs. The interiors of many of them have been thoughtlessly modernized, but some — among them the Golden Cross in Cardiff with its delightful tiled walls — are still splendidly intact. A number of the grander hotels have been turned over to other uses.

In Aberystwyth, the astonishing Castle Hotel became the University College, and the Queen's Hotel was adapted as county offices. Many distinguished buildings, however, still fulfil their original function, including several at Llandudno, The Parc Hotel at Cardiff (1884) and the Metropole at Llandrindod (1899).

Among Wales's municipal buildings, those of particular interest still in use include the town halls at Cardigan (1860), Ruthin (1865), Abergavenny (1871), Lampeter (1881) and Mold (1912). The establishment of the county councils led to the erection of a diversity of buildings, varying from the unassuming Cardiganshire County Hall at Aberaeron (an adaption of Aberaeron's town hall of 1834) to the Corinthian splendours of Glamorgan County Hall at Cardiff.

Glamorgan County Hall is part of one of Europe's most splendid complexes of civic buildings. Cathays Park was bought by the Cardiff Corporation from the marquess of Bute in 1898 with the intention that the land should provide sites not only for buildings to serve Cardiff but also for those which would emphasize Cardiff's position as the largest urban centre in Wales. The most glorious of the buildings is the City Hall, designed by Lanchester, Stewart and Rickards. Completed in 1905, the year Cardiff became a city, its dome, capped by a wonderful dragon, and its clock tower, enriched by flamboyant convolutions, are the high points of a superbly harmonious and richly detailed masterpiece. To the right of the City Hall stands the National Museum, a more squat and streamlined building than its neighbour but in some ways more aesthetically pleasing. It was begun in 1912, a year after work started on the National Library at Aberystwyth.

The museum and the library can be considered the first Welsh national buildings ever erected. Yet perhaps it could be argued that Wales's institutions of higher education were equally national in their motivation. The University

The colourful tiled façade of the Golden Cross Public House, Cardiff, which was built around 1903 (© Steve Benbow/ Photolibrary Wales).

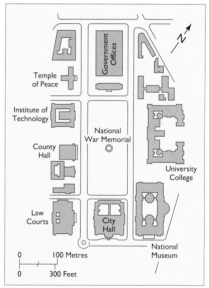

Above: Cathays Park was bought by the Cardiff Corporation from the marquess of Bute in 1898. It has subsequently been developed to become the finest civic centre in Britain. The monumental buildings are set out in such a way that the qualities of each can be appreciated in its own right.

The City Hall in Cathays Park was built in 1901–05 to designs by Lanchester, Stewart and Rickards. It is a building demonstrating the brilliance of its architects, and was to set a new standard in the emergence of great civic buildings in Edwardian Britain (© Crown Copyright (2009) Visit Wales).

The courtyard ranges of the main building at the University College of North Wales, Bangor, were built between 1907 and 1911, to designs by Henry T. Hare. It is the city's most splendid landmark.

College, Aberystwyth, the cradle of the Welsh national revival, was opened in 1872. It had to make do with J. P. Seddon's exotic hotel, but at Cardiff and Bangor purpose-built colleges were erected. The first section of the college at Cardiff, completed in 1909, was a worthy neighbour of the other sculptured white buildings in Cathays Park; sadly its library, the most beautiful room ever built in Wales, suffered in 1977 the indignity of having its lower storey floored over, with the result that its superb harmony has been ruined. The Cardiff college also acquired a building in Newport Road, a section of whose proposed quadrangle was completed in 1915; now an incongruous remnant, it represented the last fling of the neo-Gothic in Wales. Bangor was particularly fortunate in its initial building; the fine uncluttered complex designed by H. T. Hare (1860–1921) and opened in 1911 provides the city with a splendid landmark. Of all Wales's university buildings, the most appealing is the smallest — the University Registry in Cathays Park (1904), cheerfully squeezing in among its monumental neighbours.

Educational provision at the primary and secondary levels had far greater implications for the landscape. The Education Act of 1870, which laid down that an elementary school should be within reach of every child, led to a flurry of building. As much of rural Wales lacked villages, the location chosen for the school often became the focal point of the community, a phenomenon particularly observable in parts of Cardiganshire, Anglesey and the Llŷn Peninsula. Late nineteenth-century rural schools, with their high windows, railed playgrounds and sometimes crowned by a belfry, are significant features of the landscape. In the industrial areas, the rate of school construction could be very rapid; seven were built in the Rhondda between 1878 and 1881, and a further twenty-eight by 1901. Urban schools could be vast. Terrace Road School, Swansea, built in 1888, accommodated 1,455 children; Manselton School, also in Swansea, was attended by 1,212 pupils and is, as John Newman put it: 'An ingenious and dramatic composition worthy of an Elizabethan prodigy house'. Following the passage of the Welsh Intermediate Act in 1889, the building of county schools began and ninety-five had been completed by 1905. In many rural towns, the county school was by far the largest complex of buildings and by acquiring one the town immediately moved to the apex of the local urban hierarchy.

While school boards were ensuring that every child was within reach of a school, the Established Church was seeking to ensure that the whole population was adequately served by Anglican churches. During Bishop Ollivant's episcopate at Llandaff (1849–82), 170 churches were built or restored in the diocese. Some of them have dramatic locations — Christ Church, Aberbeeg, for example, which stands above the confluence of Ebbw Fawr and Ebbw Fach, and Christ Church, Ebbw Vale, which rears up above the site of the Ebbw Vale Ironworks. Rails manufactured for the Trans-Siberian Railway sustain the roof of the church's crypt. Much of the work in the Llandaff diocese was undertaken by John Prichard (1817–86) of Llangan, an example, rare until the twentieth century, of a native of Wales designing major projects in his own country. Among the highlights of the rebuilding in the diocese are the steeples, such as those designed by John Prichard at Baglan and Bridgend. Buildings employing the juxtaposition of materials of different colours enjoyed a great vogue; William Butterfield's St Augustine's Church, Penarth (1866), is a classic example of this polychrome genre.

The Education Act of 1870 laid down that an elementary school should be within reach of every child. In rural areas the new schools often became the focal points of communities. In urban industrial areas, the schools of this era could be vast. Manselton School, Swansea, was built in 1901–02, and had over 1,200 pupils.

St Augustine's, Penarth, was designed by the great Victorian architect William Butterfield (d. 1900). He produced a wonderful example of the polychrome genre fashionable at the time.

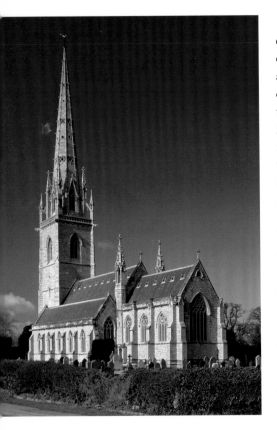

The later nineteenth century saw a new boom in Anglican church building. The best-known example in Wales is probably the so-called Marble Church of St Margaret at Bodelwyddan. It was an estate church, built at the expense of Margaret, Lady Willoughby, as a memorial to her husband. Constructed in 1856–60, the architect was John Gibson (d. 1892).

Opposite: The Anglican building boom of the later nineteenth century was vastly exceeded by the efforts of the Nonconformists. In Glamorgan alone, there was a threefold increase in the number of chapels between 1851 and 1905, with 1,229 such places of worship by the later date. Elaboration became increasingly prized, but few could compete in this respect with Tabernacl Welsh Congregational Chapel at Morriston, Swansea. Built in 1872–73, on the initiative of the local tinplate entrepreneur Daniel Edwards, this magnificent chapel has a seating capacity of 1,450.

At least an equal number of churches were restored or enlarged in the vast diocese of St Davids; there, where centuries of neglect meant that hundreds of churches were in semi-ruin, rebuilding became such a passion that in many areas — central Cardiganshire, for example — it is difficult to find a church containing any features earlier than the 1850s. The diocese's churches include the remarkable Holy Trinity, Pont-ar-gothi (1865–78), with a sumptuous interior unrivalled anywhere in Wales. Among the most appealing buildings in the diocese of St Asaph are the work of G. E. Street (1824–81), the most tireless of the architects of High Anglican churches. At Towyn, near Abergele, he designed a superb grouping of church, vicarage and school. Just 3 miles (4.8km) from Towyn stands the best known of all nineteenth-century Welsh churches, St Margaret, Bodelwyddan, an exercise in indiscriminate opulence. However, it is the diocese of Bangor which has the most intriguing building of the Anglican revival. That is St Marks's, Brithdir (1898), an art nouveau church with remarkable furnishings in beaten copper; it is one of Wales's rare post-Reformation churches with a grade I listing.

The four cathedrals were thoroughly restored, with St Davids and Llandaff in particular undergoing vast refurbishment. In 1863, the west front of St Davids was rebuilt to the somewhat bland Romanesque design of George Gilbert Scott. At Llandaff, the arcades were reconstructed, the nave roofed and a splendid south tower and spire was built to the design of John Prichard, giving the cathedral an air of consequence it had previously lacked.

So great was the activity of the Victorian rebuilders and restorers that only twelve of the thousand and more parish churches which existed in Wales in 1800 have survived untouched. Some of the rebuilding was overzealous. There must be many who have sympathy with Ffransis Payne's lament that so many 'neat edifices' had replaced the ancient churches of Radnorshire. Writing of the rebuilt church at Bronllys (1863) in Breconshire, David Verey, the author of *Mid Wales: A Shell Guide* commented: 'it must have been much nicer before'. A great deal of church building was inspired by an intense desire to ensure that Anglican places of worship should exude the devout spirit of the Middle Ages. Medievalism inspired one of Wales's most remarkable buildings of the Victorian era. That was the Anglican Benedictine monastery commissioned by Joseph Lyne (Father Ignatius) at Capel-y-ffin (1869–82), an attempt to replicate the Augustinian monastery at Llanthony.

The Anglican building campaign, though vigorous, was vastly exceeded by the efforts of the Nonconformists. By 1905 there were 1,229 Nonconformist places of worship in Glamorgan, a threefold increase since 1851; the Rhondda had 150 chapels, a number of them capable of accommodating over a thousand worshippers. In the middle decades of the nineteenth century, chapel architects were generally loyal to the tradition of the restrained pedimented gable façade, typified by Siloa, Aberdare (1855) or Tabernacl, Pontypridd (1861). Some chapels, however, acquired dignified classical porticoes — the superb Bethesda, Mold (1863), for example — or dispensed altogether with the pediment, as with the handsome Tabernacle, Cardiff (1865).

As the century advanced, elaboration became increasingly prized; Tabernacl, Morriston (1873), the most monumental of all Welsh chapels,

with its clock tower and its gigantic Corinthian pillars, is splendidly idiosyncratic. Façades became wilder, with disconcerting hybrids such as Tabernacl, Cardigan (1870), Capel y Crwys, Cardiff (1899) and Rehoboth, Holywell (1904). Welsh-language congregations emphasized the distance between them and the Established Church by not espousing Gothic, although there are some exceptions, such as Pembroke Terrace, Cardiff (1877), Woodland Road, Colwyn Bay (1879) and Ebenezer Newydd, Swansea (1896). English-language congregations had no such inhibitions and most of the places of worship they erected after about 1870 tended to be humbler versions of Anglican churches. However, some of their buildings — that of the Presbyterians at Roath Park in Cardiff (1899–1901), for example — are of considerable distinction. Roman Catholics too were Nonconformists and their buildings include what are now the three Roman Catholic cathedrals of Wales — Our Lady of Dolours, Wrexham (1857), St David's, Cardiff (1884–87), and St Joseph's, Swansea (1888) — all designed by the firm of Pugin and Pugin.

By the late nineteenth century, church and chapel building had become an almost exclusively urban activity, for, as a result of rural depopulation, the countryside was more than adequately supplied with places of worship. The growing urbanization of the population led to changed attitudes to the landscape, for rural people see the countryside as a source of livelihood, while townspeople see it as a source of recreation. Visits to the uplands of Wales, undertaken by a few intrepid seekers of the Picturesque in the late eighteenth century, had, with the growth of the railway network, become a mass activity. Places sprouted new names — Artists' Valley, Happy Valley, Torrent Walk and Panorama Walk. And it was land along Panorama Walk above Barmouth — the 5 acres (2ha) of Dinas Oleu — that became in 1895 the first property acquired by the newly established National Trust, itself an intriguing alliance of 'right to roam' radicals and Gothic-loving conservatives. The age of the preservation of the landscape had arrived.

Below right: Land along Panorama Walk above Barmouth — the 5 acres of Dinas Oleu — became in 1895 the first property acquired by the National Trust (© The National Trust).

Below: Our Lady of Dolours, the Roman Catholic cathedral at Wrexham, was designed by E.W. Pugin and built in 1857 at the expense of ironmaster and colliery owner Richard Thompson.

The age of the preservation of monuments, or, to use the current term, of built heritage, had also arrived. The Caerleon Antiquarian Association, founded in 1847 to preserve the remains of Caerleon's legionary fortress, blazed the trail. In comparison with such local initiatives, the State was somewhat tardy, but, in 1882, Parliament passed the Ancient Monuments Protection Act, which laid the foundations for what a later age would call safeguarding the physical remains of the past activities of human beings. The Royal Commission on the Ancient and Historical Monuments of Wales was established in 1908 and by 1914 it had published five county inventories, although their quality was poor compared with the Commission's more recent publications. The State began to involve itself more closely with the care of the built heritage. Some of Wales's greatest monuments — the castles at Caernarfon and Harlech, for example — had always been Crown property, but of the other great Edwardian castles, Conwy had been sold in 1627 and Beaumaris 1807. The Crown's purchase from the duke of Beaufort of Tintern Abbey in 1901, on the six hundredth anniversary of the completion of the abbey church, inaugurated a new policy. Acquisitions and those buildings already in the possession of the Crown became the responsibility of the Office of Works, thereby launching a new era in the history of the safeguarding of the built heritage of Wales.

The later nineteenth century saw the dawning of the age of the preservation of ancient monuments and historic buildings. Tintern Abbey, for example, was bought by the Crown in 1901, and the long process of conserving the ruins after centuries of neglect began.

WAR AND DEPRESSION

THE MAKING OF WALES 1914–45

For the people of Wales, as for the rest of the peoples of combatant Europe, the First World War was a devastating experience. Yet, as no part of Wales was bombed, the townscape suffered less than it would during the Second World War, although that conflict, for the Welsh, was much less of a bloodletting. Had war not broken out in 1914, employment in the south Wales coalfield would probably have peaked in 1913. The industry had already overexpanded; the war and the post-war boom led to further growth in the number of colliers employed, thus ensuring that the slump, when it came, would be far more ruinous.

The full implications were not apparent until 1925; in that year, severe depression set in, resulting in the unmaking of industrial communities which had been in the making for a century or more. Between 1923 and 1928, coal output tonnage declined from 54 million to 35 million in the southern coalfield, and from 3.4 million to 2.7 million in that of the north. Winding towers, washeries and coking plants were abandoned by the score, thus adding to the scene of desolation. Of the great ironworks, the Bessemer works at Blaenavon closed in 1900, Cyfarthfa closed in 1921, the Siemens furnaces at Ebbw Vale closed in 1925 and steel making ceased at Dowlais in 1930. Parts of the works were demolished, and many buildings of rich historical significance were left to fall into ruin.

Rural Wales, like industrial Wales, suffered grave economic difficulties in the 1920s and 1930s, although the war years themselves were a period of considerable prosperity. The agricultural depression of the late nineteenth century had led to the collapse of 'high farming'; by 1914, the proportion of the cultivated land of Wales under cereal, green and root crops had fallen to 15 per cent. Because of the need to have more home-produced food, the proportion had risen to 26 per cent by 1918, thus altering, temporarily at least, the appearance of large areas of the countryside.

More long-term in its effects upon the landscape was the consequence of the wartime belief that Britain was overdependent upon timber imports. By 1914, only 5 per cent of Wales was wooded, a figure which represented the culmination of millennia of assarting. The establishment of the Forestry Commission in 1919 began a reversal of the process, for over the following half century the amount of Welsh land devoted to commercially managed

By the eve of the First World War, the coal industry had already overexpanded, with the conflict and subsequent boom encouraging yet further growth. In 1925, when the slump and depression set in, the effects on industrial communities were devastating. At Ferndale, in the Rhondda, closures began in the 1930s (© National Museum of Wales).

Opposite: The Welsh National War Memorial in Cathays Park, Cardiff, was designed by Sir Ninian Comper. A work of 1924–28, it is a beautiful and reverent classical composition.

Following the establishment of the Forestry Commission in 1919, the amount of commercially managed woods in Wales increased sixfold over the next half century. The effect on vast swathes of the Welsh landscape is readily apparent, especially across the south Wales coalfield.

woods increased sixfold. There were criticisms that the Commission was undermining the viability of upland holdings and that its straight-edged plantations, mainly of Sitka Spruce, did nothing to beautify the landscape. Furthermore, as the trees grew, fears were expressed that they were blanketing historic landscapes. The Commission's work transformed extensive areas of Wales, above all perhaps in the southern coalfield, where a forest came to stretch almost unbroken from Margam to Rhigos. Along with suburban plantings of exotica, twentieth-century afforestation caused Wales to be one of the few countries the majority of whose trees belong to non-indigenous species.

The Forestry Commission was not alone in changing the appearance of large areas of upland Wales. In 1919, George Stapledon was appointed Professor of Agricultural Botany at Aberystwyth, where he also became the first director of the Welsh Plant Breeding Station. He and his colleagues conducted research into the grasses most likely to produce fodder for grazing animals. Hybrid grasses came to replace the native sward of tens of thousands of acres of upland Wales, giving the landscape a smoother, more controlled, appearance, and allowing the number of sheep in Wales to rise from 3.3 million in 1920 to 4.6 million in 1939.

In the immediate post-war years, there was the growing realization among landowners that owning land gave a poor financial return compared with other forms of investment. Between 1918 and 1922 at least a quarter of the landlord-owned farms of Wales were placed on the market and, over subsequent decades, the landlords' readiness to sell showed no signs of abating. Most of the farms sold by the landlords were acquired by their tenants. By 1922, 35 per cent of Welsh farmers were freeholders, compared with 10 per cent before the war. The process continued over the subsequent decades. By 1970, 64 per cent of the agricultural holdings of Wales were owned by those who farmed them, and, by then, the Welsh landed class which had dominated the countryside since the late Middle Ages, was virtually extinct. Pride in achieving freehold status is movingly expressed by a monument in a field at Ambleston, north of Haverfordwest, to John and Martha Llewellin, who 'by the blessing of God on their joint undertaking and thrift, bought this farm and hand it down without encumbrance to their heirs.' Land reformers had argued that the removal of landlordism would bring about a rural renaissance, but the decline in the prices of agricultural produce from the early 1920s onwards meant that the possibilities open to the new class of freeholders were very limited; indeed, it was not until the 1950s and 1960s that the landscape implications of the emergence of the new freeholder class became fully apparent.

The landscape implications of the decline of the landlord class quickly became apparent. Long-cared-for gardens became overgrown, park walls began to collapse, as, in some cases, did the mansions themselves — Edwinsford, for example, and Bronwydd. Indeed, so numerous would be 'the lost houses of Wales' that Thomas Lloyd's study of the subject (1986) offered a melancholy account of ruin and desolation. Some mansions were saved by finding new purposes for them, Wynnstay becoming a school, and St Brides Castle a hospital. Others eventually found security under the wing of the National Trust, in particular Penrhyn Castle (1951), Powis Castle (1952), Plas Newydd (1976) and Chirk Castle (1981). The fact that the owners of those mansions managed to retain possession of them well into the second half of the twentieth century suggests that the extinction of the Welsh landlord class should not be pre-dated. Indeed, the fourth marquess of Bute (d. 1947) held on to his vast park at Cardiff and maintained a lavish lifestyle at the castle throughout the inter-war years, and between 1928 and 1937 the American tycoon, William Randolph Hearst, spent a fortune refurbishing St Donat's Castle.

While the post-war land sales were leading to profound changes in rural Wales, economic problems were wreaking havoc in industrial Wales. The

Below: Chirk Castle was one of the great Welsh houses that eventually found security under the wing of the National Trust.

Below left: The old order did not entirely collapse overnight, and there was always the unexpected. In the inter-war years, the American tycoon, William Randolph Hearst, for example, spent a fortune refurbishing St Donat's Castle in the Vale of Glamorgan (© Crown Copyright (2009) Visit Wales).

Above: The decline in coal exports through the Bute Docks dashed all hopes of Butetown becoming a great commercial centre. Its finest monument to the aspirations of the age is the National Provincial Bank, completed in 1927.

Above right: The development of Swansea's Town Hill began before the First World War, but the much praised Townhill Estate was created between 1920 and 1929. The estate was laid out by the borough architect, Ernest Morgan, in consultation with the well-known exponent of the rus in urbe *movement, Raymond Unwin.*

collapse of the prosperity of the south Wales coalfield had repercussions well beyond the boundaries of the industrial valleys. With the colliers' purchasing power severely cut, disaster struck the woollen industry of west Wales, and, in the Teifi Valley, mill after mill became derelict. Depression also struck the spa towns of mid-Wales causing places such as Llanwrtyd Wells to have a highly melancholic air. The ports suffered in the wake of the collapse of the coal export trade. Docks at Cardiff and elsewhere became idle. The extensive areas devoted to coal sidings were no longer needed and thus many acres became available for redevelopment. Hopes that Butetown would become a great commercial centre were dashed. One of its finest buildings, the National Provincial Bank, was completed in 1927; thereafter, the district fell into depression and, in some places, into semi-ruin until the 1980s when a vast renewal project was launched.

Yet it would be wrong to present the inter-war years solely as a tale of woe and to describe their impact upon the landscape exclusively in terms of the spread of dereliction. Even in the increasingly depressed condition of Wales, there were some positive developments. The social legislation of the Lloyd George government of 1918 to 1922 brought about significant improvements. The appointment of Christopher Addison as Britain's first Minister of Health in 1919 led to legislation permitting the government to give subsidies to local authorities to build houses. Council houses brought about a revolution in the housing of the working classes. Some of the major urban centres seized the opportunity avidly. Between the wars, Newport rehoused half its population, Cardiff was active at Ely and elsewhere, and Swansea built the much praised Townhill Estate. Wrexham, where some municipal housing schemes had been undertaken before the war, was particularly progressive, and considerable building was also undertaken in the Deeside towns. Under the influence of the *rus in urbe* movement, inter-war municipalities aimed at low-density housing with semi-detached rather than terraced dwellings, extensive gardens, trees and grass verges. Their schemes were therefore prodigal in terms of land use; the built-up area of Newport doubled during the inter-war years, although the town's population grew by less than 10 per cent. In the more affluent parts of Wales, the 1920s and 1930s also saw much building of private housing, some of it in the stockbroker-Tudor and bypass-variegated styles beloved of cartoonists (Lisvane in Cardiff, Swansea's Gower Road and the suburbs of Colwyn Bay come to mind), but such developments were as nothing compared with the huge building boom in inter-war south-eastern England.

As the depression deepened, unemployment reached horrendous levels. Yet, there were always more families with earners than without, and the deflation of the period meant that those with steady incomes found their purchasing power increasing year by year. The number of private motor cars in Wales rose from 29,000 in 1926 to 81,000 in 1938, the beginnings of a revolution in mobility which would have revolutionary implications for the landscape. The coming of the lorry meant that bricks, tiles and corrugated iron could be carried cheaply to districts far away from a railway, districts which had formerly made extensive use of local materials in building. 'By 1930', Peter Smith has written, 'the last vestiges of real regional architecture had finally been destroyed.' Bus services proliferated, breaking down the age-old isolation of rural communities. Charabanc excursions allowed trippers to visit areas hitherto untouched by tourists — the further reaches of the Llŷn Peninsula, for example.

Greater mobility and the relative affluence of considerable sections of society brought about a marked increase in holiday making, a development which led to the laying out of Barry's Cold Knap and to extensive improvements at Porthcawl, Rhyl and Llandudno. For the less affluent, there were the caravan parks which were becoming major features of the coastlands of Flintshire, Denbighshire and Glamorgan. More elegant delights awaited the affluent. Among them was the holiday village which Clough Williams-Ellis

Below left: In spite of the economic depression in the inter-war years, the number of private motor cars in Wales had risen to 81,000 by 1938. Tom Norton had begun selling motor cars before the First World War and his splendid art deco showroom in Llandrindod was completed in 1911. This photograph, taken in the 1920s, shows an impressive array of vehicles assembled outside 'The Automobile Palace' (Radnorshire Museum Collection, 79.25.8).

Below: Barry's Cold Knap Lido opened on 1 May 1926 and boasted one of the largest open-air pools in Britain. This photograph was taken in the 1960s (Courtesy of Tom Clemmet).

began constructing at Portmeirion in 1926, surely the most delightful group of buildings anywhere in Wales. Portmeirion is architecture as entertainment and is proof that tourism does not necessarily ruin a landscape; indeed, it can enhance it.

Other developments did less, perhaps, to enhance the landscape. The coming of broadcasting to Wales in 1923 led to the festooning of enthusiasts' houses with aerials and eventually to the erection of skyscraper transmitters. The Central Electricity Board, established in 1926, had by 1933 constructed its grid, initiating the process which was to ensure that wide areas of Wales offered constant views of massive pylons. Wales seemed tailor-made for the production of hydroelectricity, a development which began with the construction of the Trawsfynydd Lake and the Maentwrog turbine in 1930. The inter-war years too were the period of the creation of the basic telephone network, giving rise to a fascinating wirescape and ensuring that many rural roads were bordered by an endless line of wooden crosses. The most attractive structures which resulted from the new technology of the period were the classic cast-iron telephone kiosks designed by Giles Gilbert Scott; several — including that at Llanengan — have received a grade II listing.

Delight in the Llanengan kiosk was a sign of a widening appreciation of the meaning of built heritage. In Wales between 1914 and 1945, the most significant evidence of that widening appreciation was a growing interest in vernacular architecture, signified in particular by the publication in 1940 of Iorwerth Peate's *The Welsh House*, a book which proved that the anthropological studies initiated by H. J. Fleure at Aberystwyth in 1917 and the delight of men like Peate in the craft skills of their forefathers were bearing fruit.

Nevertheless, interest in earlier evidence of human endeavour continued to be foremost in the minds of those studying the material remains of the inhabitants of Wales. In this field too academic work proved crucial. In 1920, Mortimer Wheeler became the University of Wales's first lecturer in archaeology; also keeper of archaeology at the National Museum of Wales, and later its director, the excavations he conducted at *Segontium* and Caerleon ensured that in the 1920s, Wales was at the forefront of archaeological innovation.

The 1920s was also the decade of a major development in the study of archaeological remains for which there is no surface evidence. Aerial photography first had an impact in 1924 with the publication of O. G. S. Crawford's *Air Survey and Archaeology*. Buried remains show up better on arable land, where crops are closely mown, than they do on pasture land with its lusher growth; in addition, regions prone to drought offer sharper images than do regions of regular rainfall. Thus, aerial photography is less effective in Wales than it is in regions such as East Anglia. On the other hand, buried evidence is more likely to survive intact beneath pasture land than beneath arable land, where deep ploughing can cause havoc to the fragile remains beneath the soil's surface. Decades would pass before the full implications of aerial photography were realized, but, when they were, they came to have a profound impact upon investigations into the activities of the makers of Wales.

Opposite: The holiday village at Portmeirion is surely the most charming group of buildings anywhere in Wales. The Italian-style village was the creation of Clough Williams-Ellis and was begun in 1926 (© Crown Copyright (2009) Visit Wales).

The first major project to tap Wales's potential for the generation of hydroelectricity was launched by the North Wales Power Company in the mid-1920s and four dams were constructed to create Trawsfynydd Lake. By 1930, the new power station at Maentwrog was able to generate 18 megawatts of power. In 1965, a nuclear power station was brought into service on the shore of the lake (© Crown: Royal Commission on the Ancient and Historical Monuments of Wales, 96/CS/0465).

Caerphilly Castle before the extensive restoration commissioned by John Crichton Stuart (d. 1947), the fourth marquess of Bute. The work lasted from 1928 to 1939 and transformed the appearance of the castle (Bute Archive at Mount Stuart).

Many important monuments came into State care between the wars, amongst them Kidwelly Castle in 1927.

Where the conservation of Wales's built heritage was concerned, the role of the Office of Works (the Ministry of Works from 1940) expanded significantly between 1914 and 1945. Denbigh Castle came into its care in 1914, Beaumaris Castle in 1925, Kidwelly Castle in 1927, Strata Florida Abbey in 1931, the Bishop's Palace at St Davids in 1932, Raglan Castle in 1939 and Rhuddlan Castle in 1943. Timely and essential work to shore up the buildings and to remove ivy and other intrusive plants was undertaken, but virtually nothing was done to excite the interest of the public. Guidebooks were provided, often written with admirable scholarship by authorities such as C. A. Ralegh Radford, but their layouts were dire. Public notices were confined to cast-iron plaques warning of the dangers of climbing walls — plaques which now approach the status of being historic artefacts in themselves. Improving the presentation of Wales's built heritage was one of the great achievements of the second half of the twentieth century.

In addition to the Office of Works, other owners of historic buildings were involved in conservation in the inter-war years. They included the fourth marquess of Bute, who commissioned a vast restoration project at Caerphilly Castle, and the Church in Wales, which undertook the refurbishment of the conventual buildings adjoining St John's Church, Brecon (Brecon Cathedral from 1923), thereby creating an ensemble of great charm.

Where Wales's natural heritage was concerned, the National Trust came to shoulder increasing responsibilities. It acquired a number of outstandingly beautiful areas, including the Sugar Loaf Mountain above Abergavenny, considerable stretches of the Welsh coast and some of the most rugged parts of Snowdonia. The Trust also acquired historic buildings, Skenfrith and Cilgerran Castles among them. Part of an organization which also serves England and Northern Ireland, there were accusations that it lacked concern for landscapes and buildings that had a particular resonance for the people of Wales, a marked contrast, it was claimed, with the situation in Scotland,

where its National Trust, founded in 1931, rapidly became a truly popular movement with hundreds of thousands of members. It was an accusation which the Trust, in the later twentieth century, vigorously sought to refute.

While the Office of Works and the National Trust were concerning themselves with the conservation of Wales's natural and built heritage, technical innovation was endowing the country with new icons. Of the innovations which won the most widespread acceptance in the inter-war years, the most important was the cinema. Picture palaces were the quintessential architecture of the 1920s and 1930s, with the construction of such splendours as the Carlton in Swansea and the Capitol (now demolished) in Cardiff. It was in the north-east that cinema building reached its peak. That was the result of the spirited work of Colwyn Foulkes (1884–1971), an architect who is second only to Percy Thomas (1884–1969) among the makers of twentieth-century Wales; several of Foulkes's best works have been demolished and those that survive have been mauled, but the Plazas at Rhyl and Flint still testify to his talent. Foulkes left his mark on other aspects of the townscape of north-east Wales — at Station Road and Abergele Road, Colwyn Bay, for example. However, the main town-centre development of the inter-war years was the erection of shopfronts for chain stores, building work which ensured that the commercial core of any town came to look very similar to that of any other.

The construction of places of worship, a leading building activity during the previous 900 years, took place very rarely in the Wales of the 1920s and 1930s. Some interesting Catholic churches were built — the Church of the Resurrection at Ely, for example — but the erection of Nonconformist chapels virtually came to an end, and the Anglicans built little of distinction apart from the dramatically sited second St Luke's Church at Abercarn (1923–26). There were reverential aspects to one of the most widespread activities of the 1920s — the erection of war memorials. Bangor acquired an impressive

Tryfan is one of the eleven peaks in Snowdonia for which the National Trust is responsible. The years between 1914 and 1945 saw the National Trust taking an increasingly important role in the stewardship of the natural heritage of Wales. It acquired properties in many areas of the country, including some of the most rugged parts of Snowdonia (© Crown Copyright (2009) Visit Wales).

Picture palaces were the quintessential architecture of the 1920s and 1930s. Although somewhat mauled in an unsympathetic age, the cinemas designed by Colwyn Foulkes at Flint and Rhyl testify to the talents of this spirited architect. There is also a good selection of work by Foulkes in Colwyn Bay, including this once delightful shop.

Opposite: Although it no longer stands in majestic isolation on Penglais Hill, it is still easy to understand why the National Library of Wales has been termed Aberystwyth's 'Parthenon'. The architect, S. K. Greenslade, won the competition to design the library in 1909 and work on the building began in 1911. Like most ambitious buildings in Wales at that time, it was constructed of Portland Stone — a fine, pale limestone — which accounts for its gleaming exterior (© Keith Morris/Photolibrary Wales).

memorial arch and Cardiff the circular colonnaded Welsh National War Memorial. Most towns and many villages were provided with some form of commemoration, on occasion work by distinguished sculptors such as the memorial at Llandaff designed by Goscombe John (d. 1952), and that at Chirk designed by Eric Gill (d. 1940). Memorial halls proliferated, among them Criccieth, where Lloyd George laid the foundation stone in 1922. The anti-war movement inspired the Temple of Peace, completed in 1938 at Cathays Park; designed in a streamlined classical idiom, it was one of the major 1930s commissions of the firm of Percy Thomas.

The same firm was responsible for the most splendid building of inter-war Wales — the Guildhall at Swansea. Also in the 'stripped classical' style, its restrained tower and its subtle massing of white cubes make it a building of great distinction; its quality can be appreciated by comparing it with the broadly contemporary county hall at Newport, where a not dissimilar design is handled with far less assurance. The inter-war years also saw work continuing on the completion of the first phases of two buildings which had been begun before the war — the National Museum (begun in 1912) and the National Library (begun in 1911). The library, designed by S. K. Greenslade, has been described as an interesting mixture of Parisian Beaux-Art classicism and Edwardian baroque. Like most of the ambitious buildings erected in

Swansea's Guildhall, designed by Percy Thomas and built in 1932–36, is the most splendid building of inter-war Wales.

Wales in the first half of the twentieth century, it was constructed of Portland Stone. So great was the prestige of that stone that Aberystwyth's railway station (1924) was built in an ersatz version of it. Virtually all Wales's inter-war buildings, the National Library among them, made no concessions to the international modern style of architecture. Almost the sole exception is Sully Hospital (1932–36), Wales's finest example of a functionalist building.

The Temple of Peace was the last major building to be completed in Wales before the country was again involved in war. Even before 1939, the threat of war had already had an impact upon the Welsh landscape, with the construction of a 'bombing school' at Penrhos, west of Pwllheli, and of an air base at St Athan in the Vale of Glamorgan. With the outbreak of hostilities, further military installations came to Wales, among them aerodromes at Fairwood, near Swansea, and at Valley, near Holyhead, a gunnery range at Castlemartin and camps at Tywyn, Trawsfynydd and elsewhere. Above all, a 40,000-acre (16,000ha) firing range was established west of Brecon, resulting in the pulverizing of the seven beautiful valleys of Mynydd Epynt. Pillboxes and concrete barriers to hold back tanks were erected — the first significant fortifications, apart from those built in the mid-nineteenth century along the Milford Haven Waterway, to be constructed in Wales since the castles of the Middle Ages. Among the most impressive of the structures brought into existence as a result of the Second World War was the domed gunnery

The outbreak of the Second World War led to the construction not only of military bases, firing ranges and munitions factories in many places in Wales, but also of numerous pillboxes, gun emplacements and concrete anti-tank barriers to defend the country against possible invasion. This is a beach defence gunhouse at St Ishmael, Carmarthenshire.

Above: The chapel built and decorated by Italian prisoners of war at Henllan, near Llandysul.

Above left: Bombs fell on a number of locations in Wales during the Second World War. By far the greatest sufferer was Swansea, where the town centre was devastated during the three-night blitz of 19, 20 and 21 February 1941. This photograph shows the south side of Caer Street with the roofless St Mary's Church (West Glamorgan Archive Service, P/PR/95).

training centre erected at Pembrey. A more appealing one is the chapel built by Italian prisoners of war at Henllan, an astonishing baroque building made of scrap materials. Other buildings constructed in relation to the war effort were a military hospital at Morriston and a gigantic munitions factory at Bridgend; centres of armament production were also established at Marchwiel, Glascoed and Hirwaun.

The locations of the war factories were chosen in part because it was believed that Wales was too far to the west to be subject to German bombing. The belief proved to be ill founded. At Llandaff, a land mine fell near the cathedral in 1941 and once again the building was in ruins. Elsewhere in Cardiff, bombs destroyed much of the area north of the General (now Central) Station and large sections of Butetown. Newport, Pembroke Dock and parts of Deeside were also bombed, but by far the greatest sufferer was Swansea. In the three-night blitz of 19, 20 and 21 February 1941, the entire town centre was obliterated. Further raids followed, including a ferocious one in February 1942, and, when the war came to an end, Dylan Thomas's 'ugly lovely town' was a disembowelled wreck.

The period 1914 to 1945 represented for Wales the years of the locust. The economic growth of the previous century had come to a halt and there was little hope of addressing the environmental problems industrialization had caused. The momentum of efforts to provide Wales with buildings to sustain its social and cultural life had stalled. The traditional framework of rural communities had been undermined. In 1945, the makers of Wales faced a huge challenge. The transformation of the country in the following decades is a measure of their success in meeting that challenge.

THE IMMEDIATE POST-WAR YEARS

THE MAKING OF WALES 1945–84

Between 1945 and 1984, the making, the unmaking and the remaking of Wales proceeded at a wholly unprecedented pace. Large areas of the country, rural and urban, were transformed, and by the 1980s, few viewpoints were able to offer scenes identical with those of the 1940s.

The Labour government elected in 1945 was above all determined that the appalling levels of unemployment suffered in the 1930s should not recur. In Wales, central to its hopes was a stable workforce in the coal industry, which came into public ownership on 'vesting day' — New Year's Day 1947. The National Coal Board's intention was to maintain a Welsh workforce of around 100,000, an intention realized until the mid-1950s. The Board recognized, however, that the majority of the 150 and more pits in the south Wales coalfield and the six pits in the north were hopelessly old fashioned; they would have to cease to operate and be replaced by modern collieries. Thus, between 1947 and the late 1950s, almost half the pits of Wales were closed. The removal of large numbers of pithead winding towers had a marked impact upon the landscape, as did the establishment of 'super' collieries such as those at Cynheidre (1956) and Abernant (1958).

From the late 1950s onwards, the contraction of the coal industry gathered pace, and by the early 1980s there were only thirty-six collieries in the south Wales coalfield and only two in that of the north. Little evidence of the workings of the industry was retained; indeed, at Cwmfelinfach there are few signs that the Nine Mile Point Colliery — a colliery famous in the story of the miners' struggle — ever existed. In landscape terms, the major development in the Welsh coal industry by the 1970s was the marked expansion in opencast mining. The excavations created by the 'sunshine miners' — those above Dowlais, for example, or those in the anthracite districts — represented landscape manipulation on a grand scale, and were a cause of much distress to communities in their vicinity. However, when the work is finished and the topsoil replaced, the new landscape can be very attractive. Landscape restoration became an acute issue in areas of dangerous subsidence; south of Wrexham, vast sums had to be spent in the mid-1970s to save the splendid Erddig Hall from collapse. The removal of tips also led to landscape restoration; for example, at Gelli-ceidrim in the Llwchwr Valley a handsome rounded hill came to replace a scene of desolation. Tip clearing

Workers outside Lewis Merthyr Colliery after the nationalization of the Coal industry on 'vesting day' — 1 January 1947. The noticeboard reads: 'This colliery is now managed by the National Coal Board on behalf of the people' (© National Museum of Wales).

Opposite: The headgear and winding house at Bersham Colliery Mining Museum. The headgear is the last still standing in the Denbighshire coalfield and once served the colliery's No. 2 Shaft. Bersham Colliery was the last working colliery in the Denbighshire coalfield and closed in 1986.

One of the most evocative sights in Wales — the slate mill at Ynys-y-Pandy. The building was constructed in 1855 and served the Gorseddau Quarry. The works were powered by an intenal waterwheel (© Crown: Royal Commission on the Ancient and Historical Monuments of Wales, DS2007_280_001).

accelerated following the appalling disaster at Aberfan in 1966, with much of the waste being carried to Cardiff to fill in the West Bute Dock — the spoil of an industry being used to obliterate the transport facility which had given it birth. As the coal industry declined, the rivers of the coalfield revived, with trout in the Cynon and herons fishing in the Llwyd below Garndiffaith.

Contraction in employment was equally evident in another of Wales's traditional industries — the quarrying and mining of slate. Output of slate in Wales declined from 106,000 tons in 1948 to below 10,000 by the late 1970s (the industry had peaked at 507,000 tons in 1898). As slate quarrying has a marked impact on the environment, the closure of all the major slate quarries apart from Penrhyn had major implications for the landscape. Work ended on the astonishing terraces above Llyn Peris, and quarry buildings were abandoned by the score; one of the most evocative sights in Wales is the slate mill at Ynys-y-Pandy, a ruin of almost Tinternesque grandeur.

The decline of Wales's traditional industries had long given rise to demands that alternative work should be provided. In the southern coalfield, some efforts had been made in the late 1930s with the re-establishment of steel making at Ebbw Vale and the setting up of a trading estate at Treforest near Pontypridd. After the war, such efforts redoubled. Architecturally, the most significant fruit of those efforts was the rubber factory at Brynmawr, built between 1947 and 1953. Designed by the Architects' Co-operative Partnership and engineered by the Danish firm of Ove Arup and Partners, the factory was the first post-war building in Wales to be listed. The thin-shell concrete vaults were designed to roof an enclosure of 6 acres (2.4ha), and the factory's central production area was hailed as the most elegant internal space created in Britain since the completion in 1711 of St Paul's Cathedral.

Other distinguished factory buildings erected in Wales between 1945 and 1984 include the Pilkington factory at St Asaph (demolished in 2009),

Erected in 1947–53, the rubber factory at Brynmawr was built to bring aid to the devastated economy of the south Wales valleys. It was undoubtedly a spectacular building, but following its closure in 1982 it was abandoned and allowed to fall into ruin. The factory was to become an object lesson in the problems of conservation. This photograph, taken after the factory's abandonment, shows one of the elegant thin-shell vaults (© Crown: Royal Commission on the Ancient and Historical Monuments of Wales, 990035/2).

Anglesey Aluminium's complex near Holyhead, and the now closed Dupont factory at Mamhilad, near Pontypool, originally built for British Nylon Spinners in 1947–48. Government initiative led to the construction of nuclear-powered stations at Trawsfynydd, designed by Basil Spence and landscaped by Sylvia Crowe (which began generating electricity in 1965) and Yr Wylfa (which began producing electricity in 1971). The former was decommissioned in 1991; the latter, a splendidly monumental building improbably sited at the top corner of Anglesey, is due to be decommissioned in 2010. It was government action too which endowed Wales with those massive if rather undistinguished buildings — the Royal Mint at Llantrisant and the vehicle licensing centre at Swansea. The rationalization of the tinplate industry led to the construction of two large tinplate works — Trostre (built 1952–56) and Velindre (1956) — and the closure of the handmills which had once dotted the valleys of the Llwchwr, the Gwendraeth and the Afan. With the revival of the Welsh steel industry, the country acquired vast plants at Port Talbot and Llanwern, although rationalization eventually led to the demolition of works at Shotton, Ebbw Vale and Cardiff, and to the end of large-scale steel making at Llanwern. Steel making at Port Talbot led to the construction of an iron ore terminal capable of handling ships three times the size of those able to gain entry to the older docks. Terminals in the Milford Haven Waterway can handle even larger ships, the result of the decision made in 1957 to develop the Haven for oil tankers. Clusters of oil storage tanks were erected on both sides of the Haven, thus creating an industrial landscape unique in Wales.

After the decision was taken in 1957 to develop Milford Haven to accommodate oil tankers, clusters of oil storage tanks rose on both sides of the Haven, creating an industrial landscape unique in Wales. The port is the largest in Wales, and facilities have recently been constructed to enable the handling of ships carrying liquified natural gas (© Crown: Royal Commission on the Ancient and Historical Monuments of Wales, AP_2009_0950).

The prefab preserved at St Fagans National History Museum. Prefabs were regarded as well appointed and commodious when they were first introduced to a Britain suffering from a severe post-war housing shortage (© National Museum of Wales).

Of all the post-war building activities, the most massive was the addition to the housing stock. The cessation of building during the war, coupled with losses through bombing, meant that by 1945 there was a severe housing shortage. A sustained attack on the problem had to be delayed owing to a lack of resources, but prefabricated houses offered a stopgap solution. A total of 156,623 'prefabs' were built in Britain; they could be surprisingly commodious, as can be seen from the one rebuilt at St Fagans National History Museum. From the mid-1950s, council house construction took off with the building of extensive estates such as Penlan in Swansea, Bettws in Newport and Llanrumney in Cardiff. Council estates built in the 1950s consisted almost invariably of virtually identical family houses, but in later decades a greater variety of dwellings was constructed. Every market town acquired estates, some of them very banal, but others — those at Newtown, Beaumaris and Llandrillo-yn-Rhos (Colwyn Foulkes's Elwy Road Estate) in particular — showing considerable imagination. In the south Wales coalfield, housing reached up into the moorland, thus blurring the old contrast between the built-up areas and the open mountain. Penrhys (1966–69), a housing estate built between the valleys of the Rhondda Fawr and the Rhondda Fach, is perched at an altitude of 1,300 feet (400m), as are Gurnos and Galon-uchaf in Merthyr. Wales, however, was not overendowed with those disasters of the 1960s — high-rise council blocks — although a group of them was built, astonishingly, on the wide expanse of the Hirwaun Moor; they were demolished in 2004.

The post-war years also saw the building of a large number of privately owned dwellings. Public and private enterprise together caused the housing stock of Wales to expand by 50 per cent between the 1940s and the 1980s, although the population increased by only 12 per cent during that period. Many private estates were very modest — that at Killay near Swansea, for

Cwmbran was the only town in Wales established under the New Towns Act of 1946. Its development proceeded within the framework of a master plan formulated in 1951. The architect, Gordon Redfern, was largely responsible for the design of the town centre, and he created a totally pedestrianized area served by multi-storey car parks. This photograph shows the Fairwater Shopping Centre around 1965 (© The Francis Frith Collection)

example. Other privately owned houses could be lavish, but few dwellings of any distinction were built in Wales between 1945 and 1984. Among the most interesting of them were the Round House (1964–68) at St Davids, Bryn Aberoedd (1968) at Aberystwyth, the group of houses at Little Orchard in Dinas Powys (1968), and Castell Gyrn (1977), that astonishing pastiche of a medieval tower which overlooks one of the most delectable parts of the Vale of Clwyd.

Houses were increasingly provided with integral garages, which presented major problems in creating a harmonious façade. Centrally heated, most of them lacked the chimneys which are the crowning glory of almost every house built before the later twentieth century. In the rural areas, the most intrusive development was bungalow building; the inhabitants of mid-Cardiganshire, like those of the west of Ireland, were avid bungalow lovers, the result, perhaps, of an atavistic desire to revert to the single-storey cabins of their ancestors.

Where public buildings were concerned, architects designed little in Wales between 1945 and 1984 comparable with Swansea's Guildhall or the original buildings of Cathays Park. Some of the most interesting of Wales's post-war public buildings were those erected at Cwmbran. The only town established in Wales under the New Towns Act of 1946, Cwmbran was, by the late twentieth century, the sixth largest urban centre in the country. The growth of higher education endowed Wales with a number of impressive buildings. In 1957, a new start was made in the designing and building of what was then University College, Swansea; the result was a compact group of buildings arranged around an axial approach from Mumbles Road. At Aberystwyth, the steep slopes of Penglais Hill had by the 1980s acquired a linear band of structures, including Percy Thomas's neo-Georgian Neuadd Pantycelyn (1948–60), and Theatr y Werin (1971–73), a starkly functional block designed by Alex Gordon and Partners. At Bangor, there was praise for Percy Thomas's completion of Henry T. Hare's outer quadrangle, and enthusiasm for David Roberts's Plas Gwyn. There was less approbation for the twelve-storey tower built for University College, Cardiff, in 1967, a building which involved the abandonment of the height restriction until then obligatory in Cathays Park; the restriction had been based upon the cornice line of the City Hall and had been the determining factor in ensuring the coherence and unity of Cardiff's splendid Civic Centre.

Cathays Park also acquired Alex Gordon's Welsh Office (1972–79), a building with a splendid inner court but whose outer appearance makes it 'a symbol of closed inaccessible government…of bureaucracy under siege', to quote the *Architects' Journal*. The reorganization of local government in 1974 led to the construction of not unattractive county offices, in particular those of Clwyd, West Glamorgan and South Glamorgan. County architects were responsible for some attractive schools, among them the secondary schools at Llanidloes and Llanrwst. Crematoria, virtually unknown in Wales before the war, have proliferated since 1945, with significant implications for the landscape, for the popularity of cremation means that there is no need to devote further land to cemeteries. Outstanding among the crematoria is that at Coychurch (1970). With the adoption of cremation, the commemorating of the dead with tombstones, a practice with millennia of history behind it, went into rapid decline, and it seems unlikely that future generations will lay out

Neuadd Pantycelyn — Percy Thomas's neo-Georgian hall of residence for the Penglais university campus at Aberystwyth — was built between 1948 and 1960 to a design of 1939.

Coychurch Crematorium near Bridgend, is the most outstanding of the numerous crematoria constructed in Wales since 1945. The design, by Maxwell Fry, was strongly influenced by the work of Le Corbusier. Fry sought to make crematoria more sympathetic places and he enriched the Coychurch buildings with extensive displays of stained glass.

Mold's Theatr Clwyd, which was designed by R. W. Harvey and opened its doors in 1976, was one of the many public buildings erected in Wales between the end of the Second World War and 1984 (© David Williams/Photolibrary Wales).

fascinating places such as the vast graveyard above Treorchy. Among other public buildings erected in urban Wales between 1945 and the 1980s were hospitals, leisure centres, libraries, swimming pools, theatres, concert halls and stadiums.

Post-war change was perhaps more profound in the countryside than in the urban areas. One of the major problems facing the Labour government elected in 1945 was the inadequacy of the food supply. The Agriculture Act of 1947 brought in an array of subsidies, grants and deficiency payments, which ensured that the Second World War, unlike almost all previous wars, was not followed by a depression in farming. In the immediate post-war years, agriculture was the miracle industry of Wales. Although the percentage of the employed population directly dependent upon the land halved, output in most sectors of farming doubled. Between 1950 and 1974, the number of sheep in Wales increased from 3.8 million to 6.7 million, leading to concern that the country's uplands were being overgrazed. The production of liquid milk was central to the output of the majority of the farms of post-war Wales. In 1950, the Milk Marketing Board bought 180 million gallons (820 million litres) of milk from its 30,000 Welsh suppliers; in 1970, there were only 15,000 suppliers, but they produced 279 million gallons (1,270 million litres) of milk. As the number of producers declined and the output of those who remained increased prodigiously, milk tankers began collecting the milk directly from farms, thus making redundant one of the most familiar features of mid-twentieth-century rural Wales — the roadside milk stands on which dairy farmers placed their churns.

The increasing efficiency of farmers was one of the chief keys to the transformation of the countryside. Innovation in agricultural practices meant that traditional farm buildings became redundant, and farmers, less hampered by the planning restrictions than were other entrepreneurs, erected buildings wholly out of character with their surroundings. Tall silage holders sprouted throughout dairying country, giving the slightly myopic traveller the impression that every settlement had acquired a church tower. In sheep-rearing areas, farms acquired huge sheds where lambs could be born safe from the likelihood of death from hypothermia. Hedges were torn out to form larger fields, an

The third quarter of the twentieth century saw new farm buildings sprouting across the Welsh landscape. Tall silage holders of dairy country, were often wholly out of character with their surroundings. After further changes in farming practices, many have disappeared or have been reduced in height.

activity which altered the appearance of the traditional Welsh bocage, and which posed a threat to wildlife. Improved farming methods involved heavy use of fertilizers, thus giving rise to pollution problems. The investment in machinery could only be justified if the holding were enlarged, and thus farm amalgamation proceeded apace. In 1945, Wales had about 40,000 farms capable of providing a family with an adequate standard of living; in the early 1980s, it had less than half that number, and a large proportion of the rural housing stock had been released for purposes other than agriculture. The process was aided by the continuing rise in freehold farming, which meant the absence of the restraints inherent in the estate system. Estates sustaining landed families living off the rents of their tenant farmers were virtually extinct by the 1970s, but new landlords were emerging, among them the National Trust in the upper Conwy Valley and pension fund holders in the Vale of Tywi.

With their increasing income, farmers could modernize their dwellings. In the 1960s, there seemed to be a cement mixer outside every farmhouse as occupants replaced mud walls, filled in wide fireplaces and installed metal windows, activities which robbed thousands of Welsh farmhouses of their historic meaning. Adventitious rural dwellers — those who lived in the countryside not because they had an economic role there, but because they chose to do so — constituted the majority of Wales's country dwellers by the early 1980s, a social change of deep significance. They, too, modernized their houses, and they tended to prettify them as well, thereby adding twee touches which could be highly incongruous. A high proportion of the new

The modernization of historic farmhouses and cottages has gone on at a rapid pace since the 1960s. Such modernization has sometimes robbed dwellings of their historic meaning. The new rural dwellers of recent decades have also increased this pace of modernization.

rural dwellers were migrants from outside Wales. Some of them were anxious to live in houses whose names they could pronounce; thus Berllan Dywyll became Dark Orchard and Carreg-lwyd Greystones; ancient title deeds were being cast into oblivion.

The transformation of the countryside was promoted by pressures other than the increasing productivity of farmers. Many of them emanated from the fact that the population of Wales, and of Britain, was overwhelmingly urban. One of the chief needs of those populations was an adequate water supply. Between 1952 (Claerwen) and 1976 (Brenig), Wales acquired eight major reservoirs, a development which aroused considerable controversy. Some of the engineering work was very impressive; the Clywedog Dam, the highest mass of concrete in Britain, has hollow buttresses with vaults which soar higher than those of any cathedral. The development of the electricity industry also involved considerable manipulation of the Welsh landscape with hydroelectric complexes constructed above Blaenau Ffestiniog and in the Rheidol Valley.

The greatest pressure on the countryside was caused by the demands of recreation and tourism. To meet the needs of visitors, butterfly centres, fish farms and pony-trekking centres proliferated and the number of golf courses soared. In much of rural Wales it seemed that the national motto was 'Bed and Breakfast', and many farmers found it preferable to milk fewer cows and more caravanners. Holiday camps became a significant feature of the landscape, not only at traditional resorts but also in wholly rural areas such as Penychen near Pwllheli, where Billy Butlin turned a wartime training establishment into a major holiday complex. Nature trails abounded and, with the urge to explain everything, ever larger and grander interpretation centres sprang up. The most famous beauty spots came under threat as tens of thousands of boots pounded the paths up and down Snowdon and Cadair Idris.

Central to the influx into the countryside was the growth in the private ownership of motor cars. The number of Welsh families owning cars increased tenfold between the late 1950s and the late 1970s, and the increase in neighbouring regions of England was even greater. The implications for both the rural landscape and the urban townscape were immense. Hitherto uncluttered streets came to be lined with parked vehicles; petrol stations became a recurring feature of the roadside and housing developments were obliged to cater for garages and increased access roads. Until the 1960s, drivers had to make do with the existing road system, the cause of enormous traffic jams in places such as Port Talbot. Modern road building came to Wales with the construction of the M4, which included the elegant and innovative first Severn Bridge (1966). Other distinguished examples of road engineering included bridges over the Dee at Queensferry (1960–62) and over the Cleddau near Neyland (1975), ingenious flyovers at Newport and Briton Ferry and sections of the dual carriageway between Cardiff and Merthyr. Congestion at Conwy led in 1958 to the construction of a bridge which had a disastrous impact upon the prospect of the castle and which decanted a mass of vehicles into the centre of the town.

Opposite: Between 1952 and 1976, Wales acquired eight major reservoirs. The Clywedog Dam, begun in 1964, is the tallest mass of concrete in Britain (© Jeremy Moore/Photolibrary Wales).

Modern road building came to Wales with the construction of the M4 motorway. The scheme included the construction, in 1966, of the elegant and innovative Severn Bridge (© Glyn Evans/Photolibrary Wales).

Commercial Street in Newport; the once busy thoroughfare has been successfully transformed into a pedestrian precinct (© Newport City Council).

The viaduct above Cefn-coed-y-cymmer, built in 1866 to carry the Brecon, Newport and Merthyr Railway over the river Taff, is now a poignant memorial to the great days of railway transport before the closures following the Beeching Report of 1963 (© Crown: Royal Commission on the Ancient and Historical Monuments of Wales, 99/CS/0448).

The growth in car ownership gave rise not only to ambitious road-building schemes but also to changes in housing provision and in settlement patterns. Adventitious rural dwellers multiplied chiefly because of the car, ownership of which frequently led to the suburbanization of villages — in the Vale of Glamorgan, for example, or at Abergwili near Carmarthen or Bow Street near Aberystwyth. Wales's most interesting experiment in post-war town planning resulted from the challenge represented by the car. The Queen's Park Housing Estate at Wrexham was the first example of Radburn planning in Britain; pioneered at Radburn, New Jersey, the aim was to segregate pedestrian from vehicular traffic. The Wrexham scheme was carried out in the 1950s, and versions of it were later laid out in several other parts of Wales, particularly in Newport and Cwmbran.

The same thinking inspired the pedestrian precinct movement which significantly enhanced Commercial Street, Newport, and the Queen Street and St John's areas of Cardiff. Unfortunately, the movement arose too late to affect Wales's largest town-planning scheme of the immediate post-war years — the rebuilding of Swansea. The decision to construct a dual carriageway through the middle of Swansea created a wholly disastrous townscape. Yet, compared with many English cities, the major urban centres of Wales — with the exception of Swansea — did not suffer excessively through road construction. A plan in the 1960s to drive an expressway through Cardiff was abandoned and access to Newport was skilfully handled. Elsewhere, Caernarfon was badly sliced, but other towns — Brecon, Llanidloes and Denbigh among them — came to have bypasses which offer attractive urban views. The car too was the key to the construction of out-of-town shopping centres with their pagoda-like buildings capped with vaguely ecclesiastical towers. Seen as a dire threat by town centre traders, they have the capacity — as the experience of the United States has shown — to revolutionize the relationship between a town's core and its periphery.

The great transport innovation of the post-war years was mass air travel. While British centralization means that most Welsh air travellers fly from airports near London, Wales does have one airport capable of handling international flights. The Cardiff International Airport at Rhoose has one of the longest runways in Britain (1.47 miles, 2.354km), and its vast hangar (1993), visible from most of the Vale of Glamorgan, must rank among the country's most intrusive buildings. The great transport regression of the post-war years was the contraction of the railway system. The scale of closures following the publication of the Beeching Report in 1963 meant that, by the late 1960s, Wales had a smaller railway network than it had had in the late 1860s. Railway closure was particularly a feature of industrial Wales, for, with the attenuation of the coal industry, the network of lines in the south Wales coalfield was unnecessarily dense. Abandoned lines came to be among the major features of the landscape; some poignant memorials remain — the track and tunnels in the Clydach Gorge, for example, and the splendid viaduct above Cefn-coed-y-cymmer. Nostalgia for the age of locomotion led to the reopening of several of the lines served by 'the Great Little Trains of Wales', among them the Talyllyn Railway, where restoration

began in 1951, the Ffestiniog Railway which was reopened in 1954, and the Welsh Highland Railway, which was reopened in 2009.

In the third quarter of the twentieth century, nostalgia for the past, such as that shown by steam-train enthusiasts, went hand in hand with a readiness to destroy evidence of the past. That highly acclaimed reclamation project, the detoxification of the lower Swansea Valley, cleared away most of the evidence of what had once been one of the world's most important industrial areas. In Cardiff, the Franciscan friary was built over and the heart of Butetown was ripped out. In Caernarfon, much of the interior of the walled town was demolished and at Conwy there were demands that Telford's bridge should be pulled down. Tudor Street and Flannel Street vanished from Abergavenny, one of the many market towns to suffer despoilation. In 1964, the superb façade of Ynysmaengwyn was used to hone the skills of members of Tywyn's fire service.

The authorities at Merthyr Tydfil proved to be particularly destructive. Between the 1950s and the 1970s, the town lost two market halls, the Iron Bridge, the Triangle, Dowlais House, Dowlais School, Penydarren House and Brunel's railway station. To the journalist, Mario Basini, Merthyr's 'official vandalism' was the result of the belief of local politicians that 'anything associated with the capitalist ironmasters and coalowners, the exploiters of the people, should be destroyed'. Here, there is relevance in the lines of Bertolt Brecht: 'Who built Thebes of the seven gates?/ In the books you will find the names of kings;/ Did the kings haul up the lumps of rock?'

Such thoughtless destruction sharpened worries about the fate of the built heritage. There was a belief — not totally sustained by the facts — that great houses were adequately cared for, and that priority should be given to the vernacular architecture of Wales. A key figure in that development was Iorwerth Peate, whose book, *The Welsh House* (1940), has already been noted. In 1948, he became the curator of the Welsh Folk Museum at

The built heritage of Wales suffered a number of regrettable losses in the third quarter of the twentieth century. For instance, most of the historic buildings in Abergavenny's Flannel Street, seen here in the 1950s, and Tudor Street were swept away during the redevelopment of the town centre between 1957 and 1968 (By permission of Abergavenny Museum).

St Fagans (now the National History Museum). By 1984, twenty examples of Welsh vernacular architecture had been re-erected at the museum, including a pigsty, a cockpit, a tannery, a school, and a woollen mill as well as a variety of cottages and farmhouses. Inspired perhaps by the example of the National Trust of Scotland, whose conservation of vernacular architecture at Culross and elsewhere won great acclaim, the National Trust of England, Wales and Northern Ireland began to show an increasing interest in the more modest buildings of Wales. That postage stamps in 1970 bore portrayals of stuccoed buildings at Aberaeron was an acknowledgement that, in the making of Wales, vernacular architecture out-trumps anything that can be ascribed to a more 'refined' tradition. That proposition received magnificent scholarly endorsement in 1975 with the publication of Peter Smith's *Houses of the Welsh Countryside.*

Growing concern for vernacular architecture was accompanied by important developments in the conservation of major historic monuments, with the Ministry of Works becoming responsible for an ever growing number. Following the establishment of the Welsh Office in 1964, the duties of the ministry became the responsibility of the Secretary of State for Wales. By then, the properties that had come into State care since the war included Castell Coch, Caerphilly Castle and Valle Crucis Abbey (1950), Chepstow and Conwy Castles (1953), Dolforwyn Castle (1955), Llansteffan Castle (1959) and Montgomery Castle (1963). In scholarly terms, the most important work done on Wales's built heritage between 1945 and 1984 was A. J. Taylor's study of thirteenth-century castle building (*The King's Works in Wales*, 1963, 1974), a study which revealed the extraordinary contribution to the making of Wales ascribable to the organizing genius of the Savoyard, James of St George. In scenic terms, the most striking achievement was the work of the Ministry of Works at Caerphilly, where the reflooding of the lakes surrounding the castle created a scene of memorable grandeur.

At the same time, developments in the countryside were leading to increased demands for the safeguarding of the natural heritage. Writing of the English landscape in 1955, W. G. Hoskins commented that every change it had undergone in the recent past had 'either uglified it or destroyed its meaning or both'. Although the countryside of Wales has not been assailed as vigorously as has that of much of England, anyone who has seen Epynt or Freshwater East or Morfa Rhuddlan cannot but agree that Hoskins's comment has relevance in the Welsh context. Yet, partly because of the anguished cries of people like Hoskins, efforts gathered pace in the 1950s to ensure that Wales's natural heritage should be both beautiful and meaningful.

The decade saw the establishment of three national parks — Snowdonia (1951), the Pembrokeshire Coast (1952) and the Brecon Beacons (1957) — causing 19 per cent of the surface area of Wales to receive statutory protection. Had the proposal to establish a national park in the Cambrian Mountains been successful, the proportion would have risen to almost 26 per cent; that region, however, had to be content with being an Environmentally Sensitive Area. In addition, Wales acquired five Areas of Outstanding Natural Beauty, the first of which — the Gower Peninsula — received the designation in 1956.

This thatched cockpit once stood in the yard of the Hawk and Buckle Tavern in Denbigh and may be of seventeenth-century date. It was moved to the Welsh Folk Museum (now the National History Museum) at St Fagans in 1964. More than forty historic buildings have been moved and meticulously re-erected at the museum (© National Museum of Wales).

Opposite: A quarry worker's cottage surrounded by a slate-pillar fence at Nant Peris. This fine example of Welsh vernacular architecture is located within the borders of Snowdonia National Park.

Rhossili Bay and Worms Head at the western end of Gower are well-known properties of the National Trust in Wales. By the early 1980s, some ninety years after its foundation, the Trust owned at least 85,000 acres (34,000ha) of land in Wales, as well as numerous houses and gardens of distinction (© Crown Copyright (2009) Visit Wales).

Concern about the dangers threatening the natural heritage increased following the publication of Rachel Carson's *Silent Spring* in 1962 and the broadcasting of Fraser Darling's Reith Lectures in 1969. Further protection ensued, causing Wales to have some seventy National Nature Reserves and over a thousand Sites of Special Scientific Interest (SSSIs).

While most of the land within the national parks, the nature reserves and the SSSIs was in private hands, the body with the strongest commitment to conservation — the National Trust — was the owner of the land under its care. By the early 1980s, the Trust owned at least 85,000 acres (34,000ha) of Welsh land, including much of the coasts of Pembrokeshire and the Gower and Llŷn Peninsulas, and wide stretches of Snowdonia. As was noted earlier, the National Trust also acquired pre-eminent examples of Wales's built heritage, Penrhyn Castle, Powis Castle, Plas Newydd and Chirk Castle among them. All four of those properties, Powis Castle in particular, are adjoined by gardens of distinction; following their acquisition and that of Bodnant Garden (1949) and of Erddig Hall and its garden (1973), the National Trust became as much a guardian of the horticultural heritage of Wales as of its great houses and rugged landscapes.

While the National Trust was primarily concerned with the beauty of the landscape, organizations came into being which were primarily concerned with the meaning of the landscape. Chief among them were the four archaeological trusts — Clwyd and Powys, Gwynedd, Dyfed, and Glamorgan and Gwent — established in the 1970s. Initially, the trusts were mainly involved in rescue archaeology, an urgent need as major landscape manipulation such as the construction of the M4 and

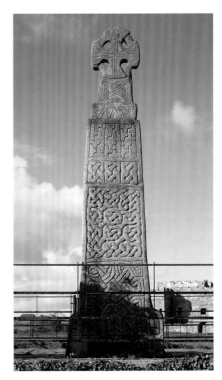

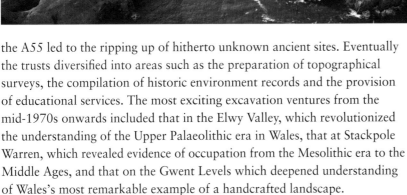

Above left: Excavations and survey work at Stackpole Warren, Pembrokeshire, in the 1970s revealed evidence of occupation from the Mesolithic era to the Middle Ages. (© Crown: Royal Commission on the Ancient and Historical Monuments of Wales, 2000/CS/0897).

Above: The Carew Cross dates from the second half of the tenth or early eleventh century. The head of the cross provided the inspiration for Cadw's logo in 1984.

the A55 led to the ripping up of hitherto unknown ancient sites. Eventually the trusts diversified into areas such as the preparation of topographical surveys, the compilation of historic environment records and the provision of educational services. The most exciting excavation ventures from the mid-1970s onwards included that in the Elwy Valley, which revolutionized the understanding of the Upper Palaeolithic era in Wales, that at Stackpole Warren, which revealed evidence of occupation from the Mesolithic era to the Middle Ages, and that on the Gwent Levels which deepened understanding of Wales's most remarkable example of a handcrafted landscape.

Increasingly, however, students of the making of the landscape came to favour non-intrusive methods of investigation rather than excavation — a process which is, by definition, destructive. Chief among such methods is aerial photography, which received a huge boost from the intensive air reconnaissance of the 1950s. In addition, there was by the 1970s a growing use of geophysical surveying, a method which allows the detection of buried structures and of even such slight remains as the organic staining caused by decayed wooden posts.

These and other innovations were widely available by 1984, when the care of Wales's built heritage became the responsibility of Cadw: Welsh Historic Monuments. Of all the consequences of the administrative devolution which began in 1964 with the appointment of a Secretary of State for Wales, the establishment of Cadw was the most serendipitous. The name means to keep or to preserve, and the choice was a disappointment to those who hoped for a title which would suggest a more proactive policy. But, as shall be seen, proactive is precisely what Cadw proved to be.

THE LAST TWENTY-FIVE YEARS

THE MAKING OF WALES 1984–2009

In 1984 the main issue under discussion in Wales was the threat to the coal industry as a significant element in the Welsh economy. In 1980, there had been twenty-eight deep pits in operation in south Wales and one in the north. Half the southern collieries were closed within two years of the end of the miners' strike of 1984–85. With the closure of Point of Ayr Colliery in 1996, deep coal mining ceased in the north; it ceased in the south following the final closure of Tower Colliery in 2008. By the early 1980s, there had been a sharp decline in the numbers employed in the steel industry, with Cardiff's East Moors Works closing in 1978 and the Shotton Works in 1979. There were further closures in subsequent years — Brymbo in 1990, most of Llanwern in 2001 and all operations at Ebbw Vale in 2002. Tinplate making ceased at Velindre in 1989. In that year, employment in the Welsh slate industry amounted to no more than a couple of hundred. Heavy industry, which had been central to the concept of Wales for 150 years, had become peripheral to the country's economy.

In landscape terms, this meant that pithead winding towers, once the defining symbol of Welsh industry, came to be seen only at mining museums. With the end of coal mining, tips of colliery waste no longer proliferated; indeed, by the beginning of the twenty-first century, almost all the coal tips in the southern coalfield had either been removed or made safe and grassed over. In the more level coalfield of the north, the Bersham Colliery tip survives as a symbol of coal mining in the Wrexham area. Furthermore, with Blaenau Ffestiniog still overshadowed by quarry waste and with the Rheidol and the Ystwyth among the most polluted rivers in Britain, the detritus of the slate and lead industries is still evident. What had been Europe's largest area of derelict land was transformed as lakes and woodlands enhanced the lower Swansea Valley. In 1995, an ambitious project was launched to clean up a 14-mile (22.4km) stretch of the once highly industrialized coast west of Llanelli; work on the 2,000-acre (810ha) Millennium Coastal Park, opened in 2002, was, at the time, the biggest land reclamation project in Britain. Docks built to accommodate the coal trade were no longer necessary. Swansea and Penarth acquired attractive marinas, but the most radical development was at Cardiff, where a barrage turned the estuaries of the Taff and the Ely into a freshwater lake.

Steel making at Llanwern. Most of the Llanwern steelworks closed in 2001, one of many indications that by the beginning of the twenty-first century heavy industry had become peripheral to the economy of Wales (© Jeff Morgan/Photolibrary Wales).

Opposite: The Senedd in Cardiff Bay was designed by Richard Rogers to house the debating chamber of the National Assembly for Wales. Opened on St David's Day, 2006, the building gives expression to the ideal of transparency in government. It was also planned from the outset as a 'green' building (© Crown Copyright (2009) Visit Wales).

The Inmos Microchip Factory (1982) at Newport reflects the predilection of its architect, Richard Rogers, to position the skeleton of a building on its outside rather than its inside.

The second Severn crossing was completed in 1996. The elegant structure consists of long approach viaducts from each bank of the estuary and a central suspension bridge with a span of 1,495 feet (456m) (© Crown Copyright (2009) Visit Wales).

While industrial and transport undertakings of an earlier age were either swept away or adapted for other uses, new undertakings were constructed. The most remarkable industrial building erected in Wales between the early 1980s and 2009 was the Inmos Microchip Factory at Newport (1982). Designed by Richard Rogers, it was inspired by his predilection, already displayed in his Pompidou Centre in Paris (1972–77), for ensuring that the skeleton of a building should be on its outside rather than its inside.

The most dramatic contribution of recent times to Wales's transport system was the completion in 1996 of the second Severn crossing, which, unlike the first, really does link the Welsh and English banks of the estuary. The 1,495-foot (456m) central span of the crossing is suspended from two H-shaped pylons by spans of taut steel stays, presenting a scene of gossamer elegance. Equally innovative, but less visible is the immersed tube tunnel (1991) which solved the town of Conwy's dire traffic problem.

It was in the field of energy production that late twentieth-century Wales was endowed with its most elaborate project. Fully commissioned in 1984, the Dinorwig hydroelectric power station is Europe's largest pump storage station. When demand for electricity is low, water is pumped from Llyn Peris (524 feet (160m) above sea level) to Llyn Marchlyn Mawr (1,880 feet (580m) above sea level); when demand is high, water is released to work generators which are located in a hall which could accommodate St Paul's Cathedral. However, as virtually all the construction is underground, it is difficult to appreciate the immensity of the project. A less elaborate, but more controversial, venture related to energy was the construction of the 197-mile (316km) Milford Haven natural gas pipeline, although this too is now underground. Wind farms, perhaps the most divisive issue of early twenty-first century

Wales, are permanently visible. By 2008, there were at least eighteen land-based wind farms in Wales, some of them located not far from the borders of the Snowdonia National Park. (The building of such constructions is forbidden in national parks.) The largest collection of turbines is at Llandinam where 104 turbines had been erected by 2000. However, they are being replaced by larger turbines similar to the 39 which came into operation at the Cefn Croes Wind Farm on the slopes of Pumlumon in 2005, which are capable of producing almost 20 per cent of the 300.6 MW of the energy output of the wind farms of Wales. The North Hoyle Wind Farm located in the sea north of Rhyl is even more productive, and is soon to be expanded. There have been discussions concerning the erection of offshore wind farms south of Porthcawl and in Cardigan Bay, and the harnessing of tidal power through the building of lagoons, although no concrete proposals have as yet been put forward. The largest project ever proposed affecting Wales's marine environment — the construction of a tidal barrage across the Severn Estuary capable of producing electricity equivalent to the output of at least two nuclear power stations — may yet come to fruition.

Of all the structures erected in Wales in the past twenty-five years, perhaps the best loved is the Millennium Stadium (1999). Dominating the centre of Cardiff, it has a capacity of 74,500 and is the largest stadium in the world with a fully retractable roof. Those in Wales whose patriotism is not wholly focused on rugby may see more significance in the Senedd, the seat of the National Assembly for Wales. Designed by Richard Rogers and opened in 2006, its translucence is a marked contrast with the forbidding character of the former Welsh Office buildings (now the offices of the Welsh Assembly Government) — a contrast which perhaps symbolizes the difference between

Above left: The Millennium Stadium, opened in 1999, provides Wales with an international sporting venue. Seating 74,500, it is the largest stadium in the world with a fully retractable roof (© Crown Copyright (2009) Visit Wales).

Above: Wind farms are some of the newest features in the Welsh landscape. These turbines are located on Mynydd Maendy, Tonyrefail (© Paul Parker/ Photolibrary Wales).

The Great Glasshouse of the National Botanic Garden at Llanarthne, Carmarthenshire, is the largest single-span glasshouse in the world. Elliptical in plan, it is 361 feet (110m) long and 197 feet (60m) wide and covers an area of 37,673 square feet (3,500 sq m). Designed by Norman Foster and Partners, it was completed in 1999 and houses a collection of plants that includes some of the world's most endangered species (© Crown Copyright (2009) Visit Wales).

the Wales of 1979 and that of 2006. In rural Wales, the most impressive structure constructed in recent years is the Great Glasshouse at the National Botanic Garden. Designed by Norman Foster and Partners and completed in 1999, it is the largest single-span glasshouse in the world. Other significant cultural additions to the built heritage of Wales made in the late twentieth and early twenty-first centuries include the completion of the National Museum (1993), the additions to the National Library (1982, 1995–97, 2004), Peter Roberts's attractive Arts Centre at Aberystwyth and The Wales Millennium Centre in Cardiff (2002–04), an ingenious armadillo-shaped building with a sparkling copper roof. Interesting local government buildings include the twenty-four bays of the county hall at Haverfordwest (1998–99) and Dewi-Prys Thomas's innovative interpretation of a fitting headquarters for the Gwynedd County Council (1980–83).

The late twentieth and early twenty-first centuries was an era of losses as well as gains. Among the losses were chapels which, by the new millennium, were estimated to be closing in Wales at an average rate of one a week; intriguingly, taverns — once the chief rivals of the chapels — were by then also closing in Wales at the rate of one a week. While taverns can be fairly unobtrusively adapted as dwellings, chapels often pose greater problems. There is something incongruous about Aberystwyth's The Academy public house (formerly St Paul's Chapel), where the wall beneath the Lord's Prayer holds the optics; however, the conversion into a dwelling of the handsome Congregational Chapel in Glendower Street, Monmouth, has been widely commended.

Wales's chief architectural loss since 1984 has been the Brynmawr rubber factory. Despite its grade II* listing, and despite the claim that it was the

The Dowlais Stables were built in 1820 to house the horses of the Dowlais Iron Company. The oldest surviving building in Dowlais, the block was admirably restored by the Merthyr Tydfil Heritage Trust in the 1980s and sensitively converted to residential use (© Crown Copyright (2009) Visit Wales).

inspiration for the Sydney Opera House, no viable reuse could be found for it; the factory was demolished in 2001 and replaced by a supermarket. Hopes that the factory's still surviving boiler house might be converted into a theatre have yet to be realized. Another loss, although a less serious one, was the King's Hall at Aberystwyth. The hall (opened in 1934), the finest art deco building ever erected in Wales, had, until its demolition in 1989, provided the resort's seafront with an admirable centrepiece.

Less obvious, but sometimes more regrettable, is the loss of a host of authentic details as buildings are thoughtlessly modified. The use of clay tiles fragmented the unity of the slate roofs of terraced houses; historic façades were covered with artificial stone cladding; the wooden frames of sash windows gave way to the horrors of polyvinyl chloride (PVC).

Yet, there should not be too much lamentation. Merthyr, once so cavalier towards its history, has admirably restored the Dowlais Stables, and throughout urban Wales developers have been obliged to preserve handsome frontages, as at Wrexham's Wynnstay Arms and Cardiff's neo-Venetian Queen's Chambers. Newport's pedestrianized streets have been embellished by delightful sculptures and mosaics, and entire historic towns — Tenby and Dolgellau in particular — have been splendidly revamped. The Welsh have rediscovered paint; that can lead to excessive exuberance (Elm Street, Cardiff, comes to mind), but the painting of the stuccoed houses of Aberaeron has created a townscape of wondrous charm.

In urban Wales, the most magnificent conservation achievement of the past quarter of a century is that at Plas Mawr, Conwy, an achievement which in 1997 won the Building Conservation Award of the Royal Institution of

Above: The severed Englishman's head emblem of the Griffith family from the plasterwork of Plas Mawr, Conwy.

Above right: The dining room at Gwydir Castle in the Conwy Valley. The carved panels, which had been removed in the early 1920s by William Randolph Hearst, have been brought back to the house, which is being carefully restored by its current owners.

Chartered Surveyors. The finest surviving sixteenth-century town house in Britain, Plas Mawr was built between 1576 and 1585 for Robert Wynn (about 1520–98). The splendid frontage that faces Conwy's High Street is merely that of the gatehouse; the gate leads to the lower courtyard which gives access to the superb great chamber, where the delightful plasterwork has been repainted in the flaunting colours favoured by opportunist careerists like Robert Wynn. Among the motifs are severed heads of Englishmen. A plaster cast of one of them was presented to Prince Charles in 2002; the precise meaning of the gift was obscure.

Almost as exciting as the work at Plas Mawr was that at another Wynn property — Gwydir Castle, the home of Robert's nephew, Sir John Wynn (1553–1627), delectably located in the Conwy Valley west of Llanrwst. In the early 1920s, the newspaper magnate, William Randolph Hearst, bought and removed the magnificent carved panels of Gwydir's dining room only a few months before the house was gutted by fire. In 1996, the panels were discovered in one of the warehouses of the Metropolitan Museum of Art in New York. Returned to Wales, they were reinstalled at Gwydir, where Judith Corbett and Peter Welford are lovingly restoring the house. Other rurally located houses where memorable work has been done include Aberglasney, Erddig Hall, Llanerchaeron, Newton House and Sker House. The most charming restoration work of the 1990s was that completed in 1998 at Tŷ Mawr, Castle Caereinion, a house whose praises have already been sung.

Perhaps the most interesting building work done in the Welsh countryside over the last quarter of a century or so has been that inspired by the ecological movement. It is a movement to which Wales has made a significant contribution, ranging from the 'small is beautiful' theory of Leopold Kohr, the self-sufficiency advocated by John Seymour of Fachongle in north

Left: The Centre for Alternative Technology near Machynlleth provides a showcase for new approaches to the responsible stewardship of the environment (© Crown Copyright (2009) Visit Wales).

Above: The kindergarten of the Nant-y-Cwm Steiner School at Llanycefn, Pembrokeshire was designed by Christopher Day and built about 1989. It is one of Pembrokeshire's noteworthy 'green' buildings.

Pembrokeshire and the concepts inspiring the Centre for Alternative Technology north of Machynlleth to the dedication to landscape expressed in the poems of Waldo Williams and in the novels of Raymond Williams. Pembrokeshire is home to many of Wales's 'green' buildings, among them the Steiner Kindergarten at Llanycefn (about 1989), the visitors' centres at Scolton (1993) and Castell Henllys (1994), turf-roofed Malator at Nolton (1998) and the tourist information centre at St Davids (2001). Elsewhere in Wales, there has been a revival in the building of clom houses, in the construction of thatched roofs and in the use of lime mortar in preference to Portland cement, together with a somewhat over-enthusiastic eagerness to build in Welsh slate.

The ecological movement was in part a reaction to what was happening in agriculture. By the 1980s, farmers were beginning to reap the penalties of their success, and the means that had led to that success — the heavy use of artificial manure, herbicides and pesticides, the draining of wetlands, the removal of hedges and the replacement of natural upland swards — were coming under increasing attack. With surpluses accumulating and the costs of agricultural incentives rising, production quotas were introduced and farming became increasingly concerned with environmental protection. Set-aside came into vogue, thus endowing the countryside with patches of land which were in the process of reverting to an older untended condition.

Much remained of the era of over-intensive farming — factory-like towers at farms, vast corrugated-iron sheds and piles of black plastic sacks holding winter fodder that had once been stored in hayricks — but the appearance of agricultural land was changing. Carts carrying manure and compost reappeared as organic farmers increased in number. New crops were planted — maize in the Vale of Clwyd and the Vale of Monnow, vines in the Vale of

This Neolithic chambered tomb in Snowdonia had been incorporated into a drystone sheepfold. Funding from an agri-environment scheme enabled the farmer to clear the tomb.

Glamorgan and the Usk Valley, and, incredibly, an olive plantation in northern Anglesey. Sensitivity came to characterize owners of woodlands as indigenous broad-leafed trees were planted in preference to Sitka Spruce.

There were those who argued that, while farmers are undoubtedly food producers, they are also, and perhaps more importantly, the guardians of the diversity of wildlife and of the beauty and the meaning of landscape. Such thinking inspired the Tir Gofal (originally Tir Cymen) schemes which supported agriculturalists for farming in an environmentally friendly fashion as well as protecting and managing historic features.

Although the last quarter of a century has seen a marked change in the appearance of both rural and industrial Wales, the dominant theme in the making of Wales during that period has been the determination to conserve the natural and built heritage, allied with the desire to ensure that the beauty and the meaning of the landscape should be the sources of enlightenment and delight to as many people as possible.

In that story, the changing role of the National Trust has been particularly significant. While the National Trust maintains its solicitude for beautiful landscapes, acquiring three quarters of the coastline of Gower and 4,000 acres (1,620ha) in Snowdonia, land which includes part of the summit of Snowdon itself, its concern that the remnants of the Welsh landowning class should continue to occupy their ancestral houses has become less dominant. Chirk Castle is no longer the main residence of the Myddelton family; the major interest at Erddig is not the story of the erstwhile owners, but that of their servants, and at Llanerchaeron, splendidly restored by the National Trust between 1990 and 2004, the emphasis is upon the total ecology of a country estate. In 1997, the National Trust abandoned the notion that North (sic) Wales and South (sic) Wales were regional parts of an England-and-Wales structure, and established a semi-autonomous organization for Wales as a whole, admittedly one dependent in part upon the subscriptions of National Trust members in England. The National Trust showed increasing interest in vernacular architecture. Its work at Tŷ Mawr, Wybrnant, the childhood home of William Morgan, completed in 1988 on the four hundredth anniversary of the publication of Morgan's translation of the Bible into Welsh, was particularly commendable. In 1991, the National Trust acquired properties at Cwmdu, north of Llandeilo, consisting of an inn, a shop, two terraced houses, a chapel, a vestry and stables. The work of the National Trust and that of the local inhabitants has created a model example of a revived rural community. In addition, the Trust's work at Aberdeunant, east of Llandeilo, has brought into being a delightful re-creation of the thatched buildings which were once so numerous in Carmarthenshire.

The National Trust was one of a number of organizations which were, by the early twenty-first century, involved with the built heritage of Wales. The work at Sker House, near Porthcawl, was led by the Buildings at Risk Trust and that at Aberglasney by the Aberglasney Restoration Trust. Castell Dinas Brân is owned by Denbighshire County Council, Margam Castle by

Tŷ Mawr, Wybrnant, was the childhood home of William Morgan (d. 1604), the translator of the Bible into Welsh. It is a property of the National Trust, which completed its commendable work there in 1988, the four hundredth anniversary of the publication of Morgan's translation (© Crown Copyright (2009) Visit Wales).

The National Trust acquired this terrace at Cwmdu, north of Llandeilo, in 1991. Working with the local residents, the Trust has created a model example of a revived rural community (© NTPL/John Miller).

The Shell House at Cilwendeg, Pembrokeshire, an early nineteenth-century Gothic folly, has been beautifully restored by the Temple Trust.

Neath Port Talbot County Borough Council, and Caergwrle Castle by Hope Community Council. Since 1984, the National History Museum has re-erected twenty historic buildings at St Fagans, including the hugely popular Rhyd-y-car houses from Merthyr and the wonderfully restored St Teilo's Church from the Llwchwr Valley. Other organizations include the Civic Trust, the Friends of Friendless Churches, the Welsh Religious Buildings Trust, the Architectural Heritage Fund, the Spitalfields Trust, the Temple Trust (which concerns itself with garden buildings) and the Wellsprings Fellowship (which is involved with the care of historic wells). While there are private owners who have behaved impeccably — the record of the Philipps family, owners of Pembroke Castle, has long been exemplary — the fate of many privately owned smaller sites is a cause for concern. Of the larger sites, the saddest case is Cardigan Castle, where the owner allowed decades of neglect to spiral into a scene of desolation which will take a decade and millions of pounds to rectify. On a happier note, there is a welcome interest from local community groups in acquiring,

Above left: Manordeifi Old Church in Pembrokeshire is one of the redundant churches in the care of the Friends of Friendless Churches.

Above: The stately Bethania Chapel in Maesteg was designed by William Beddoe Rees in 1906. The Welsh Religious Buildings Trust stepped in to rescue the building when its maintenance became too heavy a burden for its dwindling congregation (© Crown: Royal Commission on the Ancient and Historical Monuments of Wales DS_2006_118_007).

managing and promoting their local monuments. Examples include the trust set up at New Radnor to manage the magnificent motte-and-bailey castle which dominates that one-time parliamentary borough, and the group established at Knucklas — once also one of the parliamentary boroughs of Radnorshire — which has purchased the site of Knucklas's earthwork castle with the intention of promoting its community use.

While newer organizations were proliferating, the most venerable body involved in the study of Wales's built heritage was celebrating its centenary. The Royal Commission on the Ancient and Historical Monuments of Wales, founded in 1908, experienced a flowering in the post-war years. Its volumes on Caernarvonshire (1956, 1960, 1964) set new standards, and its subsequent publications, in particular Peter Smith's *Houses of the Welsh Countryside* (1975, 1988) and Stephen Hughes's *Copperopolis* (2000), were further proof of the superb quality of the Royal Commission's work in recording the built heritage of Wales.

While the Royal Commission was producing authoritative studies, Penguin Books, and later, Yale University Press, were publishing more portable volumes. The completion in 1974 of Nikolaus Pevsner's guides to the buildings of England gave rise to the term 'to pevsnerize' — to visit examples of the built heritage of England with a Pevsner volume in hand. Between 1979 and 2009, Wales was endowed with seven volumes in the Pevsner tradition, so that explorers of Wales may enjoy the greatest of all delights — to be able to 'pevsnerize' the entire country.

While the authors of the Pevsner volumes combed the country for all that is architecturally notable, new technologies were being used to comb the country for all that is archaeologically notable. By the early twenty-first century, aerial photography had developed far beyond what was available to those involved in the air reconnaissance of the 1950s. In particular, the technique proved its value during the dry summer of 2006, when much more

was revealed of the internationally important prehistoric site at Walton. Geophysical investigation had also greatly advanced. In 2003, when two Roman forts were discovered in Dinefwr Park, it proved possible to find out a great deal about them, not so much through excavation as through geophysical prospection.

In the story of the conservation and interpretation of the built heritage of Wales, a development of central importance in government terms was the setting up in 1984 of Cadw, which celebrated its quarter-centenary in 2009. The Ministry of Works, in all its varying guises, had seen its role as caring for those buildings which were its direct responsibility. Cadw's duties include the protection of the archaeological, built and maritime heritage of Wales, a task which became even more meaningful in 1999 with the establishment of the National Assembly for Wales. In 1984, there were those who expressed fears that Wales lacked the resources to go it alone, and that Cadw would not be able 'to look English Heritage [its closest equivalent body in England] in the face'. Such fears proved groundless. With its splendid logo (based upon the Carew Cross), its superb guidebooks, its impressive programme of conservation, its register of historic parks, gardens and landscapes and its exhaustive records of structures and sites, it is an institution in which all Welsh people can take pride. Sometimes, however, Cadw can give the impression of being over-meticulous. Have its officers read Walter Benjamin's *The Concept of History* (1939), where the author puts forward the wholly unrealizable proposition that 'nothing that has ever taken place should be lost to history'?

Cadw began life at Brunel House — a fitting name considering Brunel's contribution to the making of Wales. From its inception, its employees considered that raising awareness of Wales's built heritage was a major priority. Within two years of its establishment, that awareness received a huge boost through the grant of World Heritage Site status to the best known of the monuments in its care — the castles of Beaumaris, Caernarfon, Conwy and Harlech. Even more significant was UNESCO's decision in 2000 to grant World Heritage Site status to the Blaenavon Industrial Landscape, for that was an indication of the way in which the understanding of the built heritage was evolving from an appreciation of individual structures to a concern for the totality of a historic landscape.

Boosting awareness was much aided by the marked improvement in Cadw's publications. Its guidebooks, with their excellent pictures, diagrams and cutaway reconstructions, and with their emphasis upon putting the monument under consideration into a wider context, won warm praise. Imaginative depictions of monuments as they had been in their heyday — a method of presentation pioneered by Alan Sorrell — were made by Terry Ball, Ivan Lapper and Chris Jones-Jenkins. Replica medieval weapons were erected on the walls of Caerphilly, mock battles were conducted by the Ermine Street Guard at Caerleon and by the Sealed Knot at Raglan, and open-air plays were performed at Tretower and elsewhere. Three-dimensional models were created, virtual reality displays were introduced, and, by 2009, 'Bluetooth' mobile telephone technology was helping visitors to explore sites.

Opposite: Pontcysyllte Aqueduct — the stream in the sky — was the creation of Thomas Telford and William Jessop. Building work began in 1795 and the aqueduct was opened in 1805. Recently conserved, it has been nominated for World Heritage status.

Above: Beaumaris Castle, which was begun in 1295, was accorded World Heritage status in 1986 along with Edward I's other great fortifications in north Wales: Harlech Castle and the castles and associated town walls at Conwy and Caernarfon.

Internationally recognized, the World Heritage symbol designates a site of outstanding universal value.

In its mission to protect the historic environment of Wales, Cadw's most labour-intensive activity in recent years was the compiling of registers of historic parks, gardens and landscapes, lists of historic buildings and schedules of ancient monuments. Its register of historic landscapes is a European 'first'. A total of fifty-eight landscapes (thirty-six outstanding, twenty-two special) have been described in volumes which contain some of the finest aerial photographs ever published. Even more impressive is the listing of almost 30,000 historic buildings and the scheduling of some 4,000 ancient monuments. In the upland Ceredigion community of Nantcwnlle thirty sites have been protected and nine in inner-city Grangetown in Cardiff. The sites in Grangetown, which adjoins the estuaries of the Taff and the Ely, include underwater sites (a wreck and a coal staithe), an indication that conservationists are coming to grips with Wales's maritime heritage.

In its twenty-five years of existence, Cadw's most visually impressive and most capital intensive contribution has been its restoration work. Plas Mawr is the pre-eminent example, but the same attention to detail — attention to which its skill centre has made a crucial contribution — is evident in other projects. Cadw's work at Blaenavon had been virtually completed by the 1990s, but other highly promising projects are being undertaken at the ironworks at Cyfarthfa, Tondu and Wenallt. Particularly appealing is the work on some less imposing monuments; for example, Cadw grants have assisted the conservation of overgrown and burrow-riddled mottes which has allowed visitors to earthworks such as Aberlleiniog, Nevern, Glyndyfrdwy and Sycharth to have a truly enlightening experience. Conservation work has also been done on other sites that are outside State care but which are of paramount importance, Cwmhir Abbey among them. Crowning everything is what has been achieved at Wales's major medieval buildings. Indeed, by the end of the twentieth century, every issue of Cadw's magazine, *Heritage in Wales*, seemed to be announcing a new triumph — Dolforwyn, Dryslwyn, Laugharne, Montgomery, Narberth, St Quentins.

Sensitive to the accusation that far more funding had long been expended upon the conservation and interpretation of medieval buildings commissioned by the invaders of Wales than upon those commissioned by indigenous Welsh rulers, Cadw began indulging in a rather amusing ding-dong. In 2002, for example, it informed the readers of *Heritage in Wales* that it had completed its restoration work on the ('English') castle at Montgomery and the ('Welsh') castle at Dolforwyn and that work was afoot at the ('English') castle at Laugharne and the ('Welsh') castle at Dryslwyn. Perhaps it would be better if Cadw were to acknowledge that what was built in Wales in the past is now the common heritage of the entirety of the country's present inhabitants, and leave it at that.

Citizens of the larger nations of Europe cannot hope in the span of a single lifetime to get to know all the highlights of the natural heritage and built heritage of their country. But Welsh residents and regular visitors to Wales can, by the time they reach three score and ten, visit, appreciate and love all its glories. Whatever else are the virtues of Wales — and they are many — its primary virtue is that it is the right size for loving.

Dolgellau, like every one of the 869 communities in Wales, was resurveyed as part of an eleven-year programme to reassess the historic buildings of Wales and list those of historic or architectural interest.

Opposite: The motte at Sycharth is resonant with associations with Owain Glyndŵr (© Crown: Royal Commission on the Ancient and Historical Monuments of Wales, AP_2009_0058).

Further Reading

In recent years, Cadw has published a wide range of guidebooks to sites and historic landscapes, all of which contain invaluable information. Cadw's membership magazine, *Heritage in Wales/Etifeddiaeth y Cymry,* provides admirable accounts of developments in the story of the making of Wales.

M. Aston, *Interpreting the Landscape* (London 1985)

E. Beazley and L. Brett, *North Wales: A Shell Guide* (London 1971)

H. Burnham, *A Guide to Ancient and Historic Wales: Clwyd and Powys* (London 1995)

S. Burrow, *The Tomb Builders in Wales 4000–3000 BC* (Cardiff 2006)

A. Caseldine, *Environmental Archaeology in Wales* (Lampeter 1990)

N. Coldstream, *Builders & Decorators: Medieval Craftsmen in Wales* (Cardiff 2008)

R. J. Colyer, *The Welsh Cattle Drovers* (Cardiff 1976)

F. G. Cowley, *The Monastic Order in South Wales 1066–1349* (Cardiff 1977)

J. Davies, *A History of Wales*, revised edition (London 2007)

J. Davies, *The Celts* (London 2000)

J. Davies, N. Jenkins, M. Baines, P. I. Lynch, *The Welsh Academy Encyclopedia of Wales* (Cardiff 2008)

R. R. Davies, *The Age of Conquest: Wales 1063–1415* (Oxford 1991)

W. Davies, *Wales in the Early Middle Ages* (Leicester 1982)

N. Edwards and A. Lane (eds), *The Early Church in Wales and the West* (Oxford 1992)

N. Edwards, *A Corpus of Early Medieval Inscribed Stones and Stone Sculpture in Wales: Volume 2 South-west Wales* (Cardiff 2007)

F. V. Emery, *The World's Landscapes: Wales* (London 1969)

R. A. Griffiths (ed.), *Boroughs of Mediaeval Wales* (Cardiff 1978)

R. Haslam, *The Buildings of Wales: Powys* (Harmondsworth 1979)

R. Haslam, J. Orbach and A. Voelcker, *The Buildings of Wales: Gwynedd* (London 2009)

J. B. Hilling, *Cardiff and the Valleys* (London 1973)

J. B. Hilling, *The Historic Architecture of Wales* (Cardiff 1976)

W. G. Hoskins, *The Making of the English Landscape* (London 1955)

E. Hubbard, *The Buildings of Wales: Clwyd* (Harmondsworth 1986)

S. Hughes, B. Malaws, M. Parry and P. Wakelin, *Collieries of Wales: Engineering and Architecture* (Aberystwyth 1995)

S. Hughes, *Copperopolis* (Aberystwyth 2000)

G. H. Jenkins, *The Foundations of Modern Wales: Wales 1642–1780* (Oxford 1993)

A. H. John, *The Industrial Development of South Wales 1750–1850* (Cardiff 1950)

A. Jones, *Welsh Chapels*, 2nd edition (Stroud 1996)

W. Linnard, *Welsh Woods and Forests: A History* (Llandysul 2000)

T. Lloyd, *The Lost Houses of Wales*, (London 1986, 1989)

T. Lloyd, J. Orbach and R. Scourfield, *The Buildings of Wales: Pembrokeshire* (London 2004)

T. Lloyd, J. Orbach and R. Scourfield, *The Buildings of Wales: Carmarthenshire and Ceredigion* (London 2006)

P. Lord, *The Visual Culture of Wales: Industrial Wales* (Aberystwyth 1998)

P. Lord, *The Visual Culture of Wales: Imaging the Nation* (Aberystwyth 2000)

P. Lord, *The Visual Culture of Wales: Medieval Vision* (Aberystwyth 2003)

J. Lowe, *Welsh Industrial Workers Housing 1775–1875* (Cardiff 1977)

J. Lowe, *Welsh Country Workers Housing 1775–1875* (Cardiff 1985)

F. Lynch, *A Guide to Ancient and Historic Wales: Gwynedd* (London 1995)

F. Lynch, J. L. Davies and S. Aldhouse-Green, *Prehistoric Wales* (Stroud 2000)

C. Musson, *Wales from the Air: Patterns of Past and Present* (Aberystwyth 1994)

G. Nash, *The Architecture of Death: Neolithic Chambered Tombs in Wales* (Almeley 2006)

V. E. Nash-Williams, *The Early Christian Monuments of Wales* (Cardiff 1950)

J. Newman, *The Buildings of Wales: Glamorgan* (London 1995)

J. Newman, *The Buildings of Wales: Gwent/Monmouthshire* (London 2000)

D. H. Owen (ed.), *Settlement and Society in Wales* (Cardiff 1989)

H. W. Owen and R. Morgan, *Dictionary of the Place-names of Wales* (Llandysul 2007)

I. C. Peate, *The Welsh House* (London 1940)

H. Pryce, *The Acts of the Welsh Rulers, 1120–1283* (Cardiff 2005)

O. Rackham, *The History of the Countryside* (London 1986)

M. Redknap, *The Christian Celts: Treasures of Late Celtic Wales* (Cardiff 1991)

M. Redknap, *Vikings in Wales* (Cardiff 2000)

M. Redknap and J. M. Lewis, *A Corpus of Early Medieval Inscribed Stones and Stone Sculpture in Wales: Volume 1 South-east Wales and the English Border* (Cardiff 2007)

D. M. Rees, *The Industrial Archaeology of Wales* (Newton Abbot 1975)

S. Rees, *A Guide to Ancient and Historic Wales: Dyfed* (London 1992)

V. Rees *Mid Western Wales: A Shell Guide* (London 1971)

V. Rees, *South-west Wales: A Shell Guide* (London 1963)

W. Rees, *An Historical Atlas of Wales from Early to Modern Times*, 3rd edition (London 1967)

S. Rippon, *The Gwent Levels: The Evolution of a Wetland Landscape* (CBA Research Report 105, York 1996)

D. Robinson, *The Cistercians in Wales: Architecture and Archaeology 1130–1540* (London 2006)

P. Sager, *Wales* (London 1991)

M. Seaborne, *Schools in Wales, 1500–1900: A Social and Architectural History* (Denbigh 1992)

J. B. Smith, *Llywelyn ap Gruffudd* (Cardiff 1998)

P. Smith, *Houses of the Welsh Countryside: A Study in Historical Geography,* (London 1975, 1988)

I. Soulsby, *The Towns of Medieval Wales* (Chichester 1983)

R. Suggett, *Houses & History in the March of Wales: Radnorshire 1400–1800* (Aberystwyth 2005)

A. J. Taylor, *The King's Works in Wales 1277–1330* (London 1974)

J. A. Taylor (ed.), *Culture and Environment in Prehistoric Wales* (Oxford 1980)

D. Thomas (ed.), *Wales: A New Study* (Newton Abbot 1977)

R. Turvey, *Llywelyn the Great* (Llandysul 2007)

D. Verey, *Mid Wales: A Shell Guide* (London 1960)

P. Wakelin and R. A. Griffiths (eds), *Hidden Histories: Discovering the Heritage of Wales* (Aberystwyth 2008)

E. Whittle, *The Historic Gardens of Wales* (London 1992)

E. Whittle, *A Guide to Ancient and Historic Wales: Glamorgan and Gwent* (London 1992)

E. Wiliam, *Historical Farm Buildings of Wales* (Edinburgh 1986)

G. Williams, *The Welsh Church from Conquest to the Reformation,* 2nd edition (Cardiff 1976)

G. Williams, *Renewal and Reformation: Wales c. 1415–1642* (Oxford 1993)

M. Williams, *The Making of the South Wales Landscape* (London 1975)

Index of Places

All county designations follow The Buildings of Wales series. Page numbers in bold italics refer to illustrations.

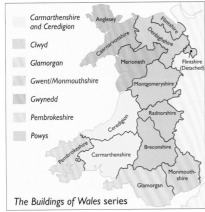

The Buildings of Wales series